FOOD and HEALING

"*Food and Healing* establishes the scientific, philosophical, ethical, nutritional, emotional, psychological, sensual, sensuous, and cross-cultural foundation on which a vibrant state of health can build."

Organica

"*Food and Healing* is like a breath of fresh air . . . nutritionally speaking, this book can be a powerful catalyst to our letting go to the wisdom of life."

The Chiropractic and Whole Health Center

"Highly recommended."

Brain Mind Bulletin

"This is a work of careful research and scholarship . . . . *Food and Healing* is a compendium of concepts, practical recommendations and personal sharing . . . a bold as well as valuable undertaking. Readers will appreciate [Colbin's] broad view and the gentleness and clarity of thought behind the words."

Macromuse Magazine

"Pragmatic, flexible, and well-informed guide to health-supportive eating . . . . The book considers the dynamics of living systems, the law of opposites, the effects on the body and feelings of different foods, the meaning of cravings, and food as medicine."

East West Journal

ALSO BY ANNEMARIE COLBIN

PUBLISHED BY BALLANTINE BOOKS

THE BOOK OF WHOLE MEALS

FOOD *and* HEALING

Annemarie Colbin

BALLANTINE BOOKS
NEW YORK

Library of Congress Catalog Card Number: 85-90882

ISBN: 0-345-30385-7

Cover design by James R. Harris
Photo by David Spindell
Text design by Ann Gold
Charts designed by Clarèse Peterson
Illustrations by Mary A. Wirth

Manufactured in the United States of America

First Edition: June 1986
10 9 8 7

This book is dedicated to
Shana and Kaila, who give meaning and
cohesion to my life;

and to
George Ohsawa, whose vision sparked mine.

Acknowledgments

Although I wrote this book initially in solitude without benefit of counsel, the final version of it would not have been digestible without the help of many dedicated people. I'd like to thank Adele Leone and Richard Monaco, my agents, for their continuous support of my work; Joëlle Delbourgo, my editor at Ballantine, who watched carefully over the development and maturing of this project; and Nancy van Itallie, who lent her expert editorial eye. My thanks to Clarèse Peterson, Dr. Rosemary Felton, Norman Porter, Richard Carlton, M.D., and most especially to Christiane Northrup, M.D., who read the first drafts of the manuscript and had valuable comments and considerations. Richard Donze, M.D., of the Philadelphia Methodist Hospital, looked over the final draft and with kind precision pointed out where facts needed clarification. My brother, Michael Polonyi, an electrical engineer, reviewed my section on systems theory. Klara Glowczewski pared my original ponderous tome down to a readable volume, and Mary Flynn and Dodie Edmands checked and rechecked all the charts, footnotes, references, and punctuation. Any inaccuracies that remain are my sole responsibility.

My thanks also to John Boyajy, who in our brief but enriching marriage taught me, among other things, that vegetarianism can actually make some people sick and miserable; to Bernie Gavzer, for moral support and marvelously accurate proofreading; and to my numerous friends who are willing to listen to me when I need them.

And finally, I want to emphasize that this book would not have been possible without the wonderful people who come to my classes or for consultations; they end up being my best teachers by sharing their experiences and reactions, and by asking the questions that send me looking for answers. This book is but a signpost on our journey together.

Contents

Part Two: FOOD

Part Three: HEALING

Foreword

This is the most profound book on nutrition I have ever read. Filled with wisdom—derived from a kaleidoscopic array of sources—Annemarie Colbin successfully integrates modern medicine, folklore, alternative healing systems, legend, myth, and common sense. The result is a mosaic pattern that is as pleasing esthetically as it is practical on a personal level.

Coming from a background of modern medicine, I, as well as hundreds of thousands of other M.D.s, was carefully educated in nutritional ignorance—indeed in disdain for food. The hospital "dietician" was not—and is not even today—a teacher of physicians. The dietician's traditional purpose in life has always been to serve as a "referral" for a patient who bothered the physician with too many questions about food. The very title of this book *Food and Healing* represents a joining of two concepts that most doctors regard as unrelated. But thanks to my patients, I have learned something about nutrition since my formal education ended. I now appreciate Mark Twain's answer to the question, "Where did you get your education?" His response: "Throughout my life—except for the years I attended school."

All doctors can learn from Annemarie Colbin what they didn't learn in school. And because of pressure from insistent patients, who now know that food is important, doctors have a new and powerful incentive to learn. Patients are increasingly aware of the aphorism that when it comes to nutrition, a doctor knows as much as his secretary—unless she has been on a diet, in which case she knows more.

But this book is important for many other than M.D.s. For those whose backgrounds are in general nutrition, macrobiotics, herbology, vegetarianism, fruitarianism, homeopathy, iridology, faith healing, reflexology, massage therapy, natural hygiene, and other food and healing systems, Annemarie Colbin has provided an opportunity to make a giant leap forward. While other books are satisfied to downgrade—and even attempt to destroy—those they regard as competitors, Annemarie Colbin instead selects judiciously and comprehensively from each system, correlates aspects of different methods, highlights interrelationships between various approaches—all with thorough documentation and clarity of expression.

Taste just a sample of the delicious morsels in this book:

- "No one diet is right for everyone all the time."
- "In the modern western belief system . . . 'it could have happened to anyone' is the consoling, guilt-absorbing response. The sick one is a victim, not responsible for the state of his health."
- "Any cure of a major disease that occurred without official medical intervention is considered 'spontaneous remission.'"
- "Could the lack of an integrated energy field in baby formulas be the reason for the high correlation of Sudden Infant Death Syndrome (SIDS) and formula feeding?"
- "The partial, fragmented, unwholesome, chemically tampered-with foods that the Standard American Diet (S.A.D.) consists of cannot, in the long run, adequately support healthy life processes . . ."
- "Forcing a sick person to eat 'to keep up his strength' overlooks the fact that digestion uses up strength too."
- "Every food philosophy has its dogma and its devils, its sin and its salvation."

In accord with the definition of intelligence as the ability to identify and correlate important relationships, *Food and Healing* is a quintessentially intelligent book. I recommend it as the state-of-the-art work in the field—second best only to a personal consultation with its author.

Robert S. Mendelsohn, M.D.
Author, *Confessions of a Medical Heretic*

Acknowledgments

Although I wrote this book initially in solitude without benefit of counsel, the final version of it would not have been digestible without the help of many dedicated people. I'd like to thank Adele Leone and Richard Monaco, my agents, for their continuous support of my work; Joëlle Delbourgo, my editor at Ballantine, who watched carefully over the development and maturing of this project. My thanks to Clarèse Peterson, Dr. Rosemary Felton, Norman Porter, Richard Carlton, M.D., and most especially to Christiane Northrup, M.D., who read the first drafts of the manuscript and had valuable comments and considerations. Richard Donze, M.D., of the Philadelphia Methodist Hospital, looked over the final draft and with kind precision pointed out where facts needed clarification. My brother, Michael Polonyi, an electrical engineer, reviewed my section on systems theory. Klara Glowczewski pared my original ponderous tome down to a readable volume, and Mary Flynn, Nancy van Itallie, and Dodie Edmands checked and rechecked all the charts, footnotes, references, and punctuation. Any inaccuracies that remain are my sole responsibility.

My thanks also to John Boyajy, who in our brief but enriching marriage taught me, among other things, that vegetarianism can actually make some people sick and miserable; to Bernie Gavzer, for moral support and marvelously accurate proofreading; and to my numerous friends who are willing to listen to me when I need them.

And finally, I want to emphasize that this book would not have been possible without the wonderful people who come to my classes or for consultations; they end up being my best teachers by sharing their experiences and reactions, and by asking the questions that send me looking for answers. This book is but a signpost on our journey together.

FOOD *and* HEALING

Introduction:
The Power of Food

Some of the best years of my life were those I spent in high school in the city of Mar del Plata, Argentina. I had a wonderful group of friends and still have strong bonds of affection with many of them. Among these is Elida, one of my closest buddies; she and I and two other girls were known as "the Four Bewitchers"— actually a name we had invented for ourselves, hoping to live up to it.

Much water has passed under the bridge since then, and Elida and I had managed to see each other only three times in the twenty years since I'd left Argentina; but we kept in touch. Imagine my delight when I received a letter from her, in August 1981, in which she told me that she was coming to New York for two whole weeks. The first week she would be alone; her husband, Pedro, would join her for the second.

She called me from her home in Rio de Janeiro a few days before her departure to ask me to find her a hotel. Instead, I invited her to stay with us. The children were away for the summer, so their room was free; they'd be returning just a day after Pedro was due to arrive, so everything would dovetail perfectly. Elida and Pedro could spend the rest of their stay in a nice hotel.

Elida was thrilled. So was I. Time and distance seemed not to have cooled our friendship. I wondered whether a week together would strengthen or weaken that old bond. How much could she have changed? I remembered her as an attractive, vibrant brunette who always gestured when she spoke and had an enthusiastic lilt to her voice. She used to laugh a lot, too. I looked forward to a week of much chatter and reminiscence, albeit with vague trepidation: How would Elida feel about the spartan vegetarian fare in our home?

Finally, she arrived, and it didn't take me too long to find that, indeed, our friendship was as strong as ever. However, I was startled by the physical changes in my friend. Elida's health was not good; she had diabetes, was taking an insulin shot daily, her hands were bloated, and she was overweight. She was often tired and was unable to walk more than a few blocks at a time. I found that there was even more to worry about.

"Why do you walk so stiffly?" I asked her at one point.

"I can't feel my feet," she said.

"What?"

"That's right, I can't. Look," she said, and showed me the nails on her big toes; they were black and blue. "I wore some tight shoes last week and couldn't tell that they were cutting off my circulation. Now I'm going to lose those nails."

I was horrified. "You have to do something! At this rate, you'll get gangrene, and soon you'll be walking around with a wooden leg!" I looked her squarely in the eye. "You're my age, and that's too young to have a wooden leg."

She giggled, but there was no mirth in her eyes.

"What does your doctor say?" I asked.

She shrugged. "Nothing. He gave me medication, but it doesn't seem to help, so I don't bother. He told me to stop eating sugar but doesn't tell me what else to do."

We just looked at each other. I could see her native vitality still shining through her ill health. If allowed to work, that vitality would help her heal very quickly.

"Well, my dear friend," I said, "there must be a reason why you've landed in my hands for a whole week. Let's see what happens after a few days of birdseed and rabbit food."

She laughed. "I'm willing to try," she said.

On the second morning after her arrival, Elida called me into her room to show me her hands. "Look," she said. They were puffed up like balloons, and she could barely remove her ring. "If I don't eat sugar, I blow up. My kidneys don't work. When I eat sugar, it acts like a diuretic and I urinate gallons, and then there is no bloat." She had spent the day before eating with us, and that meant that she'd had nothing with sugar in it.

It's not that she hadn't known about my lifestyle. Our sporadic contact had kept her up to date with my involvement in natural foods, my cooking classes, and my interest in natural healing. She had even asked for a copy of my cookbook, *The Book of Whole Meals*, and I had sent it to her. She knew as well that I had recently remarried and that my husband was a vegetarian cook also. Thus she was quite prepared for a change in her diet.

What she found was a fairly austere home regimen, enlivened with two or three weekly outings during which we partook of fish or perhaps poultry. For breakfast, there was brown rice and vegetables; for lunch, bean or lentil soup, whole-grain bread, and salad; for snacks, fruit, or rice cakes with apple butter; for dinner, a grain, beans, vegetables, salad. For Elida I added aduki beans cooked with kombu seaweed*, of which I offered her a small bowl twice daily; these small red Japanese beans are traditionally considered to be strengthening for the kidneys. Sure enough, Elida reported with glee that they were a much better diuretic than sugar.

I also decided to manifest my feelings as a caring friend and strongly admonished her to stay away from sugar and alcohol 100 percent. What I didn't tell her is that such sacrifice would be quite easy to undertake if she ate our food: When one eats no meat, one needs no sugar—if at the same time the diet includes whole grains.

Thus my friend found herself plunked, with practically no transition, into a totally different dietary mode. From a diet high in meat protein, fat, sugar, alcohol, and soft drinks, she went to complex carbohydrates (whole grains, beans, vegetables), low fat, little natural sugar (fruit was only an occasional snack), herb teas, and, at times, apple juice. Ah yes, and no milk, butter, cheese, or yogurt either.

I must say she handled the shock well. Only the first day was there a reaction—her bloated hands. But soon the aduki beans went to work, and within two days the bloating had vanished.

On the morning of her third day with us, I gave Elida a shiatsu acupressure massage. I am by no means an expert masseuse, but I know enough to do it for family and friends. One of the things I know is that if I find a pressure point that hurts, it means that energy is blocked there and I must keep on massaging it gently but firmly until it begins to hurt less. Well, when I got to working

---

* These items are available in Japansese markets or health food stores. For recipes, see *The Book of Whole Meals*.

on her feet, Elida started gasping. The mildest pressure hurt her. But I kept it up anyway as we joked about how much suffering it takes to get better.

After I finished, Elida stood up. A look of disbelief crossed her face. She stared at me. "I can't believe this," she said. "I can feel my feet. I can feel my feet!"

By the fifth day of her stay, her strong constitution had begun to assert itself. She was walking from thirty to fifty blocks at a clip. She had lost about six pounds. She had reduced her insulin intake. Her feet felt normal. And she looked radiant and felt terrific. I began to relax.

We talked a lot about the experience. Elida was amazed that she didn't *desire* sugar. "I think that it must be because of the balance of the other foods," she commented one day. "At home I go crazy if I don't eat something sweet several times a day." I explained that she was getting all the complex carbohydrates she needed for energy and brain function from whole grains and beans; in her normal way of eating she only got carbohydrates from sugar, some fruit and potatoes, and alcohol.

She also realized something else, without my really having mentioned it specifically. "I can't believe how much fat and protein we eat at home," she commented over bean salad at lunch one day. "Do you realize that among the five of us we consume close to twenty pounds of meat a week? And so much cheese! If I can convince my cook to change her cooking, not only would we all get healthier, but we'd save a lot of money as well." I nodded. She munched on her bean salad for a while, pensively. "This is a revelation," she said, "and it's so simple."

Perhaps you think, dear reader, that I will now proceed to tell you why and how spartan vegetarian food will cure everything that ails us. And so I would have done with great and earnest conviction years ago, certain of the truth and goodness of my path. But as the food philosopher George Ohsawa* pointed out so pithily, "What has a front has a back, and the bigger the front, the bigger the back." Fortunately, time, rather than intelligence or study, eventually helps us see the other side of things.

As my friend Elida healed herself on vegetarian food, so my husband, John, got sick on it. He had become vegetarian out of intellectual conviction a year and a half before we met; not much

* Author of *The Book of Judgment*, *Zen Macrobiotics*, and other works.

had bothered him in his general health, except some allergies, but he became convinced that a change in diet was in order because it made so much sense according to the books he was reading.

He made the transition to a diet of raw fruit, vegetables, salads, some whole grains, and lots of almonds and sesame seeds. That winter, 1978–79, he felt extremely cold and also became quite thin; although friends and relatives pointed out that he wasn't looking well, he insisted that he was. Yet his energy was low, his interest in work minimal, his emotions shaky; depression stalked him like a hungry ghost. He thought that he was just going through a healing crisis and stuck it out for ten months; but eventually he decided that he needed some extra protein and added more whole grains, beans, and fish twice a week. That made him feel better, though still far from great.

I myself had also been a pure vegetarian (without fish, eggs, or dairy products) from the fall of 1979 to the spring of 1980; perhaps as like attracts like, we became a couple and eventually married. At the time, John was doing daily cooking demonstrations at a large department store and soon joined me as a teacher at my school.

I clearly remember his breakfasts in those days. I'd get up, make breakfast and school lunches for the kids, eat the leftovers, and run off on errands or business. John, in addition to what I'd already cooked, would make elaborate and beautiful vegetable dishes and then sit and chew conscientiously for half an hour. I calculated that between chopping, eating, and cleaning up, he would spend two hours on breakfast. And then came lunch. And then dinner.

I loved his food. It was beautiful and delicious, for his Middle Eastern background and his training as a chef had given him a fine touch with seasonings. The kids were especially fond of his vegetable stir-fry and his bulgur* with fine noodles. We shared the family cooking, which was a blessing for me.

Yet although the girls and I did quite well on our simple fare, I could see that John did not. His energy level and his moods were always low, and he constantly felt somewhat unwell. Disconcerting as it was for me that my husband was not thriving on our wonderful, healthy food, I began to encourage him to eat animal protein more often.

"What would you *love* to eat?" I asked one day.

* A form of whole wheat that has been parboiled, cracked, and dried.

"Steak," he said, unhesitatingly. "But I don't think I should."
Ah, the brainwashing! I almost agreed; but I believe in listening
to the body's inner voice, and besides, I was curious.

"Why don't you try it," I suggested, "and see what happens."

I must confess to flapping around restlessly when he brought
in a steak and cooked it. He confessed to feeling guilty. Yet he
relished the meat and felt much better after eating it.

Little by little, John began eating fish, chicken, or duck almost
daily; every ten days or so he'd have a steak. Slowly, he grew
stronger, his moods improved, breakfast became a manageable
fifteen or twenty minutes, and he stopped worrying about his adrenals. His allergies had improved when he'd stopped eating dairy
products; now, an occasional encounter with Brie or goat's cheese
reactivated them slightly, but he didn't mind, for he loved the
cheese.

By the summer of 1983, John was working fourteen hours a
day in a restaurant and living on fresh vegetables, whole grains,
pasta, fruit, and animal protein every day, with modest amounts
of coffee, beer, and wine thrown in for good measure. He felt
better than he'd ever felt during his three years on a healthy vegetarian regimen, a fact that we both found very interesting. It
was obvious to us that his body had not reacted well to such a
diet, although many other people thrive on it. "Perhaps it's because
I'm a Leo," he joked one day. "Lions are not known to be
vegetarians."

John's experience was a lesson for both of us about the fallacy
of being stuck in *any* single, strict food ideology. Interestingly,
though our marriage eventually faltered, we both changed and
widened our approach to food because of it. He found himself
using the information he'd picked up from me to help friends and
colleagues out of their own nutritional ruts, whether they had been
too heavy on the meat, or on the cheese, or on the fruit. I became,
I think, less rigid a "health nut." After I had practiced a mostly
vegetarian way of eating for over twenty years, the thought that
meat could make someone feel better and stronger was almost
heresy—unthinkable. But one day's heresy is another day's truth,
and so balance is achieved.

Elida's case is not unusual. There is a rapidly growing number
of people who are regaining their health through simple, natural
eating. They have decided to take charge of their own health and
life. They know that doctors and healers have their place as helpers

in serious conditions, in emergencies, or when home remedies don't work. But in many conditions, violent medical intervention resembles bailing water out of a leaking boat instead of fixing the leak, whereas a change in diet may indeed fix it.

John's case is also becoming more common, as people who have made a conscious dietary change to "health food" become stuck in dogma and stop listening to the signals of their own body. What I found necessary, therefore, was to come up with a unified theory of food and healing that would take into account *all* the dynamics of their interaction, a theory that can be used to adjust new data as it comes in and integrate it with the old.

That is what this book is all about. I have written it to share with you the theoretical principles of health-supportive eating that I've applied for over twenty years, and the practical tools based on them. The first part of the book, "Dynamics of Living Systems," lays out the principles, which are based as much on Eastern concepts as on Western logic; I have found, in my own life, that a combination of the two gives an amazing flexibility of response to problems. The second and third parts, "Food," and "Healing," show how those principles can be applied practically, in our daily lives, to help us in our continual quest to heal ourselves.

I firmly believe that theory is useless if it is not based on practice. But I have also found that it is not possible to find one set of principles that applies to, explains, and helps solve all situations. Therefore I will present you with several mental models, all of which work some of the time, but none of which, I think, works all of the time. For example, if according to the "scientific-nutritional" model it seems that a week of fasting would be harmful (because a person would apparently not get the full amount of nutrients such a model deems necessary), then we'd have to switch to the "natural healing" model to explain the fact that many people benefit greatly from just such a week. Or, to use a couple of models you'll encounter later in the book, from an expansive-contractive viewpoint it seems peculiar that people who eat a diet composed largely of fruit and vegetables also crave sweets (which many do). Both are expansive, and the idea is that if you eat too much expansive food, you'll crave its opposite, something contractive, such as miso or salt. Yet from an acid-alkaline viewpoint, this sugar craving makes perfect sense—fruits and vegetables are "alkalizing"; and when eaten in large quantities, they will create a craving for sugar and flour, which are "acid forming," and thus balancing. If we insisted on organizing our food choices strictly according to the model of contractive versus expansive foods, we would try to exercise our will power and refrain from eating sugar, a foodstuff now widely regarded as harmful; but if we take into account the concept of the acid and alkaline content of foods, and see that what is missing in our diet is some acid-forming food, then we can satisfy that need by eating more whole grains and dried beans, which are acid-forming but healthful, and thereby easily and harmlessly defuse our sugar craving.

One of the most important concepts I hope to put across is that *there is no one diet that is right for everyone all the time*. It is crucial that each person contemplating a change in diet monitor his or her own body's feedback, the feelings it emits of "okay" or "not okay." (You will find specific instructions on just how to go about such monitoring, and how to interpret the signals.) However, there still are some basic principles of healthy eating that I've found to be almost universally applicable; you will find those in the chapter entitled "The Health-Supportive Whole Foods Eating Style."

I have touched on a few of the principles in my cookbook, *The Book of Whole Meals*, which has met with a most gratifying response. The book presents a simple, yet quite tasty way of cooking healthfully, and from the reactions to it I have received over the five years it's been out, the approach seems to work. In that book I included a number of recipes that are good for healing purposes, but didn't identify them as such. I didn't discuss healing explicitly so as not to distract from the subject of cooking. Still, the underlying intent must shine through, because I've had countless requests from students and readers to elaborate on how food can be a healing tool, and I've proceeded to do that here.

You will find, in this book, as well as in my cookbook, that I suggest the use of some unfamiliar Oriental foodstuffs, such as miso, umeboshi plums, and kuzu. This is because I've become familiar with them through my study of macrobiotics and find them extremely helpful at times; also, I have found no foods with similar effects in our Western dietary tradition.

Even if you can not obtain all the foodstuffs I recommend, you can still apply most, if not all, of the basic dietary suggestions to your own life. I trust you will find, as I did, that with a solid grasp of the principles you can often find ways to balance yourself even without those foods that may be hard to get. You will also find, I hope, that with its principles well understood, the eating system I advocate in this book can be self-correcting. I believe that if we take our mistakes to be not punishment but good and valuable lessons, we can continously refine our cooking and our food choices, redefine our concepts of healing and diet, and thereby renew ourselves daily. Our greatest pitfall, in this as in all other matters, lies in thinking that we have arrived at the truth and that there is nowhere else to go.

The fourteen years that I've spent teaching and consulting with people have provided me with enough positive reinforcement to know that the approach I have developed works a great deal of the time. It is not foolproof, nor are the results universally guaranteed. But it is my fervent hope that this book will provide you with a new understanding of how food works, how your body works, and what steps you can take to keep yourself in physical and mental balance. And I hope especially that it will encourage you to keep developing your own judgment and consciousness, so that you can lay claim to your full potential as a truly evolved human being.

Part One:
DYNAMICS OF LIVING SYSTEMS

One:
Health Today

HOW ARE WE?

Unfortunately, not so well. Official reports on the condition of our health proclaim loudly that "Americans today are healthier than ever,"[1] but even a perfunctory glance at the statistics tables tells us differently. Although life-expectancy rates appear to have increased, that increase is deceptive: The child born today can expect to live twenty-six years longer than a child born in 1900, but the person who has already reached forty-five today can expect to live only four or five years longer than his counterpart did at the start of the century.[2] Moreover, during the past thirty years, mortality for the fifteen-to-twenty-four age group has increased fivefold, mostly because of traffic accidents, homicide, and suicide; it is still, unfortunately, on the rise.

And is a long life necessarily a healthier life? Childhood problems that were rare a generation ago are now so prevalent that they are called "the new morbidity"[3]: learning difficulties, behavioral disturbances, speech and hearing difficulties, faulty vision, serious dental misalignment. The average child loses three permanent teeth to decay by age eleven, eight or nine by age seventeen; and 94 percent of adolescents have cavities in their permanent teeth.

Dental diseases, especially caries and periodontal disease, constitute the most prevalent health problem in the nation. Ninety-eight percent of the population is affected, and over 19 million adults have lost all their teeth. Familiarity breeds contempt, so dental problems are generally considered "normal." Yet at least one dentist refers to tooth decay as a degenerative disease that may possibly be a precursor to diabetes.[4]

Equally severe is the incidence of acute respiratory illnesses: Each year, there are an estimated 200 to 250 million cases, and some 2.4 million people (10 percent of the population) contract pneumonia.

A few more facts: Acute gastroenteritis—inflammation of the stomach and intestines—follows colds in frequency of appearance; women are diagnosed and treated for 850,000 cases of pelvic inflammatory diseases yearly; and every year there may be as many as one million new cases of genital herpes, plus several million recurrences, as well as 120,000 cases of hepatitis and 18,000 of bacterial meningitis.

Tuberculosis may have long relinquished its place as one of the leading causes of death, but there were still over 27,000 cases in 1981, 1,900 of which were fatal. Among children, TB is on the rise. Other infectious diseases may take as many as 300,000 lives yearly. The most publicized and feared disorder of all, cancer, now takes an estimated one out of every five lives, or 20 percent of all deaths, up from a 5 percent mortality rate in 1900. In the mid-1980s it trails only accidents and violence as a killer of children and adolescents, a statistic not often noted. Major cardiovascular diseases are now the cause of 48 percent of all deaths, whereas in 1900 they caused only 18 percent. At least one quarter of the population suffers from elevated or high blood pressure.

Poor health does not manifest itself only in strictly physical illnesses. There are also close to 2 million admissions to mental hospitals each year. The Veterans' Administration estimates that in 1981 close to 2.5 million people sought out-patient treatment for mental and emotional problems. An additional 1.7 million were admitted as in-patients during the same year. At any given time, as much as a quarter of the population is estimated to suffer from depression, anxiety, or other emotional disorders. Manic-depressive conditions handicap an estimated 2 to 4 percent of adults at any given time. Suicide is the ninth leading cause of death for all age groups, and more than 80 percent of all suicide cases may be due to depression.

Violence, directed toward self or others, is a major component of life in the United States and a cause of much fear and trauma. Hundreds of thousands of violent nonfatal assaults occur yearly, including instances of spouse abuse and rape. The homicide rate in this country is much higher than that of any other industrialized nation: 10.2 cases for every 100,000 people (England's is 1.0, Japan's 1.3). And there may be as many as 4 million cases of child abuse every year, at least two thousand of which result in death. All this violence is no longer viewed as purely psychological. A growing body of research links mood, violent behavior, and even criminal behavior with various physiological imbalances: an over-active thyroid, an excess of testosterone (male hormones), allergies, low blood sugar. Lead poisoning, vitamin deficiencies, and of course alcohol and drugs all alter physiology as well as mood. Behavioral problems have even been associated with a lack of natural light, insofar as light plays a vital role in the metabolism of calcium, a mineral widely regarded as "nature's tranquilizer."[5]

HOW EFFECTIVE ARE OUR REMEDIES?

The general public has a one-sided impression of the effectiveness of modern medicine and its germ warfare. The popular belief, encouraged by the media, is that we owe the disappearance of major epidemics of infectious diseases to medical breakthroughs, whereas in fact, the death rate from infection had already begun to drop several decades before control measures inspired by the germ theory were put into effect, and almost a century before the introduction of antimicrobial drugs.[6] The incidence of cholera, diphtheria, dysentery, and typhoid declined after the introduction of clean water supplies, sewage control, general sanitation, and the pasteurization of milk. According to Thomas McKeown, professor emeritus of social medicine at the University of Birmingham, England, another reason for that downtrend was an increase in food supplies and the consequent host resistance as a result of better nutrition.[7]

Almost 90 percent of the total decline in children's mortality from diseases such as scarlet fever, diphtheria, whooping cough, and measles occurred before widespread use of antibiotics and compulsory immunizations. Diphtheria, for example, took the lives of 900 out of every million children in 1900, but only 220 by 1938—and national immunization didn't start until 1942. Scarlet fever declined from over 2,300 deaths per million children in 1860 to about 100 in 1918; but sulfa drugs didn't become available until the early thirties, and immunization didn't begin until the late sixties, by which time there were barely a dozen or so cases per million. Polio vaccine appears to be the only one to have effectively lowered the incidence of a disease: The year before the introduction of the vaccine, 1954, there were 38,476 cases of polio; the year after, 1956, there were 15,140, and the year after that, only 5,485.[8] However, a similar decrease of the incidence of this disease was observed in Europe, where no mass immunizations took place. Most of the current polio cases occur in people who have been immunized.[9] Admittedly, this a highly controversial issue. Parents who immunize their children do so in the belief that they're protecting them; most scientists believe just that. It will be a while before history sorts out the facts from the myths. Meanwhile, it behooves us to keep an open mind and to explore more fully the role of nutrition in disease prevention.

It's a sad fact that despite the full-fledged war on cancer with drastic remedies such as surgery, radiation, and chemotherapy, survival rates for 90 percent of the cancer cases have not improved during the past twenty-five years. Survival rates for breast cancer, for example, were at 50 percent in a 1963 study regardless of therapies, treatments, or checkups; untreated women, interestingly enough, fared no worse than treated women. In 1979, Maurice Fot, Ph.D., of MIT, determined that 40 percent of breast cancer victims died regardless of treatment; 60 percent showed a mortality rate "only modestly different from that of women of a similar age without evidence of disease."[10]

Technically, modern medical practice is of a sophistication unequaled in history, and modern medicine's greatest accomplishments are technical ones, involving the manipulation of the mechanics of the body: orthopedics, treatment of burns, cesarean section in cases of fibroids or faulty pelvic structure, resuscitation, microsurgery to attach severed limbs, heart-valve replacements, and similar extraordinary feats. Keeping someone alive through open-heart surgery is little short of working a miracle.

Yet there is another side to the coin, and even the tremendous advances in science carry a high price. "Above all, do no harm" was the earnest humanitarian injunction given to doctors by Hippocrates; unfortunately, with the best of intentions, things have turned out so that modern technical medical intervention produces an astonishing amount of pain, dysfunction, disability, and anguish. Iatrogenic (doctor-caused) disease is the most rapidly spreading epidemic of the twentieth century; its victims are more numerous than those of traffic and industrial accidents, and perhaps even those of war-related activities. As a final irony, it costs money to be made sick by medicine.[11]

Consider: Over 2 million infections a year develop in patient-care institutions (hospitals), resulting in sixty to eighty thousand deaths. An estimated 2.5 million operations a year are performed without real medical need, resulting in some twelve thousand needless deaths under the surgeon's knife.[12] Hospitals can be dangerous places: Nearly everybody has a friends or relatives who went in for "tests" and came out much sicker than when they went in.

Trying to cure our ills, we also take some $19 billion worth of drugs each year—an expensive river of chemicals coursing through our national veins. Many of these drugs are dangerous, and many are not even effective in curing the condition for which they were prescribed.

In one study, over six hundred commonly prescribed drugs in use for more than twenty years have been found to be *ineffective*—never proven effective by properly controlled studies. Ineffective drugs are invariably harmful, as there are no benefits to outweigh the inevitable side effects.[13] Over 1 million people a year (3 to 5 percent of admissions) land in hospitals as a result of negative reactions to drugs. Tranquilizers—we take some 5 billion pills a year—bring overdosed users to hospital emergency rooms twice as often as do heroin and cocaine.

Even though by now it is popular knowledge that X rays may cause cancer, over 300 million of them are ordered yearly *without medical need*. Radiation from diagnostic X rays is implicated in cancer, blood disorders, tumors of the central nervous system, diabetes, stroke, and cataracts.

To discover the nature of our ailments, doctors send our body fluids and tissues to be looked at in specialized laboratories. But lab tests are notoriously unreliable, perhaps because of the unreliability of human perceptions: Fifty percent of laboratories licensed to perform tests for Medicare work failed in a test of the accuracy of their analyses. Therefore, thousands of people are told they are healthy when in fact they are not. Conversely, thousands of people are told that they're sick on the basis of erroneous laboratory reports; this in turn leads them to undergo unnecessary and often harmful treatment. In fact, some critics consider medical treatment of nonexistent diseases to be a major medical problem.[14] Perhaps the solution is closer than we think: In one study, 197 out of 200 people were "cured" simply by having another test done!

WHAT ARE THE LIMITATIONS OF MODERN MEDICINE?

Medical people themselves are the first to admit that the system has severe limitations. Any medical system has them; but ours seem to be particularly galling. Modern medicine is extraordinarily adept at patching people up once they're already sick; but its ability to *ensure health* is far from satisfactory.

What is it that is wrong with our medical system? One critic maintains that the problem is not the system itself, but the way in which it presents itself as the only or most effective way to treat sickness.[15] There are disorders for which the technology of modern medicine is invaluable; however, there are many others about which present medical knowledge is at a loss. Yet the prevailing attitude is, "If the doctor doesn't know, nobody else could possibly know either."

Medical practices, it is important to remember, are based on and reflect the general attitudes and beliefs of a given society. The doctor may prescribe a pill that doesn't work, but more often than not the patient asks for it—and if it's not given, the patient may become upset, feel neglected, or simply go to another doctor who will obligingly provide the pill.

Therefore, perhaps we should also ask: What is wrong with our contemporary assumptions about health and illness? It may be more revealing to examine them, rather than just the specifics of modern medical practice. I see three major errors in our belief system:

- The belief that physiological symptoms (headaches, fevers, pimples, and so on) are erroneous reactions of the body to normal stimuli.
- The belief that surgical intervention or chemical substances, whether of natural or artificial origin, can restore health by interrupting the process called "disease."
- The belief that dietary habits are unrelated to symptoms or illnesses. This belief is now in the process of being abandoned, yet I list it here because it still is held by many—for

example, by people who buy antacids for stomach distress, creams for pimples, or antihypertensive medication without at the same time changing their diet.

The most glaring error in our belief system, it seems to me, is the first: the assumption that physiological "symptoms" (headaches, sneezing, fatigue, pimples, stomachaches, backaches, and all the rest) are mistakes, that they should be corrected or "treated," and that if this is not done, things will get worse. In short, that the physical system will deteriorate *unless we intervene*. In our technologically advanced times, intervention is done with highly sophisticated technology: drugs that alter physiology and function, suppress sensation, or speed up reactions; and surgery of an increasingly complicated nature.

Consider this scenario: A man gets a stomachache after each meal. To "treat" this problem, he takes (either by prescription or by self-medication) some antacid or other nostrum. Then he gets a headache (which may or may not be a side effect of the stomach medication); to "treat" the headache he takes aspirin, which further irritates his stomach. Three years later he develops an ulcer, for which he takes another medication, plus large amounts of milk and cream (although an outmoded treatment, it is still being used today). Meanwhile, he is still taking antacids for his indigestion and eating the same way he always had. Eventually, he has an operation to remove his ulcer. He continues with his high-dairy diet. Soon thereafter he develops arteriosclerosis and high blood pressure and begins to take antihypertensive medication. The side effects of the latter include headaches, dizziness, drowsiness, diarrhea, slow heart rate, mental confusion, hallucinations, weight gain, and impotence. When his wife leaves him for a younger man, he takes antidepressants and sleeping pills. He has a heart attack and undergoes an operation to repair a heart valve. Painkillers keep him going as he slowly recuperates. A year or two later, he finds himself with an irreversible neurological disease such as ALS or Alzheimer's, and he wonders what could have gone wrong. All that's left for him to do is wait to die, which he can do in a nursing home, drugged into complaisance and painlessness.

Now let's backtrack and see what results a different approach could have produced. The underlying assumptions this time will be that symptoms are warning signals and that the body will heal itself under the direction of the immune system if we just get out of the way. When the stomachache hits the first time, the man skips the next meal, drinks some hot broth or peppermint tea, and waits till he feels fully recuperated before putting his stomach to work again. When the stomachache recurs, the man follows the same procedure; this time, however, he also takes inventory of his meals and tries to pinpoint which of the foods consumed caused his body to protest. If he thinks that it was probably the cheeseburger and ice cream, then he tries not eating them for a while to prevent further protest demonstrations. If he's right, and he gets a stomachache only whenever he has either of those foods, he conscientiously begins to avoid them.

As he is not taking antacids, he also prevents headaches—or whatever other side effects those pills may produce. But whenever he does get a headache, instead of masking it with medication, he tries to determine its cause. Let's say he finds a correlation between eating fatty meats and the onset of headaches. Therefore, he avoids cheeseburgers, cheese, and cold cuts and finds himself headache-free most of the time.

As he has no headaches and takes no aspirins, his stomach feels relaxed, and the likelihood of an ulcer is greatly diminished. Because he is on a low-fat diet, his chances of a heart attack are also reduced. Because he feels good, his sex life is satisfactory and his wife stays with him. It's more than likely that he will go through old age with a minimum of infirmities and deterioration. He lives happily until eventually he dies peacefully, in his sleep, well past three score and ten.

In the first scenario, the stomachache was treated as if the body had committed an error by having it: The intent of the treatment was to eliminate the sensation. In the second case, the stomachache was treated as if it were information about conditions in the body: The information was that there was an error in the feeding pattern, and the treatment consisted in correcting that error. When we consider the stomachache itself an error, we get medicine very different from what we get when we consider it a warning signal and search for its cause.

The first approach, that of modern Western society and medicine, isolates the symptom and divorces it from its human context. Such an approach has been in use only a relatively short time—two hundred years or so, since the Age of Reason and the scientific revolution. The core question asked by this mode of treatment is, "How can we eliminate the disturbance?" The second approach, which places the symptom within a total mind-body context, has been and is prevalent in most traditional medical systems. The core question it asks is, "What is the cause of the disturbance, and how can we alter the conditions so as to prevent further disturbances?" Depending on the social belief system, the answer can be bad food, bad thoughts, evil spirits, stress, poisons, and so on and so forth; and the treatments can be fasting, emetics, exorcism, rest, herbs, or any other traditional practices.

In the modern Western belief system, physiological symptoms are isolated phenomena, essentially meaningless and random. "It could have happened to anyone" is the consoling, guilt-absolving response. The sick one is a victim, not responsible for the state of his health. The alternate—and more traditional—approach, on the other hand, sees symptoms as expressions of the condition of the entire body, and thereby meaningful insofar as they carry indirect information. The message is that we've made a mistake, somewhere, and that we're paying for it with this particular symptom; the other side of that guilt-inducing thought is that just as we did something wrong, we can undo it. The sick one is in charge of the situation; health professionals, of any persuasion, are only his helpers and co-workers.

The second glaring error, I feel, in our assumptions about health and illness, is the notion that substances isolated from their natural context can promote healing. Many people believe that synthesized chemicals have the ability to sustain health. This makes no sense. Life can only be created by life; health only comes from an integration of our various levels of function—not from the intake of manufactured pills and potions. Drugs and medications do not heal the gaps in our health. They only interrupt the various natural processes that are often erroneously perceived as noxious, or "sickness." And they *all have side effects*, which at times are as bad as or worse than the original problem.

It is my profound conviction that a great many of our more serious health problems today stem not only from bad food or pollution, but also from the chemical treatment of minor physiological adjustments. I also include here the extensive use of antibiotics and immunizations, both of which meddle with the immune system. Unfortunately, diseases involving malfunctions or over-reactions of the immune system are turning into a veritable epidemic. They include such "common" ailments as allergies, asthma, and hay fever, as well as multiple sclerosis, lupus, Alzheimer's, ALS (Lou Gehrig's disease), AIDS, and cancer. As a large majority of our population has been subjected to both antibiotics and immunizations, it may be time to scrutinize that practice more closely.

Until recently, a third major error in our approach to health and illness was the belief that food had very little, if anything, to do with the state of our health. The stomachache was seen as an erroneous reaction to proper food, instead of a normal reaction to improper food. Furthermore, the idea that an improper diet might have something to do with headaches, fevers, skin eruptions, liver ailments, or cancer was considered totally outlandish. Little by little, this belief is now being challenged and changed. The American Heart Association has made a strong recommendation for heart patients to change their diets, and the idea that improper diet could be one of the causes of cancer is now widely accepted.

Still, the scientific understanding of the effect of food on health remains limited. Food is viewed most of the time only in terms of its nutrient content: It is "low-fat," or "low-salt," or "low-calorie." Dietary recommendations of modern nutritional science often run along the lines of "Eat X amount of calories, Z grams of protein, and less sodium and fat." If one takes all this seriously, it becomes necessary to cook dinner with the recipe book on one side and tables of food composition on the other. Not only is this far removed from the realities of the kitchen, but, as you will see in this book, the world of food and its effects on our health is infinitely more complex and interesting than that. I believe that it is an area of knowledge that, if incorporated into our medical system, can be extremely helpful to us all. Using food to stay well is a safe, effective, and generally inexpensive practice. As the costs of medical care increase, dietary management as a cost-effective alternative will become more and more attractive. Before we can do that, however, we have to reorient our understanding about the human organism, and what makes it healthy and unhealthy.

Two:
A New World View

Our civilization rests on a faulty premise, that the world is physical and mechanical, energy and matter only. We do not pay for it in our bridges, we pay for it in the quality of our lives.
— Richard Grossinger, *Planet Medicine*

In our therapies of the future, we may deal with systems rather than with organs. —Arthur Guirdham, *A Theory of Disease*

HOLISM

It has become increasingly obvious that our exciting modern life-style has made us very unhealthy. We are also coming to realize that the technical and chemical medicine developed to treat our health problems is not only often ineffective, but has many drawbacks as well. As a result, a countermovement has arisen out of our discontent, a healing movement loosely termed "wholism," or "holism," which in turn has given us "holistic medicine" and "holistic health."

A holistic view of the human body recognizes that its function is affected by a variety of factors, both internal and external, such as food, drink, exercise, emotions, stress, and so on. It recognizes that disease symptoms express a total condition of the organism. Our individual body parts are all components of an integrated physical being who also exists on social, emotional, and spiritual levels; people are part of families, tribes, societies. In terms of illness, a weakness in the heart expresses a weakness of the other organs;

an infection in a finger means a polluted condition throughout; and improved nutrition and a tonifying of the whole body will automatically lead to the healing of many different symptoms. A holistic viewpoint also considers that organ transplants can create strange and unforeseen consequences, including weaknesses in apparently unrelated organs. For example, Dr. Bernard Kornfeld, the first artificial-heart-transplant patient, did fine with his artificial heart—but died of pneumonia. From a holistic viewpoint, the removal of the heart created a general systemic weakness, which manifested itself in the fatal illness.

Modern Western medicine is generally based on the mechanistic, Newtonian view of the universe. More often than not it treats the organism as if it were a machine, recognizing mostly isolated symptoms, isolated body parts, isolated people. A weakness in the heart must be treated with drugs or surgery, infections are to be stopped with antibiotics, and improved nutrition will mostly mean weight control. Organ transplants, in this view, seem to be a perfectly rational way of dealing with malfunctions, as only the organ itself is considered sick, and the rest of the body is seen as functioning more or less normally. Dr. Kornfeld's pneumonia, in this viewpoint, was unrelated to the absence of his real heart.

The holistic viewpoint is not a new one. In fact, it has been around since the dawn of history. It is, even now, the prevalent philsophy in all societies except our own and those we've influenced. But I imply no criticism: Western thought has taken a detour through materialism, studying and analyzing the components of matter for the past three or four centuries, and has learned an enormous amount of fascinating and useful details about it. Much as holism can fail to be useful because of a lack of attention to detail, so materialism has its dangers of nearsightedness, of missing the forest for the trees. We now live in a time when the realistic insights of holism can be supported and validated by scientific studies; conversely, scientific analysis can be validated by its relevance in the context of daily experience. The time has come, undoubtedly, for a synthesis, for making whole—for healing.

True healing begins with awareness: awareness of self, first of all, to discover how we function. With awareness comes responsibility. We are the cause of our illness and can therefore be actively responsible for our own healing. True healing is not just getting rid of a headache—we can do that very simply with aspirin. It means discovering why we have a headache in the first place, how to disperse it without causing harm elsewhere—aspirin cures the headache and hurts the stomach, an exchange that has its draw-backs—and how to avoid headaches in the future.

To live up to our responsibility, we need information, both theo-retical and practical, to help us decide what to do. Let's begin by discussing the larger underlying concepts and then narrow the discussion to specific and personal areas of concern.

First, the systems theory of how our body works. It is the sci-entific support for, the validation of, holism. We need to under-stand it fully in order to practice the holistic approach to health effectively.

LIVING SYSTEMS

Concepts of how our body works changed when doctors started getting their metaphors from the work of mechanics and craftsmen with the onset of the Industrial Revolution. "The heart could be seen as a pump only when such engines began to be widely ex-ploited in sixteenth-century mining, fire-fighting, and civil engi-neering," writes Jonathan Miller.[1]

Seeing the body in terms of its mechanical functions came to be considered a much more sensible and practical approach than believing it was swayed by humors, vapors, and evil spirits. An-chored in concreteness, from the seventeenth century onward, medical knowledge advanced in great strides. With the discovery of microorganisms, the picture seemed complete: The body was a machine, run by certain inner energy, which could break down due either to external agents (toxic substances or microorganisms) or to unexplained internal malfunctions.

But the physical sciences have advanced far beyond the simple mechanics of the sixteenth and seventeenth centuries. Most of medicine, on the other hand, is still stuck in the old concept of the body as a system of pumps and pulleys, pipes and fluids. When a link is discovered between two events heretofore viewed as un-related (food and mood, for example), the cry of the scientific community is, "But what is the *mechanism*?" Although the alliance of medicine with Newtonian physics has given us a broad under-standing of how we function, it is no longer sufficient to give us all the answers we need. Not everything can be explained in mecha-nistic terms (for example, why are certain foods related with certain moods in some people and not in others?). For this reason, increasing numbers of people are rejecting mechanistic medicine as they embrace a still broader, more holistic vision. Modern physics, always on the forefront, offers several elementary concepts to support that vision; we can apply these toward building a more satisfactory model of how our bodies really work.

Thanks to precise and powerful aids to perception, such as the electron microscope and particle accelerators, physicists are finding out what mystics always knew: that the universe is more than the sum of its parts,[2] and that reality is a complex web of relationships. Analyzing its parts is not enough to grasp it. To help us understand it better, a new approach has evolved: systems theory. According to Fritjof Capra, it is an effort to describe wholes in terms of the relationships between their parts rather than in terms of the parts themselves,[3] and living systems are described as patterns of organization.

Systems theory is supported by systems analysis, which consists, to put it simply, in describing and understanding how a system works. Any set of interacting events, things, or phenomena can be a system if it has *input*, *output*, and *purpose*. In order to make sense out of its complexity, we have to build a simplified model of the system, selecting only those details we need for clarity. This can be done with an actual small-scale model in the case of man-made systems, or it can be done mentally or with charts.* As the model of the system is tested it should be continuously corrected by experience, so that it will conform as closely to reality and need as possible.

Once we understand it, we should be able to explain the system's past behavior so that it makes sense or predict its future behavior with a reasonable degree of accuracy. If our model for the system conforms to the *actual reality* of the system, our explanations will be clear and our predictions accurate. If our model happens to be insufficient or incorrect, our predictions and explanations will also be wrong, or insufficient.

Living systems can be thought of as showing four specific characteristics:[5]

- *Wholeness and order*. It is more than the sum of its parts, and the relationships between the parts more than the parts themselves determine the behavior of the system. For instance, a

---

* The construction of mental models is a technique well known and much used in the social sciences as well. Max Weber, for example, formulated his "ideal type" as a "construct of accentuated characteristics abstracted from the subject to be studied."[4]

human being can continue to function without some parts (appendix or gall bladder, for example).

- *Adaptive Self-Stabilization.* Environmental disturbances will elicit reactions from the system that attempt to return it to normal. For instance, dust will provoke a sneeze.
- *Adaptive Self-Organization.* A constant disturbance to the system will cause it to attempt to reorganize itself so as to adapt to the interference. For instance, constant noises cease to be heard.
- *Intra- and Inter-Systemic Hierarchies.* Organisms are made up of systems of lesser complexity (for example, organs, cells) and are part of larger systems of higher complexity (for example, families, tribes, nations).

Living systems are extremely complex because they consist of other systems. All higher animals, for example, include within their bodies the digestive, excretory, respiratory, reproductive, circulatory, nervous, and endocrine systems. Not only that, it is often almost impossible to draw the exact boundaries between one system and another or between one system and its environment. The digestive, excretory, respiratory, and reproductive systems, for example, intimately connect the larger system that is the body to the outside environment.

Furthermore, living systems are unstable. They are constantly exchanging energy and matter with their environment. As a general rule, they are characterized by a strong tendency to return to "normal," to a "steady state" or *balance.* But they can also be affected by input and disturbances in unpredictable ways. Disturbances, or "perturbations," when they reach a certain intensity, may trigger changes in a self-organizing living system that amount to a total reorganization.[6] Some examples: near-death experiences that totally change a person's life; drastic changes in diet that provide a dramatic new viewpoint; amino acids organizing themselves into living muscle tissue. The reorganization, incidentally, generally goes in the direction of higher order, coherence, and complexity—the opposite, in fact, of entropy, or disintegration and decay. Understanding this progression, we can begin to view stress and trouble as friendly forces, rather than destructive ones, because it is through difficulties that we have the opportunity to evolve into higher states of consciousness.

The body, then, is an organism in which many things happen at once, intertwined in such a fashion that it is difficult to determine what starts what, or which function comes after which other. In the context of a discussion of food and healing, the systems model can give us a wholly new perspective.

DISTURBANCES
(environmental chemicals, stressful influences, lifestyle disruptions, accidents, pollution, poisons, wrong or unnecessary medications, etc.)

INPUT
(air, water, food, cosmic vibrations, sound, light, touch, talk, etc.)

OUTPUT
(breath, urine, feces, speech, laughter, tears, screams, motion, work, art, etc.)

Curiously enough, although we live inside our bodies and must deal with them twenty-four hours a day, we know less about ourselves than we do about the external world. Our senses are directed outward; we have very few sensory nerves connected to the major organs that support our life, and consequently we are unaware of all the activity within. Mostly we have generalized feelings and localized pains, and sometimes vague hunches. But in order to function better, we do need to know how we function, and for that, we must perfect our conceptual model.

There are several models of the human system that try to explain how it works, from the most arcane to the most narrowly scientific. Modern medicine tends to view what goes on inside that system as would an engineer, still somehow underestimating all the factors that influence it and the complexity of those influences and interactions. The model prevalent in orthodox medical thought includes the following basic assumptions:

- The human system works correctly unless an abnormality can be detected by an observer; that is, if nothing shows in the tests, there is no malfunction, even if the patient doesn't feel right.
- Most malfunctions of the system are due to physical agents—microorganisms, poisons, pollution. Cures are effected by

destroying the pathogenic agent or removing the diseased organ or tissue. Diseases not caused by physical agents may be due to psychological factors, which are not real. Some of these factors are now acknowledged to have a physical basis in brain biochemistry, in the interactions of neurotransmitters; thus they have, so to speak, gained credibility.

- A disease will usually grow worse unless medical treatment is applied. (This assumption is often more widely held by the patient than by the doctor.) When a disease heals naturally, without intervention, it is thought of as exceptional and labeled "self-limiting" or a "spontaneous remission."
- The symptoms *are* the disease; symptoms appearing in different organs are generally not related.
- Any disease or malfunction not due to physical or visible disturbances is of "unknown origin." Psychosomatic illness is an accepted category. The reverse, a physical disturbance that affects mental or emotional functioning, is rarely considered.
- Any cure of a major disease that occurs without official medical intervention is considered "spontaneous remission," or acausal.
- The major input in the human health disease system is that of pathogenic or disease-causing elements or organisms. Food input is only indirectly related to the system's functioning.
- In the cases in which food input *does* matter, it is mostly because of erroneous quantity (too much or too little).
- The effects of the natural environment on the human system are negligible.

The holistic model of how the human system functions might include the following principles:

- Each human being has a general sense of whether his or her system is in good working order. The sense that something is wrong is usually correct.
- Malfunctions of the organism can stem from physical, psychological, or spiritual events. Cures are effected by finding the underlying cause and correcting it; the immune system takes over from there. The physical and the nonphysical are equally real.

- A healthy organism will tend to correct its own minor imbalances if allowed to do so; medical treatment may often interfere with that self-healing ability.
- Symptoms are a message from the body about its condition and its function. The same condition may give rise to symptoms of different kinds: conversely, different conditions may cause similar symptoms.
- Cures of major diseases may occur because the immune system is sufficiently strong, perhaps supported by a change in diet or by psychological or spiritual renewal.
- Food is a direct cause of the proper or improper functioning of the organism.
- Quality, quantity, stored energy, taste, color, aroma, and texture of food all have physiological and psychological effects on the organism.
- The organism reacts to and interacts with its natural environment; climate, season, altitude, and weather all affect it.

There are of course many more details in both these models; they will vary with each individual patient, doctor, healer, or diagnostician. As we consider how that interrelationship of systems that is our body functions, we must remember also that nobody exists in a vacuum. We are part of our environment, the earth, the whole universe, as is any other natural being. There are certain laws of nature that apply to us as much as they do to stones, trees, lions, and stars.

I'm referring here to something other than the basic laws of gravity and motion: to philosophical laws, encompassing all natural phenomena, that were discovered and formulated thousands of years ago and incorporated into the world's major philosophical and religious systems, including Buddhism, the Cabala, and Hermetic philosophy. These laws are so basic that they are currently considered self-evident, and thereby dismissible. However, since they organize our perceptions of reality in a coherent and holistic manner, they are definitely worth retrieving. Although these laws do not refer directly to our concerns regarding health and the body, they do apply indirectly, for they will help us understand our inner workings.

Here, then, are seven universal laws of how things work; I have culled them from Eastern and Western philosophy, and modernized them for our practical understanding:

- *Everything is one:* Everything is connected, directly or indirectly; there are no isolated phenomena, only systems that connect into larger and smaller systems. Body and mind, then, are closely interrelated.
- *Everything changes:* Nothing remains static. Energy moves constantly, within and among systems. Thus, the diet that heals us must change as we change.
- *"As above, so below; as below, so above."* There is a basic correspondence between the phenomena of life that allows us to extrapolate what we learn in one area to the mysteries of another. For example, simple geometry helps us measure distant stars; polling a few we learn the thoughts of many.
- *Everything has an opposite:* Also, everything has a front and a back. Opposites are complementary, connected like two ends of a stick or two sides of a coin, and separated by degrees. Opposites may change into one another, and often do, either gradually or suddenly.
- *Energy moves in a pendulum swing, between opposites:* All motion is the result of expansion and contraction, to and fro, in rhythmic alternation. When the swing arrives at its extreme position, it reverses direction and heads the opposite way. Day turns to night, winter into summer, the in-breath into the out-breath. The pendulum doesn't swing back to its exact departure point, but slightly off, as spirals do.
- *There are no accidents:* Every event or phenomenon has a cause, a reason for its existence. Labeling anything as a "chance happening," resulting from either randomness, coincidence, or luck, merely exposes our ignorance of the interrelationships that brought it about.
- *Magnetism manifests itself on all levels:* Opposites attract, likes repel everywhere. But also, "like attracts like" insofar as they belong to the same category, yet are of different degree. Consider hierarchies with chief and underlings, such as a flock of birds, a pack of wolves, a business corporation.[7]

Keep this set of universal laws in the back of your mind. I will refer to them regularly throughout the book, to clarify or emphasize certain points. It is not necessary to believe that these concepts are literally true. Since we're working on the construction of a mental model, we include as relevant those concepts that appear plausible, that make sense, that are "possibly true." As we test them against reality, we'll use them *as if* they were true, and every instance in which they hold up will be a small step toward confirmation. Testing concepts in this manner will keep us from losing face if they turn out to be erroneous; believing something to be *absolutely true* is the mark of the "true believer" and the fanatic, who remains inflexible and unable to adapt to error, change, and new possibilities. These laws are helpful in seeing the interconnectedness and continuity in all things—a notion central to the systems approach to health and healing.

ENERGY FIELDS

We've talked about systems, about interconnectedness, about "wholes"—but what about that mysterious "more" that differentiates a whole from the sum of its parts? Many theorists have attempted to answer that question. I would like to present those ideas that I personally have found most intriguing and helpful.

Sometime in the late 1920s, Harold Saxton Burr, Ph.D., professor of anatomy at Yale University School of Medicine, began to study the electric properties of living organisms. In 1932 he published his first paper on the "electrodynamic theory of development." Three years later, with F. S. C. Northrop, he published "The Electro-Dynamic Theory of Life" in the *Quarterly Review of Biology*. During the following twenty-one years he would see another fifty-eight of his own papers on that subject published in the most prestigious science journals in the country.[8]

What Dr. Burr demonstrated, through the use of highly sensitive instruments, is that plants, animals, and human beings possess electromagnetic force fields, or energy fields. These fields both determine and are determined by the form and condition of the organism to which they belong. Apparently, it is also this field that is responsible for keeping the organism recognizably "itself," regardless of floating electrons or constant cellular turnover.

More recently, British biochemist Rupert Sheldrake, Ph.D., consultant plant physiologist at the International Research Institute in India, shook the scientific community with a new idea: He postulated the existence of a field that determines the *form* of living systems before they actually grow the material parts comprising it. Sheldrake calls that the morphogenetic field, which is not to be confused with an electric field. It depends on form, not electrical charge, although it does have an actual effect—it can be "tuned into"—through both time and space.[9]

There is nothing mystical about this energy field, even though it might indeed be related to the halo traditionally depicted around the heads of saints. In fact, voltmeters can measure it at the surface of the organism, as well as at a short distance from the surface. It can also be detected by a photographic process called Kirlian photography. And some people (more than you'd think!) are actually able to see this field; they call it the aura. My daughter was able to do this when she was in kindergarten and drew some wonderful portaits of me with green and, to my chagrin, even red halos.

Whatever they sense, voltmeters, Kirlian photographs, and aura readers all agree on one crucial point: The force field *fluctuates*. It is never static. It becomes weaker or stronger, brighter or duller, larger or smaller. These changes both reflect and are reflected by the condition of the force field's corresponding organism. This is as true for trees and flowers as it is for dogs and people.

With this and all the preceding information in mind, we can arrive at a loose definition of a whole living organism, or system: It is an aggregate of physical elements and parts, *plus* an organizing energy field that makes the separate parts cohere and establishes them as a system. What influences the force field of an organism to change? To a greater or lesser degree, everything. One of the laws of nature, as we've seen, is that "everything changes," and we know that living organisms change faster than anything. Not only do they undergo roughly predictable large cycles (birth, growth, decay), as well as smaller ones (respiration, digestion, sleep), but they are also changed by the continuous movement of their component parts and elements. The energy field is influenced by these inner fluctuations and influences them in turn; where the changing starts, and where it stops, is impossible to say.

The energy field of an organism is also influenced by external factors: food, light, wind, temperature, atmospheric pressure, cosmic rays, and so on. (This is not a one-way street, however. Changes have been measured in the earth's magnetic field that we've caused by the blinking of an eye.[10]) Everything, then, has an influence on us, on our energy field, either subtle or obvious. We can dismiss some influences as not important; others, especially if bothersome, we may want to investigate further. And as our own energy field is influenced by food, it's worth our time to explore what in turn influences food's energy field, and how.

Things that we didn't think made much difference—such as cooking methods or the freezing of foods—may turn out to have, as I hope to show you, a dramatic influence on us. Nonquantifiable properties of food, accessible to our senses and our intuition, though not to our science, can spell the difference between illness and health.

It's up to us, then, to become aware of these subtle influences so as to make positive choices toward healing. What I propose to explore now, and in the remainder of this book, are the various ways in which food as a system influences the human system. It's a model I have been using and refining for the past twenty-five years, and I have found it to be highly responsive and useful for describing, explaining, initiating, and predicting changes in health. By no means is this model the only one that works, nor is it complete or foolproof; much more correcting and refining needs to be done. But it is a helpful tool, and I hope you will be able to put it to work for you.

THE LIFE FORCE IN FOODS

The mechanistic worldview describes food in terms of its chemical components—proteins, carbohydrates, fats, minerals, vitamins. The systems view, based on science and on the holism of our everyday sensory experience, sees food in terms of its relationships—context, properties, effects, taste, aroma, origin, direction of growth, color, texture—as well as its chemical properties. One viewpoint does not negate the other; it is like looking on the world with two eyes, where one eye sees things slightly differently from the other. When we put both viewpoints together, we get three-dimensional vision.

We can see, then, that the outer and inner environments of a living system, or organism, are linked by food. Food is the external internalized, and the qualities of the food consumed will invariably have an influence on the condition of the organism. But what is food if not other organisms—plants or animals—that were once alive?

Insofar as plants and animals are themselves living systems, when they are used as food they still have some of their original qualities as systems. That is, they are an aggregate of physical elements plus an energy field. Live plants and cut plants of course don't have exactly the same type of energy field; the more time that elapses from the moment of cutting, the more the field of the cut plant changes, until eventually it disintegrates and the plant itself decays.

It seems to me a reasonable possibility that we derive nourishment not only from the macro- and micro-nutrients in foods, but from their energy fields as well. Just as the physical nutrients nourish our physical body, the subtle energy of foodstuffs (bio-energy, force fields, chi, ki, prana, name it what you will) nourishes our own energy field. If we accept this hypothesis as part of our working model, then we must pay at least as much attention to the bio-energy (or force field) in foods as to their nutrient composition.

I have applied this viewpoint for many years now and have found it to be a very helpful one. It explains why canned or frozen food, for example, even if it contains most of the nutrients present in fresh foods, still feels neither as healthful nor as satisfying. It's impossible to be a healthy vegetarian on frozen potatoes and canned peas.

The systems view also supports the notion that it is healthier—or less stressful—to eat locally grown and seasonal foods whenever possible. As our link with the external environment, food harmonizes us with that larger system. Foods imported from faraway places or other climates will tend to connect us with the energy of their environment of origin. Thus a tropical fruit connects us with the tropics: eating pineapples in New York in the winter would prepare us for sun and heat by cooling us off, thereby creating the desire to take a trip to Hawaii. Many a conscientious fruitarian has found our Northern winters extremely hard to take.

The most obvious variables that affect the energy fields of foodstuffs (and hence those of people who consume the foodstuffs) are fragmentation, temperature, methods of preservation, chemical additives, and irradiation. Let's take a look at each of these.

Whole Food and Fragmented Food

As mentioned earlier, in the systems approach we work with the concept of wholes and with the idea that parts of living systems are also in themselves smaller systems, or wholes, with their own energy fields. Living systems "tend to form multileveled structures of systems within systems."[11] In the ecosystem, the living creatures that comprise it are designed to subsist by consuming what the environment provides. We humans are integral parts of this system and are bound by its rules; we are built to breathe the air, drink the water, eat the plants and the animals. Through this energy exchange with our environment, we keep our own systems in a more or less steady state.

If, however, instead of eating a vegetable in the shape in which it grows, we consume it in fragmented form, its separate components split apart, we are not following the natural scheme of things. When we consume wheat germ, white flour, and bran separately, it is not the same as eating them in their natural, integrated, and properly balanced state as whole wheat. In the first case we don't interact with the natural system; in the second case we do.

This, then, is the major difference between whole foods and partial or fragmented foods. Whole foods are simply fresh, natural, edible things, as close to their natural state as possible: fruits, fresh vegetables, unrefined cereal grains, beans, nuts, seeds, sea vegetables. Animals can be eaten whole by one person at one sitting if they're small enough (smelts, oysters, sardines, soft-shell crabs, small fowl), or by a whole group or tribe over a few days' time, as is done by hunting communities. Whole foods provide not only certain amounts of basic nutrients in the natural proportion to each other; the nutrients in them are also bound together by that subtle energy that animates all living systems. Whole foods, then, give us not only nutrition, but energy—"wholesomeness," that is.

Partial, or fragmented foods are often called "refined," as if stripping foods of some of their coarser elements makes them more worthy of attention and respect. Partial foods include all those split up at the cellular level; the most commonly used are white flour, white rice, and sugar. These "foods" have all been separated from other parts of their original plant—bran, germ, water, pulp. Current understanding is that they are not quite "wholesome," which is literally correct.

Certain other foods that are generally considered "wholesome," or healthful, are in fact not whole: wheat germ, bran, molasses, juice, skim milk, butter, decaffeinated coffee, gluten-free wheat flour, and even the hallowed tofu (soybean curd). Meat is also not "whole," for it represents only the muscle of an animal; bones are left behind. Oils and fats, essential or nonessential, are partial foods; and vitamin supplements, regardless of their sources, are so, too.

Nature—our nature—abhors an imbalance. If we consume small amounts of partial foods (white flour or sugar), we can counterbalance them with small amounts of other partial foods (wheat germ or meat). But the higher the amounts of these foods in our daily diet, the wider the swing of the pendulum: The more un-balanced substances we have to compensate for, the stronger will be our feeling of uncenteredness.

As an illustration of our natural tendency to return to center, or wholeness, consider the curious saga of wheat consumption. First, a hundred or so years ago, it was discovered that stripping the bran and germ off the wheat made the flour not only whiter and fluffier, but also longer-lasting; soon, we were eating white bread. Then, early in this century, food-conscious people such as Sylvester Graham found that the discarded wheat germ contained a considerable amount of nutritive elements and suggested we add it to our meals; soon, we were eating white bread and putting wheat germ in the meat loaf. Finally, in the early seventies, Dennis Burkitt, M.D., of London, noticed that traditional peoples who ate large amounts of unrefined whole-grain cereals, such as corn and millet, had almost no diseases of the digestive tract. Noting that probably half the Western world is constipated, food reform-ers, following Dr. Burkitt's lead, identified bran as the bowel-saving element; soon, we were eating white bread, putting wheat germ in the meat loaf and adding bran to the morning orange juice—except for those who simply went back to eating the whole wheat in pasta, bread, or cereal, as in centuries past.

In some ways, juggling parts to rebalance the whole does work. You can relieve the constipation caused by white flour by eating bran. Yet, though the symptom of imbalance may be eliminated, the body is more stressed by such a juggling act than it would be if its owner stuck to the whole grain and avoided the constipation problem altogether.

Fragmentation affects foods not only on the cellular, but also on the chemical level. When wheat is refined into white flour, for example, not only does it lose its bran and germ, but some twenty nutrients are also lost or greatly reduced. Enriching the flour—which entails returning four of those twenty nutrients—does not solve the problem. Not only are the added nutrients fewer in number than those present in the original whole wheat; they also lack the energy they had when they were simply part of a living, growing plant. It's like cutting off your arm and then fitting you with a prosthetic one—it may have the same form and fulfill some of the same functions, but it is hardly as good as the original. Isolating the components of a living organism and then remixing them will not re-create the living organism.

The logic, to me, seems obvious: *Added nutrients do not contribute to a live energy field.* It is even possible that some of these chemically isolated substances may disrupt or drain it. In short, "fortified" foods are not necessarily sufficient to sustain life adequately. One researcher reports that a strain of rats fed a synthetic diet with all known nutrients present seemed to live in good health; but in the second and third generation they lost their ability to multiply, and eventually the strain died out.[12]

Another area in which it is vital to consider how fragmentation affects the energy field of a food is infant feeding. The major difference between breast milk (or even cow's or goat's milk) and commercial formula is that the milk is the product of an organism, and therefore has an organizing energy field. Formula, on the other hand, is synthesized; the components are simply placed together, as in the foods given rats in the experiment just mentioned. A great deal of power is required from the organism to overcome the energy deficiencies of such unwhole food and to unfold in a normal manner. Many organisms cannot muster the strength, as the sorry state of our children's health testifies.

Could the lack of an integrated energy field in baby formulas be the reason for the high correlation of Sudden Infant Death Syndrome (SIDS) and formula feeding?* Could there be a connection between the feeding of these synthetic foods and the increase in learning disabilities, which are generally the result of an incorrect processing of electrical impulses?

It is practically impossible to prove scientifically that a child reared on formula would have been healthier if raised on breast milk. However, mothers who have raised one child on formula and one by nursing notice a vast difference. One of my students said her bottle baby had a lot of infections and allergies, whereas her nursling rarely became sick. Man-made, synthesized "foods," and especially infant formulas, will invariably be defective, for they miss the natural life energy that the real thing has.

Faulty formulas have caused speech delays, convulsions, and poor growth. The *New York Times* of November 1, 1982, reported that a TV appearance by two women whose children had suffered from these problems because of faulty formulas brought 65,000 letters in response from parents with similar experiences. And as I finished the first draft of the above paragraph, another story broke in the *New York Times* regarding a massive recall of infant

* Another high correlation of SIDS is seen with routine childhood immunizations, especially the DPT vaccine.[13]

formula that was found to be deficient in vitamin B_6. Such a deficient formula could lead, the *Times* said, to "permanent injuries, including brain damage, cerebral palsy, and mental retardation."[14] The situation was discussed at length in my cooking class that day; coincidentally, one of my students had fed her child that very same formula. Indeed, he had developed a serious neurological defect that impaired both his learning and his behavior.

How many more defects in formulas could still be undetected? How many more mistakes will we discover we have made by trying to override the natural system? Clearly a problem exists. We do not get real mother's milk—and all its health-giving effects—by isolating, juggling, mixing the physical elements present in the real thing. There will inevitably be unpleasant consequences when we tamper with the products of nature, of living organisms, where parts are joined in optimum harmony, interrelating, supporting, depending upon one another in a manner not yet fully understood by science.

The Effects of Food Temperature

Among all animals, only humans heat their food. The interesting thing is that it is also only humans who think, speak, and write. And all human societies, to a greater or lesser extent, use fire in meal preparation. Cooking, in fact, is a universal human custom.

We will discuss the different aspects of cooking in chapter seven. Now I simply want to consider temperature, how it affects the energy field of the foods we consume, and thus how it affects us. Foods that are served hot, cold, or at room temperature all have a different effect on how we enjoy them as well as on our energy level.

First, remember that life needs warmth to unfold. We have an inner warmth (98.6° F) that allows our vital processes to move along smoothly. Heat raises energy, and our inner heat feeds our energy. We keep both of them going by "burning up" foods during digestion and metabolism; more specifically, by breaking the chemical bonds between carbon atoms, and between carbon and hydrogen atoms, and absorbing the heat released by that breakdown process. Hot foods, which provide additional heat, will support our metabolic activities even more, especially when the weather is cold and we need to counterbalance its effects. Heat raises the energy level of foods, and so our own.

In a cool environment life slows down. Witness the hibernating polar bear, and the casserole in your refrigerator that doesn't grow mold as easily as it would if you had left it out. It follows that cold foods slow down our metabolism, as well as counteracting our bodies' inner heat.

I've long been puzzled—mostly because I don't share it—by the attraction most Americans feel for icy cold drinks and foods. The only way I can explain it is by bringing in the law of opposites: If the system desires cold, there must be a lot of heat somewhere.

But where would that excess heat come from? If food is the fuel that provides us with calories (or rather, with heat measured in calories), then probably the food that people eat in this country creates an excess of internal heat. It is too high in calories. And what part of the diet would be the main source of all that heat? Considering that protein and carbohydrates each provide four calories per gram when metabolized, while fat provides nine calories per gram, and considering, too, that fat contributes over 40 percent of the calories in the American diet, it is not farfetched to speculate that fat may be the main source of excessive inner heat. Furthermore, even in the coldest regions of the country people live in springlike temperatures all year round, thanks to central heating. They have therefore little use for all that extra heat— unlike the cowboys of the last century who slept under the stars with one thin blanket and whose breakfast of fried bacon and eggs made great sense. Today Americans need to "cool it," and one way is with ice-cold drinks.

When people eat less fat and more vegetables, cold fare may not only be unnecessary, it could even have a negative effect. Food and drinks consumed straight out of the refrigerator, where they have been isolated from the larger natural force fields, have a very low energy level; hence they tend to lower energy, sometimes to the point of irresistible sleepiness. The presence of sugar—because it is a partial food whose own energy field has been disrupted—can intensify that effect. However, the energy of refrigerated foods can be raised again by heating, stirring, tossing, adding strong flavorings such as fresh garlic, lemon, onions, herbs, spices, or by any other active motions of preparation.

If you want to test this notion of the importance of temperature to the energy level of foods, just start your day with a cup of lukewarm coffee or tea. Does it give you the same boost as your usual hot cup? Or, on two consecutive days, try eating two different kinds of lunch and observe how energetic you feel in the afternoon. On the first day eat only unadorned leftovers straight out of the fridge; on the second day cook up a nice hot meal from scratch. You may be in for a surprise.

The Effects of Food Preservation

Most human communities need to stash away food for the times when it is scarce. Without a doubt, stored food is not the same as that which has been freshly picked or killed. But is the difference favorable or harmful? How can we judge the effects of food preservation methods on the nutrient and energy content of foods and hence on our health?

Traditional techniques of food preservation are cold storage, drying, salting, fermenting, pickling, and smoking. What these methods have in common is that they require only natural "technology": cold weather, sun, salt, time, fire. They work by slowing down the growth of spoilage bacteria through cold, through the removal of water, or by the creation of lactic acids by friendly microorganisms. Foodstuffs preserved in these ways often end up with increased nutrient density.

Let's take a quick look at each of these natural methods.

COLD STORAGE
Laboratory tests show that some of the more volatile food nutrients, such as vitamin C, will break down and diminish in warehouse storage,[15] but in general it seems to have little serious adverse effect on hardy vegetables. Similarly, if the cold storage is outdoors, in a cold cellar or porch, and the food is surrounded by fresh, moving air, we can assume that its energy field will diminish somewhat but not excessively.

Cold storage in a refrigerator—a closed box with an electrical current running through it—can probably alter the energy field more dramatically, mostly because of the insulation: The foodstuffs need cooking, stirring, and other active motions to be re-energized and kept from tasting flat and lifeless.

DRYING
This is probably one of the oldest food preservation techniques. Laboratory tests show that thiamine and other water-soluble vitamins suffer losses of no more than 10 percent, except for vitamin C, which can diminish by as much as 20 percent.[16] I found no studies on the fate of carbohydrates in dried foods, but a simple taste test tells us that the loss of water increases the relative con-

centration of these nutrients (raisins are sweeter than grapes), or turns sugar into starch (as in what happens when corn is dried so that it can be ground into cornmeal). It is possible that even though the absolute quantities of some nutrients may be diminished by drying, the general ratio of nutritive elements to volume increases, which would account for the generally stronger flavor of dried foods. This may also be behind the popular impression that dried fruits, vegetables, and meats are strengthening.

I have found no studies on the difference between sun-dried and commercial hot air and other drying processes. Perhaps the difference in vitamin loss is negligible; however, according to our model of living organisms, there probably is a great difference in the unmeasurable energy level of sun-dried foods and that of tunnel-, spray-, and drum-dried foods. The sun, after all, is the original source of all light, heat, and energy on our planet—our main battery charger. (Those of us who are old enough may remember that clothes dried under the sun feel very different—fresher, cleaner—from those dried in a dryer.)

SALTING
This method preserves food by inhibiting the development of toxin-producing bacteria. Traditionally, it was feasible only in those communities where either sea or land salt was easy to obtain. Today it is most often used for meats, and especially for fish, either in conjunction with drying or by immersion in brine. Nutrient density will be increased with the former method, but decreased with the latter. In many traditional communities salting is still widespread; but wherever a more "modern" diet is followed, with its unbalanced large intake of sodium, salting is less popular. For those who must restrict their salt intake, it can indeed be harmful.

PICKLING OR FERMENTING
These two food preparation and preservation techniques are popular in all major cultures. They give us not only wine, bread, and cheese, but also miso, tempeh, shoyu, idli, and poi-poi—and let's not forget pickles and sauerkraut. During the fermentation process, in the presence of salt or a mold culture, microorganisms develop that alter the composition of vegetable or animal foods by increasing the amount of lactic acid present in them. This in turn changes the food's taste and aroma, making them both stronger and more distinctive, and sometimes more sour.

Although there may be some loss of vitamins and water-soluble minerals during pickling and fermenting, the overall influence of fermented foods on our health is quite favorable. They are easy to digest, and some are even used as digestive aids; this is why we get, for example, pickles or sauerkraut with sausages or processed meats. Indeed, modern research has shown that nutritional values of foods, especially the B vitamins, are actually enhanced by fermentation.* Miso and tempeh (both cultured soybean products) have been shown to have antibacterial properties, and therefore can also be effective as disease-preventive agents.[18] In addition, both tempeh and natto (another cultured soy food) show manyfold increases in vitamin B_{12}.[19] We can safely assume that all that microbial activity in fermented food also increases the food's energy level.

SMOKING

This ancient food preserving technique has generally been used in conjunction with drying. It is most commonly applied to meats and fish. Smoking preserves foods through the action of the antioxidants and bactericides present in the wood smoke; unfortunately, these are at times accompanied by minuscule quantities of other compounds that can be toxic and even carcinogenic.[20]

Modern technology has given us additional methods for preserving our foodstuffs: freezing, canning, chemical preservatives, irradiation. What these methods have in common is that they require a more complex backup system than the traditional ones: special containers, electricity, sophisticated laboratory techniques, and machines. While the traditional methods are not associated with any danger, except perhaps for smoking, technological methods clearly appear to cause health problems—witness the fairly frequent cases of botulism from home or factory canned foods and the carcinogenic effects of many chemical preservatives. The nutritive density of vegetables is generally lowered by dilution or blanching in hot water or air, the preparations necessary for freezing and canning. And irradiation increases the presence of free radicals, chemical elements associated with the development of cancer.

* Beatrice Trum Hunter points out that "fermentation may produce desirable enzymes, synthesize desirable constituents such as vitamins, and may also result in a more favorable amino acid balance in the food."[17]

FREEZING

When foodstuffs are frozen, the water within them turns to ice. The blanching, drying, storage, and thawing involved cause a 20 to 25 percent nutrient loss in fruits and vegetables. This may not seem so bad (after all, 75 percent to 80 percent of the nutrients are retained), but there is an aspect of freezing that has generally been ignored: What happens to plant cells when the water in them freezes? We can only assume that, much like a water bottle forgotten in the freezer, the cells will burst. This is the reason why frozen untreated vegetables are mushy and limp when thawed. As instructions usually call for them to be cooked without thawing, we rarely get to see them in that stage; if we did, we might question closely whether they're fit to eat or not. In effect, frozen vegetables appear to have been destroyed at the cellular level.

We cannot assume that such cellular destruction has no effect on the consumer. Throughout nature, form is just as important as content and is closely related to function. Male and female hormones provide a dramatic example of the importance of form. The only difference between them is the placement of one oxygen molecule; that is, they have identical content, but in a different spatial arrangement.[21] Change that arrangement, or form, and you change the function and the effect.

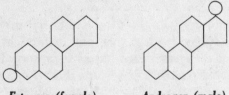

Estrogen (female)   Androgen (male)

Just as cooling does, freezing lowers the energy level of foods. Try being a vegetarian—or just imagine being one—on steamed frozen vegetables, and you'll get the picture. Not surprisingly, children, who are very sensitive to energy fields, often balk at eating vegetables if these are frozen or canned—unless, of course, there's sugar in them. Most children prefer raw or cooked fresh vegetables to frozen ones.

Frozen foods have a seriously diminished energy field. It is not uncommon for people to become very sleepy after eating a meal that includes foods that had been frozen. Recently, one of my students asked me why she would have fallen asleep right after lunch. I inquired, "Did you eat at home or out?" At home, she said. "Did you cook from scratch?" No, she said, "I defrosted my mushroom and barley soup. That's all I ate." "Did you have any reaction when you made it originally?" "No," she said, "no problem." It seemed obvious to me that the freezing would cause her sleepiness, especially because it has happened to me enough times. At this time, the only foods that I find can be frozen without diminishing my energy are clear stock, tempeh, butter, and, once in a blue moon, bread.

CANNING

Food is canned by first heating it to at least 240°, then sealing it hermetically. As the food cools, a vacuum forms within the container, and the consequent absence of oxygen keeps bacteria from multiplying and spoiling the food.

Canning lowers nutrient values considerably. Canned frozen orange juice concentrate has four times less calcium (could that be why we drink both milk and juice for breakfast?) and almost ten times less iron (could it be a cause of anemia?) than fresh juice, while canned green peas lose about 70 percent of all their original B vitamins. Yet what I find even more significant is the lack of oxygen in canned foods. Oxygen is the carrier of life, and without it food, and everything else, is dead. Canned food, therefore, offers us little or no life energy.

A few times I've had the experience that, after eating something straight from a can—sardines or canned fruit—I had trouble thinking clearly and writing, sometimes for as long as two days. As thinking is an electrical activity, I can only assume that something in my electrical or energy field had gone awry. The feeling I had was one of blockage: Energy didn't move through me, as it usually does, but seemed to be blocked by insulating covers above and below me. Canned food, of course, is insulated as well, and on all sides at that; no energy moves through it at all. It seems to me quite possible that such a lack of energy would have a slowing or blocking effect on my own energy field, if only by not charging it. Thus, if I am engaged in a lot of physical activity, an occasional sardine or tunafish sandwich doesn't bother me. But if I'm writing, I stay away from these to prevent writer's block.

CHEMICAL PRESERVATIVES
AND OTHER FOOD ADDITIVES

Although during the past twenty-five years food additives have been the subject of countless books and articles warning of their dangers, the point cannot be made too often. There is perhaps no other single thing we do to food that affects its nutrient content and life-sustaining energy—and hence our health—as negatively as the addition of chemicals.

The problem is widespread. In one of the earliest books on the problem, William Longgood wrote,

> Virtually every bit of food you eat has been treated with some chemical somewhere along the line. Dyes, bleaches, emulsifiers, antioxidants, preservatives, flavors, buffers, noxious sprays, acidifiers, alkalizers, deodorants, moisteners, drying agents, gases, extenders, thickeners, disinfectants, defoliants, fungicides, neutralizers, sweeteners, anticaking and antifoaming agents, conditioners, curers, hydrolizers, hydrogenators, maturers, fortifiers, and many others.
> These are the tools of the food technician—a wizard who can beguile, deceive, and defraud. . . . His alchemy can make stale products appear fresh, permit unsanitary practices, mask inferior quality, substitute nutritionally inferior or worthless chemicals for more costly ingredients. These chemicals almost without exception perform their mission at the cost of destroying valuable vitamins, minerals, and enzymes, stripping food products of their natural life-giving qualities.[22]

Dr. Chauncey Lake, past president of the American Association for the Advancement of Science, warned in 1963 "that general use of new chemicals in large quantities has created a new hazard—subclinical poisoning—so insidious that physicians cannot connect the poison with the ailment."[23]

Dr. Jacqueline Verret, the FDA research scientist who first alerted the nation to the dangers of cyclamate and thalidomide, wrote, "That things are this bad is not something your government is officially likely to tell you. There is not likely to be a press release from the FDA's public information office saying, 'nothing's left that's fit to eat,' or 'Whole population being slowly poisoned.' After all, in most cases it was the government that allowed things to get into such a sorry state, and it does have a self-protective stake in the affair."[24]

No one knows the exact number, but it is estimated that even today, despite the growing consciousness about the dangers of chemicals, there are over five thousand, maybe even up to seven thousand, additives still used to enhance the appearance, color, aroma, texture, flavor, keeping qualities, and other details of both prepared and natural foods. Yes, natural foods too. Oranges are dyed to look more orange, for example, and the lettuce of salad bars is sprayed with potassium bisulfite so it won't wilt. And this despite the fact that chemical additives have been linked conclusively to many diseases, from allergies to cancer, as well as blurry vision, aching backs, and hyperactivity in children.*

Generally, preservatives such as BHT and BHA are added to foods in the form of gelatin beadlets and work by blocking the access of oxygen to nutrients and microorganisms, in effect eliminating life processes within the food substance. And that's where problems may arise.

Just as the various spoilage processes are halted by chemical preservatives, so can the processes of natural function be interrupted as well. Rudolf Hauschka, a German scientist, scholar, and researcher at The Clinical Therapeutic Institute at Arlesheim, and disciple of Rudolf Steiner, the founder of anthroposophy, has set forth an extremely helpful concept that clarifies the basic difference between the natural and the artificial, and explains why the latter is so harmful to life, especially in the case of coal and petroleum-derived chemicals. He points out that for as long as humanity has existed, its life has been sustained by the world of plants, both directly and indirectly. Plants give us food, fuel, shelter, construction material, fibers for clothing, oils, sweeteners, flavors, colors, aroma, and medicinal substances.

Interestingly enough, we get almost the same elements from coal and petroleum: fuel for heating, construction materials (plastics), fibers for clothing (nylon, Orlon, and so forth), mineral oil and cream (Vaseline), saccharin, artificial flavors, colors, perfumes, and synthetic medicinal drugs.

But coal and oil are what's left of trees that lived millions of years ago—plants long dead, entombed within the bowels of the earth, paralyzed at a biological zero point. And from that point, says Hauschka, "human ingenuity takes hold and conjures forth a synthetic mirror-image of the natural world. Contrasting the two realms, we get the impression that the upper one is the realm of dynamic biological reality, the scene of a ceaseless harmonization of the living polarities of earth and heaven, giving rise to an endless range of metamorphoses. The underworld of coal tar chemistry, on the other hand, seems—figuratively speaking—like a ghostly reflection of the dynamic creativity of the cosmos."[25] The "natural" plant world above carries life—things grow and change, are

* For a thorough discussion of chemical additives, see the updated edition of *Eater's Digest—The Consumer's Fact Book of Food Additives* by Michael Jacobson, director of the Center for Science in the Public Interest.

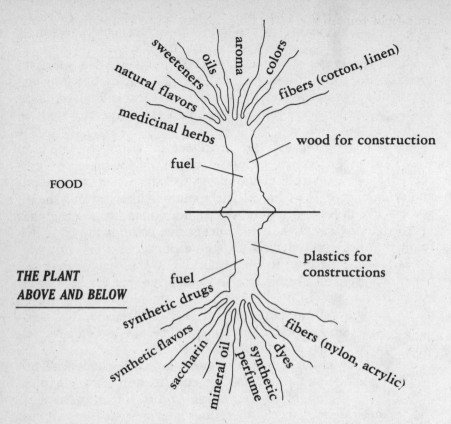

FOOD

**THE PLANT
ABOVE AND BELOW**

born and die. The "artificial" oil world below is dead: No change occurs in its elements without human technological manipulation. Substances from this realm, then, *will not support life.* In fact, they will probably block the harmonious flow of a live energy field. If we ingest artificial foodstuffs, our life processes will be undermined by not being supported. It may be significant that cancer, that frightening epidemic of our time, is a disease in which the life process (the buildup and breakdown of cells) has become deranged.

The frequent mutations and birth defects traced to the use of artificial chemicals can be understood if we accept the idea that an energy field precedes the development of the fetus. This is a concept explored at length by a number of scientists. One researcher found that he was able to record on a voltmeter the electrical potential at different points of a salamander embryo. The one constant factor during the growth and development of the embryo, he discovered, was its electromagnetic field; not only did this field remain stable throughout the differentiation and multiplication of cells, but it also didn't short out in the liquid medium inhabited by the embryo (a battery would have!).[26]

The morphogenetic field postulated by Sheldrake (which wouldn't short out because it's not electrical) is subject to deformation by mechanical collision and by electrical and magnetic fields.[27] As the morphogenetic field determines the specific growth pattern of an embryo, abnormal changes in that field, such as those created by inappropriate or noxious foods or chemicals, could conceivably create similar changes in the embryo. These changes would then translate into birth defects.

All this may explain why rats fed that synthetic diet (see page 40) seemed to do well themselves, but lost the power to reproduce in later generations and eventually died out: Their energy fields didn't get enough nourishment, and they were unable either to generate or to support new energy fields that would, in turn, develop into baby rats.

Will such a fate be ours too—a slow dying out, rather than a big nuclear bang? Infertility or problems with conception occur in a growing number of people today. And we can't say that we haven't been warned: Over five thousand years ago it was written that "the sins of the fathers will be visited upon the children unto the third and fourth generation." If our "sins" are the breaking of the laws of nature, it's unlikely that we'll escape the promised effects.

IRRADIATION

The latest technological invention to immortalize (read "preserve") our foodstuffs comes from the Department of Energy. It seems that cesium-137, a nuclear waste by-product of the manufacture of nuclear bombs, can be put to use in irradiating foods. The foods themselves will not become radioactive, even at the suggested levels of 100,000 rads. However, they could if they're overexposed. When foods are thus exposed to ionizing radiation, they will not ripen or sprout; some insects, viruses, and bacteria will also be killed, and therefore apparently the food will not spoil.

However, according to Kathleen Tucker of the Health and Energy Institute in Washington, D.C., microorganisms can develop resistance to radiation over time; some of them could even mutate into dangerous new strains. Also, some bacteria (such as salmonella and those that cause meat to appear or smell spoiled) may be killed well before the more resistant botulism bacteria. In that manner, fish or chicken meat that appears edible could in fact be seriously contaminated with botulism. Also, "radiolytic products," or "free radicals" are created in foods by the radiation process; it may be necessary to monitor them continuously for toxicity.

A few studies have been conducted on the effects of irradiated foods. Children fed irradiated wheat showed blood abnormalities called "polyploids";[28] mice fed irradiated chicken had seven times fewer offspring than those fed cooked chicken; and a relationship was found between the radiation dose and an increase in deaths in a strain of fruit flies fed irradiated foods. At this writing, the FDA does not require the labeling of irradiated foods, an unfortunate information blackout. However, all is not totally hidden: Fruit treated with radiation may become brown or mushy, or ripen abnormally; sometimes it will bruise easily, or develop black spots. Food irradiated in sealed plastic containers may develop a bitter, metallic aftertaste.

All things considered, preserving foods with irradiation appears to cause a lot more problems than it solves. It also could expose workers to lethal doses of radiation in the event of an accident; it causes problems in waste disposal; and nobody knows how such a peculiar way of dealing with the food we eat could affect our energy, our childbearing capacity (the mice didn't do so well!), and our possibilities of getting cancer.

I think drying is better.

NUTRIENTS IN PROPORTION

We have all been bombarded with countless articles, books, and lectures on the subject of vitamins, minerals, protein, carbohydrates, and fats. These elements, which are given form by the morphogenetic field of the system to which they belong, have been the focus of nutritional study for the greater part of this century. Yet although information on recommended quantities of nutrients abounds, I have seen very few comments on something I consider much more important: the *proportion* in which these nutrients occur in food.

The general scientific approach to nutrition—and this includes both medical nutrition and the "natural" approach that relies heavily on vitamin supplementation—stresses only the *quantity* of nutrients. It sees the body as a mechanism, or machine, and food as an aggregate of separable particles called nutrients. It considers that in order to run efficiently, this body-machine simply needs certain quantities of specific nutrients. The context in which these nutrients are supplied—whether they are consumed as part of food or in the form of supplements—and their relationship to one another, is of little if any consequence. Nutritionists who apply the mechanistic, scientific viewpoint believe it doesn't matter if you get your vitamin A by eating a carrot—or by popping a vitamin pill. Measurable quantity is all.

This approach to nutrition is deeply ingrained in us. No lecture on nutrition seems complete without a recommendation for taking certain amounts of vitamins or minerals, and we talk about grams of protein—we who have never weighed a protein in our lives—with the same certainty with which we consider pounds of meat.

But trompe l'oeil optics has taught us that by looking differently at something we see different things.

With the systems approach, we can look at the picture of nutrients in foods and see not their quantity, but how much of each is consumed in relation to another. What proportion of nutrients is optimal for human health? Let's look first at the one and only food that is designed specifically to meet the nutritional needs of a human being: mother's milk. All other foodstuffs—fruits, grains, leafy greens—we share with our fellow creatures, but human mothers produce the one food that is perfectly tailored to the requirement of human children. Following is a chart of its nutritive elements and the porportional relationship between them. The main point here is to get a general sense of *MORE* and *LESS*.

In 100 grams (100,000 mg) of	MINERALS and VITAMINS 120 mg	PROTEIN 1,100 mg	FATS 4,000 mg	CARBOHY-DRATES 9,500 mg	% WATER 87.5
MOTHER'S MILK	▫	▪	▪	▪	▪

Note that the proportion of minerals to proteins, proteins to carbohydrates, and carbohydrates to water is uniformly around one to eight and one to nine. This elegant progression is broken by the proportion of fats, in a four-to-one relationship with proteins, and a one to two-and-a-half relationship with carbohydrates.

Two surprising facts emerge here. First: in this perfect food for infants, which makes them double their birth weight in six months, the amount of protein present is only slightly over 1 percent. Nature doesn't seem to think that we need large amounts of protein. Second, there is four times more fat than protein in mother's milk. (I find it interesting that the modern American diet derives 12 percent of its calories from proteins and 45 percent from fats in quite a similar relative proportion.)

What is the relationship between the proportion of nutrients in mother's milk and the proportion of nutrients which adults need? My research has led me to believe that, with the exception of the high fat content needed for an infant's growth, mother's milk contains a nutrient balance very similar to that on which adult bodies thrive. This similarity manifests itself throughout our adult lives: when the necessary proportion of nutrients is not met, self-corrective mechanisms kick in, and our bodies crave the missing nutrients. If we don't obtain them, illness may result. This tendency of the body to seek nutritional balance will be illustrated throughout this book; it is one of the core concepts of my approach.

Let us compare the nutrient balance of some of the more popular foods with that of mother's milk. All values are given in milligrams, so you can see the proportions more easily. Fiber isn't included in the calculations, since mother's milk has none, and we're only trying to make a simple comparison of the relative proportions of nutrients by weight. Neither are vitamins; they are present in such small amounts that they could be lumped with the minerals and yet not change the numbers appreciably.

NUMBER OF MILLIGRAMS OF NUTRIENTS IN 100 GRAMS OF SOME FOODS*

MILLIGRAMS

In 100 grams (100,000 milligrams) of:	MINERALS and VITAMINS	PROTEIN	FATS	CARBOHYDRATES	% WATER
Mother's Milk	120	1,100	4,000	9,500	87.5
Cow's Milk	406	3,500	3,500	4,900	87.4
Sugar (granulated beet or cane)	5	0	0	99,500	.5
Grapes, green seedless American (Slip Skin)	194	1,300	1,000	15,700	81.6
Apple, whole raw	133	200	600	14,500	84.4
Potato, baked with skin	604	2,600	100	21,100	75.1
Lettuce, iceberg	233	900	100	2,900	95.5
Collards, steamed	498	2,700	600	4,900	90.3
Kale, steamed (leaves and stems, cooked)	507	3,200	700	4,000	91.2
Turnips, sliced, steamed (boiled)	304	800	200	4,900	93.5
Carrots, diced, cooked	126	900	200	7,100	91.2
Kidney Beans, canned, cooked	625	7,800	500	21,400	69.0
Lentils, cooked	396	7,800	TRACE	19,300	72.0
White Bread, enriched	799	8,700	3,200	50,400	35.5
Rolled Oats, cooked (oatmeal)	346	2,000	1,000	9,700	86.5
Brown Rice, cooked	440	2,500	600	25,500	70.3
Fish, Cod, broiled	1,006	28,500	5,300	0	64.6
Chicken, broiled, no skin	611	31,600	400	0	63.8
Beef (T-bone steak, broiled)	600	19,500	36,400	0	36.4

* Source: USDA Handbook No. 8

NUTRIENT PROPORTIONS IN FOODS

	MINERALS AND VITAMINS	PROTEIN	FATS	CARBOHY-DRATES	% WATER
MOTHER'S MILK	▪	◻	◼	◼	◼
COW'S MILK	▪	◼	◼	◼	◼
WHITE SUGAR				◼	
GREEN SEEDLESS GRAPES	▪	◻	◻	◼	◼
WHOLE RAW APPLE	▪	▪	◻	◼	◼
POTATO BAKED WITH SKIN	◻	◻	▪	◼	◼
ICEBERG LETTUCE	▪	◻	▪	◻	◼
STEAMED COLLARDS	◻	◼	◻	◼	◼
STEAMED KALE	◻	◼	◻	◼	◼

STEAMED TURNIPS					
COOKED CARROTS					
COOKED KIDNEY BEANS (Canned)					
COOKED LENTILS					
ENRICHED WHITE BREAD					
COOKED ROLLED OATS					
COOKED BROWN RICE					
BROILED RED SNAPPER					
BROILED CHICKEN (No Skin)					
BEEF STEAK					

Notice that the fat content in most foods except beef is lower than the protein content. If we remember that in mother's milk the fat content is four times that of protein, we can perhaps explain in part the attraction most people feel for butter, fried foods, mayonnaise, and so on. However, before tossing our latest low-fat diet to the winds and running for a butter and peanut butter sandwich, let's consider this: Only mother's milk derives 40 percent of its calories from fats. Nature provides that proportion for infants, but for adults much less is indicated. As almost everyone knows by now, evidence points overwhelmingly to high-fat diets contributing directly to obesity and either directly or indirectly involved in cardiovascular disease, hypertension, arteriosclerosis, hernia, gallbladder disease, and diabetes. High fat consumption, from both vegetable and animal sources, is also implicated in some cancers.

The charts of cooked grains, beans, and vegetables exhibit a certain consistency: They all contain minerals, proteins, carbohydrates, and water. These nutrients also increase in that order, in other words, there are always more proteins than minerals, more carbohydrates than proteins, more water than carbohydrates. Sugar, on the other hand, looks like this:

	MINERALS and VITAMINS	PROTEIN	FATS	CARBOHY-DRATES	% WATER
WHITE SUGAR				▨	▪

Clearly, sugar is deficient in nutritional elements. It is 99.5 percent carbohydrates. (It is instructive to remember that sugar is a *fragmented* plant food, derived from sugar cane.) If this substance is eaten, the missing elements will have to be found elsewhere, or the body will show deficiency symptoms. High-density protein foods, vitamin and mineral supplementation, and large amounts of water will be needed to balance the intake of refined sugar. A low-protein or vegetarian diet that includes a high proportion of sugar-sweetened foods can thus cause a serious nutritional deficiency. Considering water alone, it is interesting to note that if we eat 100 grams, or 100,000 milligrams (about 3.5 ounces or 9 tablespoons) of pure refined sugar, theoretically we need about 28 to 30 ounces—almost a quart—of water to counterbalance it. Did you ever notice that sweets make you thirsty? Here, by the way, lies the secret of the popularity of "soft" drinks: When they're ice-cold, they numb the taste buds while the liquid fools them into thinking that thirst is being quenched, but the seven teaspoons of sugar in each can or bottle create a need for more water—and thus keep us reaching, endlessly and greedily, for more of these phony drinks. A few swallows of room-temperature soda pop show up their true taste and nature.

Let's now take a look at meat:

	MINERALS and VITAMINS	PROTEIN	FATS	CARBOHY-DRATES	% WATER
BEEF STEAK	■				

Although meat contains water, it is only double the amount of protein. Compare that with cooked beans, for example, which contain about thirteen times as much water as protein. Now we can see why diets high in protein recommend drinking eight or more glasses of water a day to "flush out the kidneys." Vegetarians need much less additional water in their diets because plant foods already contain a very high proportion of it.

From this viewpoint, we can also understand why a diet of meat and sugar strikes a balance of sorts, and why meat creates a craving for sugar—and *vice versa*: Sugar is pure carbohydrate and has no proteins, minerals, or fats, whereas meat is high in proteins and fats and contains no carbohydrates. They dovetail, complementing each other, which is why people can actually live on hamburgers and candybars. It is a precarious balance, to be sure, lacking the stability offered by whole foods, with their natural progression of nutrients; thus it is easily tipped over into physical and mental disorders, such as tension, depression, anxiety, colds, stomach ailments, heart disease, and other problems.

We can draw a few preliminary conclusions from the preceding considerations. If we accept that the correct proportion of natural nutrients—except fat—roughly parallels that present in mother's

MEAT AND SUGAR: COMPARISON OF NUTRIENTS BY WEIGHT
*(per 100 grams, edible portion)**

	MINERALS and VITAMINS	PROTEIN	FATS	CARBOHY-DRATES	% WATER
WHITE SUGAR				■	▫
BEEF MEAT	▫	■	■		■

* Source: USDA Handbook No. 8

milk and that our bodies are built to live on foodstuffs that supply that proportion, we can see first of all why different peoples can live well on natural diets vastly different in the quantity of basic nutrients. For example: Both the Hunzas of Asia, near Tibet, and the Vilcabambans of Ecuador are healthy peoples. Studies of their diets, however, have shown that the Hunzas consume on the average 50 grams of protein and 354 grams of carbohydrates daily, whereas the Vilcabambans consume 35 to 38 grams of protein and 200 to 260 grams of carbohydrates. The total *quantity* of food varies between the two groups, but the proportions of nutrients are the same: Roughly one part protein to seven parts carbohydrates.

We can also safely assume that, following the tendency of all living systems to return to a base-line balance, our bodies will try to compensate when they are presented with any one nutrient out of proportion. For example:

• Excess minerals or even vitamins (in the form of supplements, salt, concentrated foods, or herbs) will cause a need for more fats, proteins, carbohydrates, and water—in short, more food. Everyone knows, that, among other things, salt creates thirst; but it can also create artificial hunger. Vitamin pills and mineral supplements may be necessary at times when there is a depletion in the body, usually as a result of the consumption of fragmented foods; but when taken without a specific need for them, they may, as does salt, provoke the "munchies," and could bring on an undesired and unexpected weight gain.

- High-protein foods will call for salt and other minerals, such as calcium. If not enough minerals are consumed or absorbed, the protein will actually deplete the body of minerals. (Research at the University of Wisconsin shows that high-protein intake reduces the body's calcium stores.[29]) A high-protein regimen will also require large amounts of fluids, and the regular consumption of refined carbohydrates. This is why when you give up meat, you should also give up both sugar and white flour—something that many people do not realize, except for feeling that their meatless diet is somehow awry. You may also have noticed that meat doesn't go well with brown rice, and the two are rarely served together: The reason is that a disproportioned food (meat) and a well-proportioned one (brown rice) don't complement each other according to this model. Theoretically, a meal with 30 grams of protein would also demand about 230 to 250 grams of carbohydrate (seven or eight times as much). If the carbohydrates are not supplied by bread, beans, grain, or starchy vegetables, a craving for a sugared dessert is almost inevitable. This concept may explain why people who eat a carefully measured, dietetically correct "nutritious" meal low in calories (that is, low in fat and starches) so often indulge in a rich dessert. The usual rationale is psychological: "I've been so good that I can afford a treat." The true reason may be physical; if enough complex carbohydrates have been supplied by the main meal, dessert often becomes less attractive.
- Refined carbohydrates (white sugar and white flour), if not accompanied by enough protein and minerals in the diet, will draw on the body's own protein and mineral reserves and thereby weaken it; dental caries and impaired nervous functioning (both often a result of calcium imbalance or deficiency) are two of its most immediate effects. This may be the reason why sugar and milk are automatically paired: The excess protein and calcium in the cow's milk (its nutritional composition is very different from that of mother's milk; see page 54) balances the naked carbohydrate.[30]

In the case of deficiency symptoms in an apparently well-nourished individual, it may be helpful to look not only at what his or her diet may be lacking, but also at what it may have in excess, in the form of disproportioned foods or single-element substances. Deficiencies need not be absolute; they can be relative in terms of excesses elsewhere, as when an intake of too much of one B vitamin raises the need for all the other B vitamins, or, as mentioned above, when a high sugar intake creates a calcium deficiency. In such a case it may be simpler to reduce the food or substance in excess rather than increasing the deficient elements.

Whenever I've presented these concepts to my classes, incidentally, there have always been several positive responses. Not everyone reacts in the same way, but in a group of thirty or forty people there are always three or four who get hungry from too much salt, three or four who have put on weight while taking vitamins, or who couldn't stay on a high-protein diet without going carbohydrate-crazy. And of course everybody knows that milk and cookies go together . . .

Three:
Food and the Law
of Opposites

A MATTER OF BALANCE

Recent scientific developments, as we have seen, no longer support a mechanistic view of the universe, which sees everything in terms of more or less independently functioning parts. We now know that the whole world is one big system comprised of myriads of other interconnecting systems. We also know that the energy within whole systems is always moving and that it moves in specific patterns. Yet a given system remains stable within that movement—that is, *balanced*. Remaining in or attaining balance is today one of our most earnest concerns in the area of nutrition and health. Often I hear people say, "I'm not exactly sick, but I feel off-balance," a vague description that is nevertheless intuitively clear to most of us.

To help us in our quest for equilibrium, we must understand the concept of opposites. All energy, according to natural laws, moves in a pendulum swing between opposites, as day turns to night, for example, and night to day. It is an extremely *dynamic* concept, applicable to almost any situation, and we see it at work everywhere around us. Heat alternates with cold, noise with stillness, joy with sadness, sweet with salty, all in full turn. It is, we must remember, a value-free concept. In any pair of opposites, one side is neither better nor worse than the other—only radically different.

Ancient religions and philosophies understood how opposites

rule the relative world. The word *religion*, in fact, is thought to derive from the Latin *re-ligare*, "to reunite"; and indeed, the major religions have as their goal the unification of opposites, such as body and spirit, male and female, human being and God. This goal is expressed in their well-known symbols, which usually consist of two interconnected opposing designs:

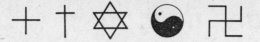

RELIGIOUS SYMBOLS

Chinese philosophy is based on a carefully thought-out system of dealing with opposites, called the yin-yang theory. Basically, it is a classification of opposite categories, extremely detailed and comprehensive, that can be applied to practically any field of endeavor (chemistry, biology, anatomy, medicine, diet, movement, art).

The original Chinese concept of the formation of the universe is based on the division of substance into a "lighter" and a "heavier" part. That is, the Primary One was divided into two opposing forces, eventually to be reunited again. The Chinese philosophers then gave the names *yin* and *yang* to the components of that duality.[1] Originally *yin* meant "the shady side of the hill," and *yang* stood for "the sunny side of the hill." Thus, *yin* represented the cool, dark element, and *yang* stood for the hot, light element. The *I Ching*, or Book of Changes, uses the terms "the yielding" and "the firm" instead of *yin* and *yang*.[2]

From these original, basic meanings *yin* and *yang* took on a host of others, and certain aspects of the theory were eventually imported to the West. As applied to food and health, they became greatly popular, although in a modified version, largely due to the work of a scholar known as George Ohsawa (his Japanese name is Sakurazawa Nyoiti). During the late 1940s and '50s, he began lecturing in Europe and the United States about food and health, using the principle of yin-yang—the play of opposites—as the basis of his approach. He termed his system *macrobiotics*, intending it to mean "the art of longevity."

What interests us most in Ohsawa's macrobiotic philosophy is his classification of foods into relative stages of yin-ness (expansiveness) and yang-ness (contractiveness). Alcohol, sugar, and fruits were on the furthest extreme of yin, while meat and salt were on the furthest extreme of yang. Grains, most notably brown rice, were placed in the middle, as the most balanced food. Health-ful eating meant always, continuously, striving for a balance be-tween the opposites of the yin and the yang, the expansive and the contractive. Since in the working out of his theory Ohsawa partially—and purposefully—reversed the original Chinese defi-nitions of yin and yang, thereby creating some confusion, I will not use those terms in this book and will say instead "expansive" and "contractive."*

Ohsawa's dietary recommendations were extremely radical at the time he started teaching. He suggested people completely avoid meat, sugar, dairy, white flour, canned foods, artificial ad-ditives, tomatoes, potatoes, eggplant, peppers, coffee, and tropical fruits, and adopt instead a diet based on whole grains, beans, soy products, and fresh vegetables. Yet many who followed his rec-ommendations healed themselves of all manner of illnesses, in-cluding hemorrhoids, skin rashes, acne, dandruff, asthma, and even (in a case well known to me, where radiation treatment had already failed) Hodgkin's disease. Whether Ohsawa's theories are universally applicable or not, one thing is clear: They have had

---

* In traditional Chinese cosmology, yang stands for, among other things, sun, heaven, day, fire, heat, dryness, light; it tends to expand, to flow upward and outward. Yin stands for moon, earth, night, water, cold, dampness, darkness; it tends to contract and flow downward. Yang ascends to heaven, yin descends to earth. Yang has also traditionally stood for Heaven, the male creative energy, whereas Yin was seen as Earth, the female, receiver and transformer of Heav-en's creative energy. Ohsawa, because he felt it would make more sense to West-erners to conceive of the earth as the active, creative (yang) force, and heaven as the passive, receptive (yin) element, partially reversed the old theory in pop-ularizing it: the earth-bound, contractive force he associated with yang, and the heaven-bound, expansive forces with yin. Some people have found this confusing because in Ohsawa's macrobiotic classification heat is then associated with con-traction (both called yang), whereas cold is lined up with expansion (both called yin), a system that does not agree with daily experience.

	YANG	YIN
	sun	moon
	day	night
	fire	water
	heat	cold
	dryness	dampness
	light	darkness
	male	female
(Traditional)	Heaven	Earth
	expansive	contractive
(Macrobiotic)	Earth	Heaven
	contractive	expansive

some very positive results. I have found some of them particularly helpful, especially the application of the general theory of opposites to food and healing. Carefully and cautiously applied, it can help us make correct choices in food and find remedies for whatever ails us. Here is how:

Let's begin by noticing that living systems and energy fields maintain themselves through a continuous give and take, buildup and breakdown, expansion and contraction. That which sustains both the systems and their energy fields must also encourage these opposing forces or tendencies. Food does just that. It expands or contracts us, heats or cools us, acidifies or alkalinizes us. The pendulum swing of our metabolism between those and still other opposites is what keeps us more or less stable; but let one of these elements grow out of proportion, let the pendulum dally too long to one side, and balance is disrupted. We feel unwell. It's as simple as that.

Most of the time, balance is maintained automatically. However, there are times when we consciously wish to aid the automatic processes—when we don't feel quite right, for example. Then, to act appropriately, to make conscious choices that will help us rebalance ourselves quickly, we need to have a clear mental picture of the various kinds of food opposites.

By knowing which foods are the opposites of others, you can quickly undo any simple health problem that arises from excessive reliance on one category. For example, if you've been eating only raw foods for five years and you're not feeling as well as you'd like to feel, you can go to the opposite and start eating cooked foods. (Curiously enough, our bodies often tell us what to do: we get yens, cravings, deep longings. It is important to learn not to ignore these cravings simply because they may not fit into some nutritional plan or theory.) The sets of opposites that most directly apply to food are: Quantity-Quality, Expansive-Contractive, Acid-Alkaline, Warming-Cooling. Let's look at each set in turn.

QUANTITY AND QUALITY: A LOT AND A LITTLE

A simple example: If you've stuffed yourself at a banquet and are all puffed up and expanded, by abstaining from food the next day (fasting is the opposite of eating a lot), your body will, following the law of the pendulum, contract naturally and regain its proper shape.

EXCESS FOOD ———————————— FASTING

STUFFED STOMACH ———————————— RAVENOUS HUNGER

This is obvious. I'm not telling you anything you don't know, simply reminding you of what you do know. And we all know that the above are extremes. Swinging from extreme to extreme can indeed keep us balanced, but it will be a violent balance. Its most dramatic expression is the classic binge-vomit cycle of the bulimic or anorexic sufferer. It is more sensible—and much healthier— to maintain balance by moving between less extreme positions:

MODERATE FOOD ———————————— NO SNACKING

STOMACH 80 PERCENT FULL ———————————— GOOD APPETITE

The above is the range within which most healthy people keep themselves. Interestingly enough, moderation and frugality in the quantity of food consumed are often responsible for the good health of people who pay no attention to what they eat. My favorite example is that of my friend Mort Glankoff, the founder of *Cue* magazine, who at eighty-three is in better health than many a younger man; yet he chain-smokes, drinks both liquor and coffee, eats in restaurants all the time, and laughs at my "healthy" diet. His secret is that he orders half portions, eats only what he wants (which can be half of that), and doesn't hesitate to leave food on his plate. As he never stuffs himself, his system can always handle whatever he eats and thus remains balanced.

Quantity, said George Ohsawa, changes quality. In atomic physics there is a specific volume of material known as critical mass, below which certain reactions cannot take place. We could say that there is an optimum quantity at which a certain quality becomes manifest at its peak (the opposites quantity and quality are thus also functions of each other).

WRONG QUANTITY ———————————— WRONG QUALITY

RIGHT QUANTITY ———————————— RIGHT QUALITY

Applying this idea to food, we can see that, in fact, food of perhaps not the very best quality can keep you going if not eaten in excess, and food of the best quality will become harmful if consumed in the wrong quantity—either too much or too little. Both excess and deficiency can turn health into sickness, medicine into poison.

EXPANSIVE AND CONTRACTIVE

As George Ohsawa taught, foods can be classified into those that have an "expansive" effect, and those that have a "contractive" effect. Please note that I am using the words *expansive* and *contractive* metaphorically. For example, if I get a headache from an "expansive" food or drink (for example, ice cream or alcohol), I can quickly tip the imbalance by taking in something "contractive" (for example, salty food). But whether my tissues expand thus compressing my blood vessels after I've eaten ice cream or vice versa I cannot know for sure; whether the salt contracts me or not I cannot measure. What is important is that the headache does go away, and there are no negative side effects. From a practical viewpoint, then, such a classification is quite useful, whether or not it reflects the *actual* effects of various foods.

To classify foods as either contractive or expansive, a number of factors have been taken into account (see the chart on the next page). Even though I appear to make a clear distinction between expansive and contractive tendencies, I want to stress that there is no really sharp division between them. There are only small differences from one step to the next, and larger ones from extreme to extreme. In short, the triangle represents a graduated scale. When we apply the concept to food categories, we get the general classification as seen on page 70.

EXPANSIVE/CONTRACTIVE FACTORS IN FOODS

	FLAVOR	DIRECTION OF GROWTH	SPEED OF GROWTH	CLIMATE OF ORIGIN	MOISTURE CONTENT
EXPANSIVE	SPICY	UPWARD (leaves)	FAST	HOT	WATERY, MOIST
	SWEET	HORIZONTALLY UNDERGROUND			
		HORIZONTALLY ABOVE GROUND (squash cabbage)		TEMPERATE	
	SOUR				
	ASTRINGENT				
	BITTER	DOWNWARDS (roots)			
CONTRACTIVE	SALTY		SLOW	COLD	DENSE, DRY

Drugs
Alcohol
Fruit juices
Aromatic herb teas
Vegetable juices
Tea/Coffee
Sugar
Spices
Fats and oils
Tropical fruits
Temperate fruits
Sprouts/lettuce
Fast-growing vegetables
Tubers
Bitter greens
Sea vegetables
Winter squashes
Roots
Nuts
Beans
Grains
Fish
Fowl
Beef
Eggs
Tamari
Miso

CONTRACTIVE   Salt

Each category also has its graduations, and sometimes more expansive foods of one category are on the same level as more contractive ones of another. For example, although plant foods are more expansive than animal foods generally, some fish can be more expansive than cooked grains. Read the chart on page 71 horizontally as well as vertically. Please note that this listing of foods and drinks is not a static list. Any one food or drink will have various expansive and contractive features. For example, there are upward-growing large leaves with a bitter taste (Swiss chard), or downward-growing large roots with a sweet taste (carrots), and so on. For this reason you may at one time experience a foodstuff as more expansive, at another time as more contractive. But on the whole the list should provide you with solid guidelines and is generally applicable.*

* These lists are based on information from the works of George Ohsawa, Herman Aihara, and Michio Kushi, as well as on my own experience.

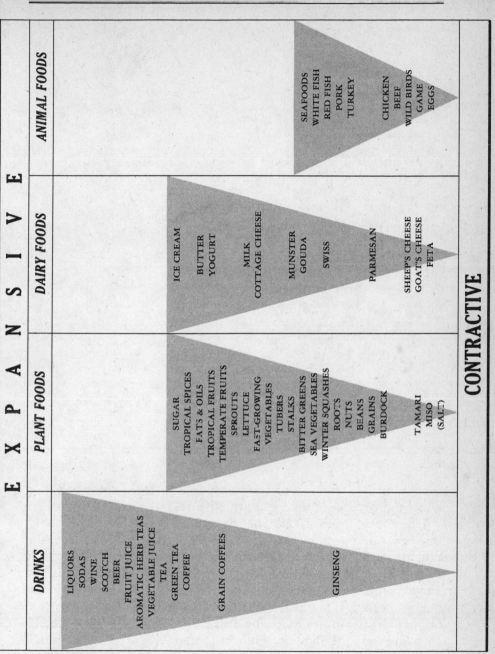

EXPANSIVE

DRINKS	PLANT FOODS	DAIRY FOODS	ANIMAL FOODS
LIQUORS	SUGAR	ICE CREAM	SEAFOODS
SODAS	TROPICAL SPICES		WHITE FISH
WINE	FATS & OILS	BUTTER	RED FISH
SCOTCH	TROPICAL FRUITS	YOGURT	PORK
BEER	TEMPERATE FRUITS		TURKEY
FRUIT JUICE	SPROUTS	MILK	
AROMATIC HERB TEAS	LETTUCE	COTTAGE CHEESE	
VEGETABLE JUICE	FAST-GROWING		CHICKEN
TEA	VEGETABLES	MUNSTER	BEEF
GREEN TEA	TUBERS	GOUDA	WILD BIRDS
COFFEE	STALKS	SWISS	GAME
	BITTER GREENS		EGGS
GRAIN COFFEES	SEA VEGETABLES		
	WINTER SQUASHES	PARMESAN	
	ROOTS		
	NUTS	SHEEP'S CHEESE	
	BEANS	GOAT'S CHEESE	
	GRAINS	FETA	
	BURDOCK		
GINSENG			
	TAMARI		
	MISO		
	(SALT)		

CONTRACTIVE

more quantity (overeating)	boiling
more variety	steaming
raw food	sauteeing
quick cooking	broiling
open pot	baking
cooked food	deep frying
less variety	pickling
closed pot (incl. pressure)	
slow cooking	
less quantity (up to fasting)	

In addition, cooking or food preparation techniques will also affect the expansiveness or contractiveness of foods (see above).

These techniques are used not only to make food more palatable and easier to digest, but also to bring the extremes closer to center and harmonize different foods with the seasons. For example, a thick bean soup simmered a long time with carrots and onions has a more contractive effect than a cold bean salad with grated raw carrots, scallions, and parsley; with the same basic ingredients you can prepare a wintery, warming dish and a summery, cooling dish, changing only the mode of preparation and a few flavoring ingredients. When all these variables are taken into account, cooking becomes a truly fascinating endeavor.

You can also affect your level of activity and your mental state by following this concept. Note, for that, the following:

ACTIVITY

hyperactive
overactive
busy
active
persistent
stable
quiet
passive
catatonic

MOTION

disjointed
loose
flexible
firm
solid
rigid
immobile

MENTAL STATES

confused
spacy
unable to concentrate
chattering
active
open
clear
concentrated
narrow-minded
mentally rigid
arrogant
fanatical

To support any one state, it often helps to eat food from around the same zone. For example, for physical activity, eat more fruit, greens, tubers, stalks, fish, fowl. To curb an excess, consuming foods from the opposite zone is at times helpful: the hyperactivity from sugar can be counterbalanced or eliminated by eating grains, beans, salty foods, animal protein.

Please remember that this whole classification, though useful, must be taken only as a broad generalization. It's a sort of relativity theory: different foods are *more* or *less* expansive or contractive than others. In order to maintain balance, we need both kinds; neither is better or more desirable than the other. It is important to keep that in mind.

ACID AND ALKALINE

Although nutrition books frequently refer to "acid" and "alkaline," the concept of acidity and alkalinity remains one of the most incompletely understood in nutritional science. Understanding it, however, is crucial to knowing how to keep ourselves balanced.

First, some basic facts. Acidity and alkalinity are properties exhibited most clearly in fluids. They are opposites, in the sense that we have defined earlier: necessary and complementary to each other, two faces of a coin, neither one being "better" or "worse" than the other.

The main characteristic of acids is that they contain a large proportion of hydrogen ions (H+), which have a positive electric charge. Hydrogen atoms normally have one proton in their nucleus and one electron spinning around it; as with all elements, the number of protons and the number of electrons are usually equal. When the number of electrons is either larger or smaller, the atom is called an ion.

HYDROGEN ATOM AND ION

These hydrogen ions are "hungry" atoms, always looking to replace their missing electron. When the proportion of these H+ in a given fluid is large enough, the fluid will become *acid* and corrosive: It will "eat" the electrons of other substances.

Alkalis, or bases, contain a large proportion of hydroxyl ions (OH−). As opposed to the hungry H+ ion, the OH− ion carries an *extra* electron and looks to donate it. Thus, when an OH− meets an H+, they bond, neutralizing each other by forming H_2O (water) and a salt. For example: HC_1 (hydrochloric acid) + $NaHCO_3$ (sodium bicarbonate) becomes → NaC_1 (salt) + H_2O (water) + CO_2 (carbon dioxide).

To find out the level of acidity or alkalinity in a fluid or tissue, we usually focus only on the concentration of H− present. This figure is given by the famous "pH," which means "one Part of Hydrogen ion per 10^n." This is what that means:

In distilled water at 22° C, there is one gram of Hydrogen ions (H+) and one of hydroxyl ions (OH−) for every 10,000,000 liters of water; the proportion is thus $1/10^7$, or 10^{-7}. The pH of water is thus 7. Acids have a higher proportion of H+. For example, beer has a pH of 4.5, which means that there is 1 gram of H+ to 150,000 liters of fluid. Stomach acid, which is very corrosive, has a pH of 1.1, or 1 gram of H+ to just 10 liters of fluid.

The important thing to remember is that *when the numbers go down, the acidity goes up*. Because water has equal amounts of H+ and OH−, it is considered neutral. A pH under 7 is considered acid, while a pH over 7 is alkaline.

ACID-ALKALINE SCALE

ACID		NEUTRAL			ALKALINE
stomach acid	wine	water	blood	sea water	baking soda
pH 1	3.5	7	7.5	8.1	12

Is this relevant to our body? Immensely so. The pH of our blood plasma must remain at a constant between 7.35 and 7.45. The slightest deviation in either direction spells trouble. An acid pH of 6.95 results in diabetic coma and death, while an alkaline pH of 7.7 causes tetanic convulsions and eventual death. The more acid pH of the blood slows the heartbeat, whereas a more alkaline plasma speeds it up.[3]

Clearly, maintaining the correct pH level of the blood is vital, and the body has several mechanisms to ensure its homeostatic balance. When the level of acids in the bloodstream is raised by the movement of the muscles and oxidation of protein and starches, these acids are then

- Broken down into water and carbon dioxide, to be eliminated through kidneys, skin, and lungs
- Utilized by the stomach for digestion as hydrochloric acid (ever notice how a walk after dinner improves digestion?)
- Neutralized and excreted as salts by the kidneys
- Neutralized or buffered by the presence of minerals left behind by the metabolism of alkalizing foodstuffs.

From a nutritional standpoint, foods are classified as either acid-forming or alkalizing according to the effect they have on the body, not according to their own intrinsic acidity or alkalinity. Thus, many foods that taste "acidic" (grapes and citrus, for example) are considered alkalizing because they leave an alkalizing residue upon being metabolized: the organic acids that affect the taste buds are dissolved and converted into carbon dioxide and water, while the minerals that are left behind serve to neutralize body acids. This is true, in fact, of most fruits and vegetables, as well as sea vegetables (dulse, kelp, hiziki, nori), all of which are high in buffering minerals (sodium, potassium, calcium, magnesium, iron). Coffee, when it is not decaffeinated, can also be alkalizing, for caffeine is an alkaloid; the rest of the coffee is highly acidic. Salt, because of its sodium content, is an alkalizing element as well.

Bland-tasting foods, on the other hand, (for example flour, fish, and grains), are often, though not always, acid-forming: when metabolized, they leave sulphuric, phosphoric, and hydrochloric acids behind. The only vegetable foods that are acid-forming are cranberries, plums, and prunes. I would like to add raw tomatoes *with seeds* to that list, as they sometimes provoke acidic reactions, such as mouth sores or bumps on the tongue (well-cooked, seeded, salted tomatoes seem more alkalizing). Sugar and other concentrated sweeteners, starches, grains, flour, fats, and most animal protein foods also create an acid condition upon being metabolized. The exceptions: potato and kuzu (kudzu) starch (see page 254 for more on this food) are alkalizing, and so at times are raw milk and cheese, because of their calcium content.*

In chemistry, the alkalis, or bases, are also known as acid-buffers; they cushion the corrosive effects of acids. Thus we can say that the alkalizing foods will buffer the acidifying ones. In addition, there is a category of foods that belong in a separate "buffer" category, for they can produce either effect: they will render the acid less acid by their mineral content, and the alkaline less alkaline by their protein content. These are dairy and soybean products (cream, yogurt, milk, cheeses, tofu), which combine well with either category of food. Butter, which has been found to be neutral (neither acid nor alkaline) also belongs in this category.

Just think: We put butter on bread (acid) and cream in the coffee (alkaline); we eat fruit (alkaline) with yogurt; we add tofu to both grain (acid) and vegetables (alkaline), and melt cheese over meat (acid)—trying, in effect, to bring the extremes closer together and keep ourselves in balance.

What is the relationship between the acid-alkaline and the ex-

---

* Unfortunately, pasteurization diminishes the available calcium in milk[4], thereby also lowering its alkalizing qualities. Pasteurized milk and milk products can therefore be viewed as more acid-forming[5], a fact that may contribute to the widespread incidence of tooth decay in American children. The acidifying effects of cookies (flour and sugar) are probably not adequately buffered by the pasteurized milk that accompanies them (raw milk would probably be better). It is interesting to note that even though processed milk products are less effective as buffers, they are still used as such in the standard American diet.

pansive-contractive sets of opposites? Is acid expansive or contractive? And what is alkaline? Both are both. Sugar is an expansive acid-forming food, whereas meat is a contractive acid-forming one. Fruit is alkalizing and expansive, whereas salt is alkalizing and contractive.[6] We can see these relationships more clearly on the chart below.

Which is "better," acid or alkaline? William Howard Hay, originator of the Hay Diet, which became popular in the 1930s, suggested a ratio of 20 percent acid-forming to 80 percent alkalizing foods by volume. Arnold Ehret, more radical and an ardent proponent of raw foods, would have us eliminate *all* acid-forming foods from our diet, on the grounds that "the blood is alkaline,"[7] yet acids are as much part of our metabolism as are alkaline substances; naturopath Paavo Airola states emphatically that our bod-

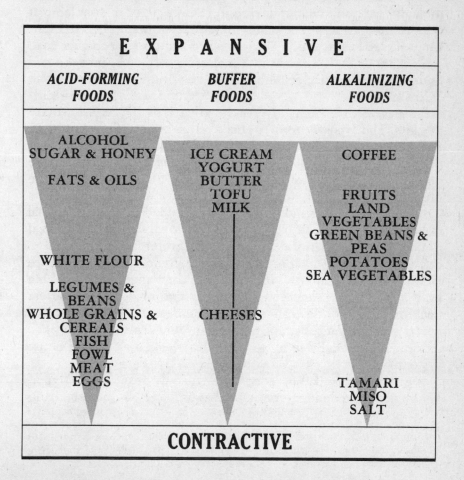

EXPANSIVE

ACID-FORMING FOODS	BUFFER FOODS	ALKALINIZING FOODS
ALCOHOL SUGAR & HONEY	ICE CREAM YOGURT	COFFEE
FATS & OILS	BUTTER TOFU MILK	FRUITS LAND VEGETABLES GREEN BEANS & PEAS POTATOES SEA VEGETABLES
WHITE FLOUR		
LEGUMES & BEANS WHOLE GRAINS & CEREALS FISH FOWL MEAT EGGS	CHEESES	TAMARI MISO SALT

CONTRACTIVE

ies need *both* kinds of foods. If we remember that opposites are complementary and necessary to each other, Dr. Airola's statement makes perfect sense.[8]

In what proportion, then, should acid-forming and alkalizing foods be consumed? As in all dietary matters, the correct proportions in each meal will vary with each individual metabolism, the amount of physical activity, other foods eaten earlier, and possibly with the depth and speed of breathing (deep breathing alkalizes the system). Hay's recommendation, for example—one part acid-forming to four parts alkalizing—is appropriate for people who are physically very active (creating a lot of acid) and need to alkalize themselves. Less active people can handle more acid-forming food, perhaps one to two, or even one to one, at times.

How do we know when our acid-alkaline balance is off? Fortunately, we don't need a degree in chemistry, or even a lab test (by the time an acid or alkaline imbalance shows up in a lab test, we're in serious trouble). What we need to do is heed the small signs that our body gives us as it makes adjustments to keep itself balanced, and rectify an imbalanced condition in time to avoid aggravating it.

It's easier to become overacidic than it is to become overalkaline. The foods we tend to gorge on are sweets, flour products, fats, and meats, all of which are acid-forming. When we become overacidic, we awaken with a sticky-sour taste in the mouth. To get rid of it, we almost automatically run for the coffee or the orange juice, both of which do indeed have an alkalizing effect. The sour taste in the mouth should be heeded as an alarm signal indicating that the body has an acid overload. If this condition is not corrected by diet or deep breathing (preferably with exercise, because too much deep breathing alone could cause hyperventilation and overalkalinity), the acids will draw minerals out of the body's own tissues, thereby creating a state of demineralization. Lack of sufficient minerals will first manifest itself in nervous or emotional imbalances, then perhaps in dental problems, broken nails, and eventually in a more serious weakening of the entire system.*

A serious overalkaline condition can only result from hyperventilating or extended vomiting. Eating large amounts of fruits

---

* Alice Chase, M.D., states that alkalizing buffer foods "could prevent demineralization of the bones, muscles, and nerves . . . and protect the body from dangerous acid saturation."[9]

and vegetables, if we don't balance them with grains or protein foods, can also cause a temporary alkaline excess; but this condition is usually promptly remedied by the subconscious wisdom of our bodies, which sends us in a pendulum swing on a cookie binge. Many of my vegetarian students have reported going through just such an experience.

It is reassuring to know that we do indeed have such a subconscious guardian of our health, that our body always tries to return of its own accord to its correct form and balance. Even collectively we share that trait, for ethnic dietary systems are invariably balanced in the acid-alkaline sense. For example:

THE WESTERN DIET

ACID	BUFFERS	ALKALINE
Sugar	Butter	Coffee
Flour	Milk	Fruit
Eggs	Cheeses	Salad, potatoes
Meat		Salt

THE JAPANESE DIET

Rice	Tofu	Scallions,
Fish	Miso	Daikon, burdock
	Soy Sauce	Sea weeds

THE ITALIAN DIET

Pasta	Cheese	Cooked tomatoes,
Veal		garlic, zucchini,
		eggplant

THE YOGIC DIET

Honey	Milk products	Fruit
Nuts		Vegetables
Bread		

Specific nutritional programs often exhibit a similar intrinsic sensitivity to the subtle acid-alkaline relationship. For example, from an acid-alkaline viewpoint it makes sense that

- Popular high-protein diets (acid-forming) that allow a minimum of alkalizing vegetables also forbid the acidifying carbohydrates (sugar, flour, and grain), yet allow coffee and salt, both alkalizers.[10]

- Raw-food diets (alkalizing) allow honey and nuts (acid-forming), yet forbid coffee and salt (both alkalizing).
- A diet such as macrobiotics that is high in whole grains (acidifying) also recommends the frequent use of seaweeds (strong alkalizers because of their mineral content) and salty condiments.
- A high protein and sugar intake (such as in the standard American diet) requires a high intake of calcium (buffering mineral) to forestall bone demineralization from its acidifying effects.

You may find that many other nutritional traditions or customs begin to make a lot more sense when you keep in mind the model of acid-alkaline opposites. For example: What is behind the common practice of adding a pinch of salt to the flour in baked goods? Why does sugar balance both coffee and salt? Why do people put salt on meat? (Notice that from an expansive-contractive viewpoint, such practices seem unbalanced.) Why do people eat meat and potatoes? Or mix tuna and vegetables?

I'm refraining at this point from giving you suggestions about what you should or shouldn't eat, and I'm certainly not advocating the consumption of sugar, salt, and coffee. My goal is to help you understand how food works. Once you do, you will be able to decide for yourself whether you should eat more acid-forming foods or more alkalizing ones, simply by attuning yourself to the signals of your own body. For pointers on this, see chapter seven, in part two of this book.

Let us now explore a third set of opposites: hot and cold.

WARMING AND COOLING

Traditional healing systems have always recognized temperature as one of the major influences on our health. Both inner and outer temperatures are taken into account. In Chinese medicine, for example, complaints such as arthritis, colic, and diarrhea are associated with cold, while headaches, sweating fits, and circulatory troubles are associated with heat.[11] External temperatures are seen as having not only a temporary effect: In some cases the heat or the cold are said to remain "trapped" inside, causing continued disturbances. One of my students, who is Chinese, wrote a paper about "hot" and "cold" foods as used by her mother and grandmother: Meat, fried foods, spices, and tropical fruits were considered "hot," and forbidden if someone had a fever; seasonal fruits and vegetables, soupy rice (congee), and pears were considered "cold" and were used to treat fevers.[12]

The Ayurvedic medicine of India holds that one of the main properties of foods is that of *virya*, or the ability to warm or cool the body. These warming or cooling effects occur regardless of the temperature or composition of the foods; they seem to have to do with a form of energy that has been called "the nonnutritious compounds or properties"[13] of the foodstuffs in question.

Laboratory analysis of components cannot tell us much about the total effect of the system called "food" upon the system called "person." In fact, most of the time one person cannot even tell with 100 percent accuracy how another person will feel or react after eating a certain food. Therefore, certain very subtle effects of food can only be noted by careful self-observation. Below is a list of warming and cooling foods that feels right to me.* It is quite possible that you may disagree with me on some of these; it all depends on how your own body reacts. The most important thing here is that you should recognize the validity of the concept and learn to work with it.

COOLING FOODS	WARMING FOODS
Raw fruits	Cooked and dried fruits
Raw vegetables	Cooked vegetables
Cucumbers	Cabbage
Summer squashes	Winter squashes
Citrus fruits	Coconut
Raw tomatoes	Tomato sauce
Papaya	Avocado
Leafy vegetables	Root vegetables
Soybeans	Tempeh
Tofu	Lentils
Mung beans	Kidney beans
Sea vegetables	Potatoes
Bulgur	Yams
Corn on the cob	Oats

* This list agrees in some parts with the Ayurvedic listing given by Ballentine, and in some other parts with the work of naturopath and acupuncturist John Garvy. Above all, however, it reflects my own sense of which foods are, in the final instance, warming or cooling.

COOLING FOODS	WARMING FOODS
Rice (brown or white)	Kasha
Ice cream	Barley
Yogurt	Cornmeal
Milk	Butter
Sprouts	Cream
Egg white	Aged cheese
Lobster	Nuts and seeds
Clams	Egg yolk
Crabs	Fish (cooked, fried)
Sashimi (raw fish)	Poultry
Pork	Beef
Coffee	Organ meats
	Chocolate
	Kuzu

Flavoring, herbs, and spices have warming and cooling qualities of their own and will affect the foods with which they're used accordingly.

HERBS, SPICES, FLAVORINGS

COOLING	WARMING
Curry	Garlic
Turmeric	Ginger
Dill	Cumin
Parsley	Caraway
Hot peppers	Basil
Coriander leaf	Thyme
Pickles	Oregano
Tamari	Bay leaf
Shoyu	Black pepper
White sugar	Coriander seed
Salt (holds cold)	Cinnamon
	Cloves
	Vanilla
	Miso
	Brown sugar
	Salt (holds heat)

At first glance, the classification of some of the herbs and flavorings may seem paradoxical: Curry, after all, tastes "hot." Yet our concept of the pendulum swing, or that of one thing turning into its opposite, supports what modern science tells us: that the final effect of "hot" spices is indeed cooling. Curry, hot peppers, and the like all grow in a hot climate; they feel initially hot to the taste because they expand the capillaries, thus allowing blood to rush to the surface of the skin. This action provokes perspiration; and when perspiration evaporates, the effect on the body is cooling. To test this, simply eat a spicy Indian meal in the middle of winter and then go out for a walk in the minus 15° wind—you'll feel chilled to the bone.

Ginger is spicy too, but being a root, it is more contractive (see Expansive-Contractive Chart, page 69) and helps hold the heat; hot peppers, on the other hand, are expansive and disperse it. The effects of ginger appear to be consistently warming if we are to go by the personal experience of those who try it. One of my students, for example, discovered recently that adding ginger and garlic generously to her soups and stews helped her overcome a feeling of inner chill that had plagued her for years.

Contractive foods, as a rule, hold the heat and thereby are warming. Heat, however, expands; and we need to eat something hot when we're too contracted from the cold, so as to expand into balance. Expansive foods disperse the heat, and therefore are, as a rule, cooling. But when we get too expanded from the summer heat (plus expansive foods), then we may require something as drastic as a frozen dessert or a chilled drink to contract toward balance again. If we eat only moderately expansive foods in the summer (cool blanched vegetables, bean and grain salads), we won't need the chilled dessert.

Sugar and salt are both warming and cooling. Their crystalline structure holds the temperature applied to them and even intensifies it: Hearty, hot soups are more so when properly salted; and ice cream is made at home with the help of ice and salt. Curiously enough, cold foods taste best when sweet or sour, hot foods when salty or spicy.

COOKING TECHNIQUES

COOLING	WARMING
Steaming	Boiling
Stir-frying	Sautéeing
Pickling	Frying
	Baking
	Dry roasting

It's a good idea to learn to use foods and cooking methods to regulate body temperature and to counterbalance the weather of the season. Notice that we have several warming-cooling elements to consider: the actual temperature of the food; the intrinsic subtle "hot" or "cold" energy ascribed to it by Oriental culture (see preceding pages); the temperature of the environment; and the law of the pendulum, which turns everything into its opposite, a phenomenon very clearly noticeable in the matter of temperatures. As the sensation of body temperature is highly subjective, you have to explore slowly and carefully your own reactions to what you eat.

BUILDUP AND BREAKDOWN

There is one very obvious set of opposites that occurs not in foods (although it is affected by them), but in our bodies: the buildup and breakdown activity of our metabolism.

Both Chinese philosophy and Western physiological science note that well-being results from the harmonious interaction of the buildup and breakdown forces in the body. An excess of either one checks the excesses of the other; the body exists at the conjunction of the two.*

During the metabolic process, we use the foods we eat to create more cells, repairing and building up our bodies; this is called *anabolism*. Much nutritional advice revolves around how to get enough material to support this process. But, lest we turn into giant blimps, we must also have an effective breakdown activity, known as *catabolism*: This process will ensure that used cells, waste matter, and metabolic by-products can be split up, broken down, and eliminated from the body.

Buildup uses or stores energy, and breakdown releases it. Thus, we grow and repair while we rest; and we break down and release energy during our daily activity and movement. The metabolic cycle is as follows: Breakdown needs rest as a balancer, rest promotes buildup, buildup demands activity as a balancer, and activity promotes breakdown.

Proteins, carbohydrates, and fats are the major building materials of our metabolism; buildup foods, therefore, are meats, dairy, eggs, beans, and grains. Fruits and vegetables will support the elim-

---

* Walter Cannon, M.D., Nobel Laureate, writes this of the human body: "The structure itself is not permanent, but is being continuously broken down by the wear and tear of action, and is continuously built up by the processes of repair."[14]

ination processes in our bodies and help in the breakdown of our cells and the expulsion of waste matter. Water plays a role in both buildup and breakdown. It must be retained in the body and circulated, and at the same time it must wash out waste matter and dead cells.

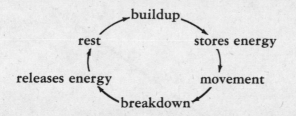

BUILDUP ELEMENTS	BREAKDOWN ELEMENTS
Proteins	Minerals
Carbohydrates	Vitamins
Fats	Fiber
Water	Water

BUILDUP FOODS	BOTH/NEUTRAL	BREAKDOWN FOODS
Meat	Grains/flour	Vegetables
Fowl	Water	Salads
Nuts and beans		Fruit
Milk		Sea vegetables
Eggs		
Cheese		

HELPERS
Salt
Sugar

I've placed grains in a "neutral" position, that is, supportive of both buildup and breakdown, because they contain both protein and fiber. They seem to aid the buildup of matter as well as its breakdown. I have seen people lose quite a bit of weight upon switching to a whole-grain regime; then, once a satisfactory balance has been reached, grains maintain weight at a steady level, supporting whatever buildup is necessary.

Salt and sugar are helpers in both processes. Salt causes the body to retain water and this process is essential to keep the body's

SEA
ORG
CO
FLA
FOOD CATEG

GRA
BE
VEGETA

FRU
ANI
FO
MO

SEASON: Spring
ORGANS: Liver/Gall Bladder
COLOR: Green
FLAVOR: Sour
FOOD CATEGORY: Fats
GRAINS: Wheat, Rye, Oats, Barley
BEANS: Lentils, Green Split Peas
VEGETABLES: Sprouts & Leafy Salads Green Peppers, Green Squash, String Beans, Broccoli
FRUITS: Tart Fruits
ANIMAL FOODS: Chicken
MOODS: *Positive*—Planning & Decision Making *Negative*—Impatience, Anger

NOURIS

WOOD

PENETR

NOURISHES

WATE

SEASON: Winter
ORGANS: Kidney/Bladder
COLOR: Black, Blue, Deep Purple
FLAVOR: Salty
FOOD CATEGORY: Salt
GRAINS: Kasha
BEANS: Black, Kidney, Pinto, Ad
VEGETABLES: Seaweeds
FRUITS: Blackberries, Blueberries Concord Grapes, Watermelons, Cranberries
ANIMAL FOODS: Bluefish
MOODS: *Positive*—Willpower, Vitality *Negative*—Fear

THE FIVE
PHASES OF FOOD

umer
rt/Small Intestine

er
ulants (Coffee, Cigarettes,
ohol, Bitter Chocolate)
ow Corn
Lentils
er Greens (Kale, Mustard
ens, Chicory, Escarole,
delion, Etc.), Tomatoes,
lions
wberries, Apricots

b, Shrimp
tive—Commanding
ction, Joyfulness
ative—Anxiety,
essive Laughter

IRE

NOURISHES

MELTS

EARTH

DAMS

NOURISHES

CUTS

METAL

RISHES

SEASON:	Late Summer
ORGANS:	Stomach/Spleen, Pancreas
COLOR:	Orange, Deep Yellow
FLAVOR:	Sweet
FOOD CATEGORY:	Sweets
GRAINS:	Millet
BEANS:	Chickpeas
VEGETABLES:	Winter Squash, Yams
FRUITS:	Sweet Fruits
ANIMAL FOODS:	Swordfish, Tuna, Pheasant
MOODS:	*Positive*—Imagination, Sympathy *Negative*—Worry

SEASON:	Autumn
ORGANS:	Lungs/Large Intestine
COLOR:	White
FLAVOR:	Spicy
FOOD CATEGORY:	Proteins
GRAINS:	Rice (Brown & White)
BEANS:	Soybeans, Tofu, Navy Beans
VEGETABLES:	White Onions, Cabbage, Turnips, Celery, Radish, Cauliflower
FRUITS:	Pears
ANIMAL FOODS:	Cod, Flounder, Haddock, Turkey, Beef
MOODS:	*Positive*— Creative Order *Negative*— Melancholy, Grief

form; only in excess is it undesirable. Paradoxically, salt also helps in breakdown by stimulating the kidneys to eliminate; I've often seen people who eat lots of salt and who are very skinny. Sugar helps in the buildup process in conjunction with flour and dairy products; however, it is also a factor in breakdown, because it causes hyperactivity. Many children on a high-sugar diet, boys especially, are extremely thin (another reason for that may be that sugar inhibits the release of growth hormones).*

It is important to remember that both buildup and breakdown processes are necessary to life. A dietary approach that emphasizes buildup foods while neglecting the breakdown foods is certain to cause problems of accumulation. In the opposite case, when breakdown foods are in excess, there may be problems of deficiency and, in severe cases, even malnutrition.

FIVE-PHASE THEORY

A more complicated, yet more detailed, model for understanding balance is that offered by the Chinese Theory of the Five Elements, or Five Phases. It is based on the notion that the life energy moves in specific cycles that are chartable and thereby predictable. As it moves, the energy passes through five changeover points, which have been called Wood (or "Tree" energy), Fire, Earth, Metal, and Water. One phase feeds or nourishes the next one; but in order to keep the energy from getting too strong, each phase also controls or holds back the opposite.

Each phase is associated with specific seasons, organ systems, colors, flavors, moods, foods, activities, and emotions. There is a tremendous amount of detail in this model, and it would be too complex for the purposes of this book. It needs, in fact, a whole book of its own; please refer to the reading list for the titles already available.[15] I will be using some of the concepts of this model without specifically identifying them, especially in the sections entitled "Can Health Food Make Us Sick?" (chapter nine), "Cravings and Binges," (chapter ten), "The Effects of Food on Mood" (chapter thirteen), and "Home Remedies" (chapter twelve).

---

* Sugar consumption prompts the pancreas to release large amounts of insulin, which remains in circulation long after the sugar is metabolized. According to Durk Pearson and Sandy Shaw, insulin suppresses the release of growth hormone and thereby may impair the immune system.

Part Two:
FOOD

Every man should eat and drink, and enjoy the good of all his
labour.   —Ecclesiastes

Food is the most intimate consumer product.   —Ralph Nader

Four:
Modern Diets —
A Reevaluation

*Thou art wearied
in the multitude of thy counsels.*

Isaiah 47:13

We have looked at various models that explain the properties of food that affect us above and beyond their quantity of nutrients and calories. Let us now reevaluate the common dietary practices from this new perspective. I would like to limit the discussion to those diets that are relevant to our contemporary lifestyles: the standard American, the recommended American, specialized diets (the Pritikin diet, high-protein diets, low-calorie diets), the fortified natural-foods diet, the vegetarian diet in its various versions, and macrobiotics. In the following chapter I will examine what I like to call the Health-Supportive Whole-Foods Eating Style—my own choice, and the way of eating that I feel is most flexible and workable in our society.

THE STANDARD AMERICAN DIET

This is a difficult diet to define, as there have been no works written specifically about it (except for those that decry it). Let's take as an example of our basic Standard American Diet (S.A.D.) the fare served in coffee shops throughout the country. It represents, I feel, the middle ground between TV dinners and martini-and-steak lunches.

Generally speaking, the diet is based on esthetics and technology. Foodstuffs are considered appropriate or inappropriate first because of their appearance, aroma, and taste; and, second, according to the number of their component material parts, or nutrients (vitamins, minerals, proteins, and so on), as identified and quantified in laboratory studies. Technological methods are applied to the preservation of foods (canning, freezing, chemical preservatives), and their effects are noted only on flavor and appearance. The S.A.D. rejects the age-old premise that food affects health greatly and in a multitude of ways. In tandem with modern Western medicine, the only health effects it attributes to food are those of obesity or malnutrition—that is, variables that can be measured in numbers. Intrinsic qualities, being nonquantifiable, are ignored.

IT CONSISTS OF:

- Meat (especially hamburgers and hot dogs), chicken, eggs, bacon, cold cuts, some fish (especially canned tuna)
- Milk, cottage cheese, butter, ice cream, and other dairy products
- Refined wheat products (bread, cake, cookies, pasta) and other refined grains with sugar, preservatives, flavorings, and synthetic nutrients added (as in breakfast cereals)
- Tomatoes, potatoes, lettuce, green beans, peas, carrots, celery, corn, spinach, peppers, cucumbers, and a few other vegetables, often canned or frozen
- Sugar in desserts, candy, jellies; as an additive to many foods, such as bread or ketchup; or added directly, as in beverages or breakfast dishes
- Fruit: citrus, apples, grapes, bananas, watermelon (in the summer), strawberries, and a few others
- Peanut butter, potato chips, and other snack foods high in fat, salt, or sugar
- Chemical additives in canned, frozen, and commercially prepared foods, such as soups, salad dressings, and ready-to-eat and heat-and-serve foods
- Artificial or imitation foods: margarine, "whipped toppings," "diet" foods with artificial sweeteners, "bacon bits," "nondairy whiteners," and so on
- Stimulating beverages: coffee, soft drinks (with or without

caffeine and heavily sweetened with sugar or artificial sweeteners), alcoholic beverages
- Orange juice and other fruit juices

IT FORBIDS: Nothing.

IT IGNORES:
Whole-grain cereals (except token amounts of whole wheat), beans (except for some lentils, navy beans, and split peas in soup), many vegetables (for example, kale, chard, rutabaga, kohlrabi, collard greens), sea vegetables (except in industrial uses, such as agar for jelling).

THE S.A.D. TABLES OF OPPOSITES

CONTRACTIVE	EXPANSIVE
Salt	Sugar
Eggs, bacon	Juices, fruits
Meat, chicken, fish	Lettuce, potatoes, tomatoes
Hard, salty cheeses	Coffee, alcohol
	Yogurt, milk, cottage cheese

WARMING	COOLING
Fats	Ice cream
Meat	Fruits, lettuce
Black pepper	Cayenne, paprika
Tomato sauce	Raw tomato
Salty cheeses	Yogurt, milk
Chocolate	Soft drinks
Bean soup	Pickles

ACID-FORMING	ALKALIZING
Sugar	Coffee
Bread, pasta	Juices, fruits
Meat, fowl, fish	Lettuce, vegetables
Fats	Salt

NUTRIENT PROPORTIONS
According to the *Dietary Goals* report, Americans, on the average, eat 42 percent of their calories in fats, 12 percent in proteins, and 46 percent in carbohydrates, of which more than half (24 percent of the diet as a whole) is sugar.[1] Two-thirds of their caloric intake, then, is derived from fats and sugar.

PERCENTAGES OF CALORIES OBTAINED FROM VARIOUS NUTRIENTS IN THE STANDARD AMERICAN DIET

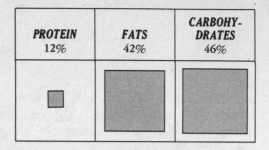

PROTEIN 12%	FATS 42%	CARBOHY- DRATES 46%

BALANCE

It is attained by counterpointing incomplete, or partial foods (see "Nutrient Proportions in Foods," page 52): meat (no carbohydrates) with sugar (no proteins), or white flour (very little proteins), and so on. Because so many foods in the S.A.D. are not whole foods, and the complementary relationship of partial foods is seldom precise, balance is extremely precarious.

EFFECTS

There has never been in the history of humanity a dietary system quite like this one. It is a very young diet, maybe a couple of hundred years old in some of its elements (bacon and eggs), thirty or forty in others (freeze-dried coffee, breakfast cereals, powdered artificial drinks). One of its interesting effects is the same as noted in traditional societies that have abruptly changed their eating habits: Because the food eaten by the children is often different from what their parents ate in their own youth, and the food consumed by pregnant women is totally different from what their own grandmothers traditionally ate, intra- and extra-uterine environmental influences are overriding heredity.[2] The physical aspect of younger generations is changing so dramatically that often children do not resemble their parents but look more like their unrelated peers. Comparing photographs of youngsters in the 1930s with contemporary children, we can observe a general narrowing of the face and jaws (with attendant orthodontic problems), most pronounced in boys. Many children and teenagers today *look* weak and are in fact often sick. The general vitality of the population is diminishing at an alarming rate. The partial, fragmented, unwholesome, chemically-tampered-with foods that the S.A.D. consists of cannot, in the long run, adequately support healthy life processes, and this is becoming more and more obvious. Even when followed only in moderation, the S.A.D. appears to cause a great deal of sickness, both physical and nonphysical. The physical problems are largely problems of accumulation and excess, for the S.A.D. is based on buildup foods. Heart disease, cancer, diabetes, and hypertension—all related to specific eating habits—"are epidemic in our population."[3]

The nonphysical health problems that plague us—delinquency, criminal behavior, hyperactivity, schizophrenia, depression—may be connected, in part at least, to the fragmented foodstuffs of the S.A.D., especially sugar and chemical additives. Imbalanced foods, whose natural, original energy fields have been disrupted, cannot properly sustain our own system in a stable balance.

General character traits may relate to diet as the chicken relates to the egg: They are either caused by it or the diet is chosen to support them. But perhaps the S.A.D. supports the general traits of this society: Aggressiveness, disregard for nature and a desire to dominate it, alienation, one-sided materialistic values, a disregard for the transcendental, and the perception of the physical as the only valid reality. On the other side of the coin, there is also efficiency, creativity, reliability, rugged individualism, entrepreneurship, and a constant desire to improve.

There is always much that we can learn when we are trying to overcome our difficulties and our mistakes. America has long been the land of growth and opportunity, where one can materialize one's dreams if one works hard enough—and not only materialistic dreams, but all kinds. One of my own dreams is that we eventually come up with an American dietary system that will bring a maximum of positive results and a minimum of unwanted disease.

THE RECOMMENDED AMERICAN DIET

I make this a distinct category, because the U.S. government, as well as the medical and nutritional scientific community, have fairly well-defined guidelines regarding what is healthful to eat. The Recommended American Diet (R.A.D.) is different from the S.A.D. and from traditional ethnic diets in that it is not a spontaneously evolved way of eating, but one based on intellectual, rational guidelines. This is a distinction it shares with vegetarianism, macrobiotics, high-protein diets, supplementation programs, and the rest of the theoretical approaches to food. They all distinguish between a wrong and a right way of eating, thereby creating the notion of nutritional sin, as well as salvation.

The R.A.D. has two aspects: a quantitative and a qualitative one. It recommends certain quantities of nutrient elements and also certain qualities of foods, or "food groups."

IT CONSISTS OF:
- Lean meats, fish, chicken, turkey
- Skim milk, yogurt, low-fat cheeses, polyunsaturated oils
- Pasta, bread, cereals, either enriched or whole grain; unsweetened or low-sugar breakfast cereals
- All vegetables, raw, steamed, baked; fresh, canned, or frozen
- Sugar in modest amounts; artificial sweeteners are not discouraged
- All fruits, fresh, canned, or frozen; heavy syrups are discouraged
- Diet foods with artificial colors, flavors, and sweeteners are not discouraged
- Coffee, tea, juices; little alcohol

IT RECOMMENDS:
- Reduced fat intake
- Reduced salt intake
- Reduced sugar intake
- Increased intake of whole grains, beans, vegetables, fruits
- Skim or low-fat milk products instead of whole or full-fat ones

IT FORBIDS: Nothing. It does disapprove of high fat, high salt, and highly processed foods.

IT IGNORES: Sea vegetables.

THE R.A.D. TABLES OF OPPOSITES

CONTRACTIVE	EXPANSIVE
Meat, fowl, fish	Juices, fruits
Eggs	Potatoes, tomatoes
Hard cheeses	Yogurt, skim milk
Cooked foods	Raw vegetables

WARMING	COOLING
Meat	Fruits, juices
Black pepper	Cayenne, paprika

WARMING	COOLING
Cooked tomato sauce	Raw tomato
Bean soups	Raw vegetables
Baked foods	Steamed foods

ACID-FORMING	ALKALIZING
Pasta, bread	Fruits, juices
Fish, fowl, meat	Cooked and raw vegetables

NUTRIENT PROPORTIONS

The Recommended American Diet would derive 30 percent of its calories from fats, 12 percent from proteins, and 58 percent from carbohydrates. Of the latter, 43 percent would be complex carbohydrates (starches) and only 15 percent simple carbohydrates (fruits and refined sugar). (See the chart on page 100.)

BALANCE

These recommendations are widely translated into meals that emphasize raw and steamed, cooling foods, very low fat and salt content, and with a respectable amount of protein most often supplied by fish or fowl. When the meal contains pasta, bulgur, brown rice, or other grain, it will probably feel fairly balanced and give rise to few cravings. If it has little or no starches, then it will create a strong desire for sweets, promoting what in the restaurant trade is called "cross-ordering": a healthy, low-fat entrée followed by a rich, sugary dessert.

COMMENTS

The recommendations based on *quality* are generalized as The Four Food Groups, or the Basic Four, namely,

- The Meat Group: beef, pork, veal, lamb, fish, fowl, eggs, as well as dried beans, peas, and nuts
- The Milk Group: milk, cheese, yogurt, and ice cream
- The Fruit and Vegetable Group: dark green and deep yellow vegetables, citrus or other fruits, and other vegetables, including potatoes
- The Bread and Cereal Group: breads and cereals, either whole grain, enriched, or restored

Lately, another category has been added, comprised of often-used but nonnutritive foodstuffs:

- The Sugar, Fats, and Alcohol Group

In this classification, foods are not actually grouped according to quality, but by their similar nutrient content. Thus, meat and beans are together because they are both protein foods; they are hardly of similar quality. Perhaps the meat group should be called the Protein Group. And, following the same reasoning, the others would best be named the Calcium Group, the Vitamin Group, and the Carbohydrate Group.

It is interesting that milk and milk products, which in fact are a single product category, get a whole group to themselves. (I have found even more peculiar the classification of ice cream—a high-fat, high-sugar concoction—as a regular food, to the point of its being recommended as a "good calcium source.") People who are allergic to milk products or who for one reason or another choose to forgo them, then appear to reject a whole food group, and thereby a whole class of nutrients. This is not the case; the nutrients found in milk products can be found in many other foodstuffs, both vegetable and animal.

We trip over semantics here. Vegetarians who eschew meat do not appear to reject a whole food group, because there are alternatives in that group, such as beans and nuts. The same opportunity for choice exists in the Fruit and Vegetable Group and the Breads and Cereals—these are broad definitions that give us choices.

What, then, are the alternatives for milk products? Curiously enough, they are the leafy greens and grains that, in some form or another, comprise the diet of milk-producing farm animals. In addition, such foods as nuts, seeds (especially sesame), and sea vegetables contain appreciable amounts of calcium, usually the only major nutrient for which milk products are recommended. (For further comments on calcium, see chapter six.)

It should be noted that there are no provisions for foods containing iodine or vitamin D in the food-group concept. To remedy this lack, I would suggest—instead of iodized salt and vitamin D–irradiated milk—sea vegetables, parsley,* and sunlight.

In some form, the idea of food groups as guidelines is not such a bad idea. In the next chapter I will give my own version of the food groups, so that you can use the concept in both a broader and a more individualized manner.

---

* Parsley contains ergosterols, which are Vitamin D precursors and convert into that vitamin in the body.[4]

The well-established Recommended Dietary Allowances
(R.D.A.) of the Food and Nutrition Board of the National Academy of Sciences, National Research Council, represent the *quantities* of nutrients suggested for optimum health. The figures vary
according to age, sex, and conditions of pregnancy or lactation in
females; they are also periodically revised upward or downward
according to prevalent scientific opinion.

As general guidelines, the R.D.A. may have a broad value, but
for many of us they are difficult, if not impossible, to act upon.
This is because, first, they are nonspecific to the individual; second, when we cook dinner, we don't boil protein, fry calcium,
sauté riboflavin, or bake carbohydrates. Instead, we cook beans,
fish, zucchini, barley. In its original, most reactionary form, the
R.D.A. accepted the consumption of the necessary amounts of
vitamins, minerals, proteins, fats, and carbohydrates regardless of
the form or quality of the food in which they were found. That
is, cake and brown rice, both "carbohydrates," were considered
virtually interchangeable from a nutritional standpoint. No significant difference was admitted between whole wheat and
bleached white flour or between fresh and canned vegetables. As
late as 1971, Leo Lutwak, M.D., a physician, professor of clinical
nutrition, biochemist, and nutrition consultant to NASA, was pub-
licly quoted as saying, "Nutritionally, it doesn't make any difference whether you eat white, brown, stone-ground, or any other
kind of bread."[5] Today, we know that such a position is erroneous.
When the human system interacts with a foodstuff system, it does
make a difference whether the carbohydrates come from a cookie,
a banana, brown rice, or split pea soup. The R.D.A. has evolved
accordingly.

Probably the biggest influence in the evolution of the R.D.A.
was the report on the "Dietary Goals for the United States," put
out by the Select Committee on Nutrition and Human Needs of
the U.S. Senate, in 1977. These are not only easier to understand
and follow than the R.D.A. chart—especially if we act upon their
suggested "Changes in Food Selection and Preparation"—but they
are nutritionally sounder, as they stress not only nutrient quantity
but also quality, the *type* of food from which we get our nutrients.

Their major suggested changes are as follows:

- Increase consumption of fruits, vegetables, and whole grains.
- Decrease consumption of meat and increase consumption of
  poultry and fish.

- Decrease consumption of foods high in fat and partially substitute polyunsaturated for saturated fat.
- Decrease consumption of butterfat, eggs, and other high-cholesterol sources.
- Decrease consumption of sugar and foods high in sugar content.
- Decrease consumption of salt and foods high in salt content.

COMPARISON OF THE PERCENTAGES OF CALORIES OBTAINED FROM VARIOUS NUTRIENTS IN THE STANDARD AMERICAN DIET AND THE RECOMMENDED AMERICAN DIET*

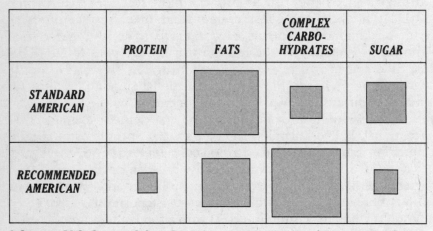

	PROTEIN	*FATS*	*COMPLEX CARBO-HYDRATES*	*SUGAR*
STANDARD AMERICAN				
RECOMMENDED AMERICAN				

* Source: U.S. Senate, Select Committee on Nutrition and Human Needs, *Dietary Goals for the United States*, 1977

Healthy People: The Surgeon General's Report on Health Promotion and Disease Prevention, published by the U.S. Department of Health, Education and Welfare, echoes the aforementioned recommendations when it suggests that Americans would probably be healthier, as a whole, if they consumed:

- Only sufficient calories to meet body needs and maintain desirable weight
- Less saturated fat and cholesterol
- Less sugar
- Less salt
- Relatively more complex carbohydrates, such as whole-grain cereal, starchy vegetables, fruits

- Relatively more poultry, fish, and legumes (for example, beans, peas, peanuts) and less red meat.

The report continues:

> . . . The processing of our food also makes a difference. The American food supply has changed so that more than half of our diet now consists of processed foods rather than fresh agricultural produce. . . . Increased attention therefore also needs to be paid to the nutritional qualities of processed food.

EFFECTS

It is difficult to assess the effects of this dietary approach because its boundaries are imprecise and its adherents difficult to identify. The recommendations are obviously sensible, although for some they may be too mild and for others much too strong. It seems to me that if present trends continue, the R.D.A. and the fortified natural-foods diet (see page 111) will eventually become almost parallel.

In addition to the S.A.D. and the R.A.D. there are a number of other diets—much more specialized—often known by the names of their proponents, that swing our metabolic pendulums this way or that. Let's take a look at the better-known ones.

THE PRITIKIN DIET

Nathan Pritikin, the late scientist, inventor, and founder of the Pritikin Center in Santa Monica, California, discovered a way to cure his own cardiovascular ailments through diet. He did this by simply cutting down drastically his consumption of fats and salt, reducing his intake of animal protein and sugar, and increasing his consumption of complex carbohydrates. He then systematized his experiences and introduced his approach to food and exercise to the general public through his best-selling books. The Pritikin Center can point to numerous cases of remission of hypertension, atherosclerosis, diabetes, constipation, and other common modern health problems.

IT CONSISTS OF:
- Whole grains, beans (except soybeans)
- Vegetables: fresh, canned, or frozen (except avocados and olives)

- Fruit: fresh, cooked, canned, or frozen (except coconut), and unsweetened; small amounts of dried fruit (limited because of its high sugar content)
- An average of about three ounces daily of lean meat, skinless chicken, or fish
- One glass of skim milk and two ounces of nonfat green Sapsago cheese or creamed cottage cheese are permitted daily
- Linden tea
- Egg whites if desired

(Exercise is also an integral part of the Pritikin Program, but we will not be commenting on that for the purpose of this book.)

IT FORBIDS:
All fats, oils, avocados, olives, salty meats, fish, poultry, full-fat dairy products, and soybeans; table salt and prepared foods containing it; refined carbohydrates, such as sugar, honey, molasses, fructose, and bleached white flour; white rice and pasta except in very limited amounts; caffeinated drinks (coffee, tea, cola, and so on); whole eggs and egg yolks; alcoholic beverages and soft drinks.[6]

IT IGNORES: No major foodstuffs.

PRITIKIN TABLES OF OPPOSITES

CONTRACTIVE	EXPANSIVE
Grains	Raw fruits
Cooked vegetables	Raw vegetables
Beans	Tomatoes, lemon, spices
Meat, fish, fowl (when used)	Egg whites

ACID-FORMING	ALKALIZING
Grain, fish, fowl, meat	Fruits, vegetables

WARMING	COOLING
Cooked grains	Salads
Cooked beans	Raw fruit
Meat, fish, fowl	Steamed vegetables

NUTRIENT PROPORTIONS
This dietary approach suggests only 10 percent of calories be obtained from fats, 10 to 12 percent from proteins, and 80 percent from complex carbohydrates, quite a radical change from the S.A.D.

PERCENTAGE OF CALORIES PROVIDED BY VARIOUS NUTRIENTS IN THE PRITIKIN DIET

PROTEIN	*FATS*	CARBOHY-DRATES
▪	▪	▉

BALANCE

Since it calls for whole foods, the Pritikin diet is essentially balanced. Some imbalances might occur with an overreliance on expansive warm-weather produce (salads, fruits, tomatoes) in a cold climate; some people might feel cold as a result. This could very easily be remedied by the use of hot dishes, hearty soups, and stews with beans, grains, and root vegetables.

EFFECTS

There is no better counterbalancer to the excesses of the S.A.D. than the Pritikin Program. We can think of it as a "minus" diet, one that because of the lack of, or very small quantities of, certain elements (salt, protein, fat), causes the body to use up whatever excesses of those elements it has, excesses that, if allowed to remain, can cause much trouble and disease. The diet can often bring excellent healing results for people suffering from such disorders of excess as obesity, heart disease, hardening of the arteries, high blood pressure, diabetes, and hypoglycemia. Dramatic recoveries have been reported: people barely able to walk after heart attacks who were walking several miles daily after six months on the diet, blood pressure dropping, insulin requirements diminishing, and even pounds being lost at a steady rate. In addition, the seasonings and the cooking methods used in the Pritikin regimen generally have expansive qualities, quite appropriate if used to balance the tightening, contractive, congestive S.A.D.

If adhered to for too long, however, past the point where it balances original excesses, the Pritikin regimen may have certain drawbacks. The total lack of added fats in what is a mostly vegetarian diet could cause a deficiency of fat-soluble vitamins, such as A and D, as well as of fatty acids essential to metabolism. This lack can, and often does, cause chilliness. Fat keeps our body temperature comfortable. A certain level of fat intake appears necessary for the production of energy from the breakdown of acetates, an intermediate product in metabolic heat production.[7]

Because the diet is not only expansive but also cooling, it is most appropriate in (a) warm weather; and (b) under conditions of metabolic overheating, when people feel warm most of the time and are attracted to cold foods and drinks. When these conditions are not present, faithful adherence to the regime will cause a general cooling of the system, nonphysical as well as physical: Emotional warmth can be lost together with a warm inner feeling. Interestingly enough, many people on long-term very low-fat diets "are notably irritable, fidgety, nervous, and depressed."[8]

COMMENTS

A no-salt, no-fat approach works best with the 10–12 percent allowable animal protein included. It definitely has negative results when followed in a "vegan" (zero animal foods) diet, for the food will be too loose and watery. I myself am not a pure vegan all the time, but I do eat a fair amount of my meals without any animal protein, not even dairy; whenever I've tried cooking such meals with absolutely no salt or oil, I've found them deeply unsatisfactory. Only a little bit of these elements restored the balance. If I didn't use that little bit, I found that after four days of completely salt-and-fat-free cooking, I would go on a binge of salty miso soup, bread and butter, and salt-cured olives.

Something similar happened the first time I taught a salt-and-fat-free cooking class. I had used fairly expansive foods, including tomatoes and lettuce, and plenty of sharp seasonings. Several people who carried an excess of dairy and protein in their bodies reacted wonderfully to the meal, reporting afterward clear heads and, in the case of one dancer, easy and flexible movements. But a few people, who already had been eating mostly natural and vegetarian foods for some time, went into a spin and took almost a week to come out of it: One went running for eggs, bacon, and sausages, while another headed for a Japanese restaurant that evening and drowned all her tempura-fried vegetables in soy sauce. A fat-free diet also requires high amounts of complex carbohydrates, needed for fuel. Counterbalancing these reactions took them the rest of the week.

Several concepts already discussed in this book shed light on the blind spots of the Pritikin Program: (a) the pendulum-swing concept; (b) the "eat as your environment dictates" concept; and (c) the understanding that canned and frozen foods in a regime low in animal protein are not at all satisfying.

If the Pritikin program has the most dramatic effects with seriously ill people, it seems reasonable to view it as a medicinal diet. That means that when the patient has recuperated, the diet must be modified, swung back, so to speak. The program followed in Pritikin's Longevity Centers allows for that, with a strict Regression (healing) and a wider Maintenance diet. (The book, *The Pritikin Program for Diet and Exercise,* does not mention these two variations.) If this swing back isn't done consciously, then there will be "cheating," an unconscious balancing move. In fact, allowances for "cheating" are made in the book, thus recognizing the need for it.

A further drawback is that although a large proportion of raw vegetables, salads, fruits, and spicy or sour-tasting dishes in one's diet is appropriate in warm weather, in colder weather we need stronger, heartier cooking. Eventually some added fat will be required in the cooking to allow for a defense against the cold.

Finally, as we saw earlier (chapter one), commercially processed foods are not only low in energy, they can be energy draining as well. This fact is even more noticeable in a low-fat, low-protein regime, for there isn't much excess against which to draw. Relying on canned and frozen produce could prevent or block feelings of energy, strength, and clear health. In a Pritikin-style diet, then, it would be advisable to consume only fresh vegetables and fruits for optimum feelings of well-being.

From all of the foregoing we can conclude that a strict Pritikin regime is excellent to counterbalance the excesses of the SAD; a modified Pritikin approach, low in but not devoid of fats, low in but not devoid of salt, with reasonable amounts of whole grains, beans, fresh vegetables, and lean animal proteins, can be an excellent health-supportive regime for most people in our society. Such a regime, in fact, is one that many doctors are beginning to suggest to their patients.

HIGH-PROTEIN DIETS

The high-protein, low-carbohydrate diet is probably over one hundred years old already and appears in a number of versions.[9] The best known of these are the Stillman, the Mayo Clinic (not associated with the real institution), the Calories-Don't-Count, and the Atkins diets. The sole aim of these regimes is to bring about a loss of weight, although Dr. Atkins also claims cures of a number of ailments.

THEY CONSIST OF:
- All forms of animal protein: meat, fish, chicken, pork, eggs, cheese, milk (skim or whole), yogurt, and so on
- In the case of the Atkins diet, generous amounts of fats: cream, butter, bacon, mayonnaise, oils
- Citrus fruits; yellow, green, and nonstarchy vegetables; lettuce
- Small amounts of sweet fruits
- Very low amounts of starchy fruits and vegetables
- Coffee, tea, diet sodas
- Eight to ten glasses of water daily
- Artificial sweeteners
- In some cases, vitamin supplements

THEY FORBID:
- Fats (on the Stillman diet)
- All foods containing sugar or white flour, white rice, corn, whole grains, pasta, starchy vegetables, root vegetables, beans, peas, and legumes
- Sweet fruit juices (with rare exceptions)
- In some versions, alcohol

THEY IGNORE: Sea vegetables, tofu, fermented soy products

HIGH-PROTEIN TABLE OF OPPOSITES

CONTRACTIVE, WARMING, ACID-FORMING	EXPANSIVE, COOLING, ALKALIZING
Meat	Lettuce
Fish	Vegetables
Chicken	Citrus
Eggs	Coffee
Pork, bacon	Water
Hard cheeses	Cottage cheese

NUTRIENT PROPORTION
By definition, the proportion of protein in a high-protein diet is much greater than that in the average diet (see chart, next page). Relative carbohydrate levels are too low, and the proportion of water must be kept high by a large fluid intake.

APPROXIMATE PERCENTAGES OF CALORIES PROVIDED BY VARIOUS NUTRIENTS IN HIGH-PROTEIN DIETS

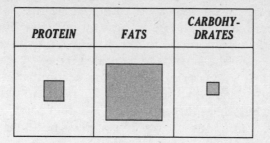

PROTEIN	FATS	CARBOHY-DRATES

BALANCE

It's very difficult, for most people, to be balanced on this kind of diet. Protein must be balanced by minerals (calcium), fats, carbohydrates, and water; the contractive substances in the diets need the expansive ones. But the high-protein diets, as prescribed, do not provide enough of these balancing factors.

EFFECTS

A high protein intake demands a very large amount of water for metabolism (see the table of Nutrient Proportions in Foods, pages 56–57). This water can be obtained by drinking, but it can also be siphoned from body tissues. As a result, these diets cause a loss of water weight, a well-known fact that accounts for their initial success. For people whose metabolism tolerates animal protein well, the weight loss can continue and be quite effective. The large amounts of animal protein can make others energetic at first, but then very high-strung and tense. A third group will react in yet another fashion, with sleepiness, lethargy, sluggishness, or a general heavy feeling. The relatively low carbohydrate level will sooner or later provoke a bread or sugar binge.

The diets are strongly tilted toward contractive, warming, and acid-forming foods. For a sedentery lifestyle (itself "contractive") pursued in a centrally heated environment, they generally prove to be unbalanced and cannot be tolerated for long. Eventual reactions are strong cravings for expansive, cooling carbohydrate foods, such as sugared desserts, ice cream, fruits. If those aren't needed, the next choice may inevitably and necessarily be alcohol. Of all the dietary strategies that my students have explored, these high-protein, low-carbohydrate ones were found to be most self-defeating, almost impossible to follow for long, and received the most negative votes.

LOW-CALORIE DIETS

These diets are an attempt to counterbalance the buildup effect of the Standard American Diet. They are not very different from the latter in the quality of the food consumed, only in the quantity. They are based on the general concept that if energy (calorie) input is less than energy (calorie) output, the accumulated excess will be burned up as the body draws on it for fuel. An example is the Weight Watchers Diet, based on the "Prudent Diet" of Dr. Norman Jolliffe. Variations of the diet appear periodically in most fashion and women's magazines.

Like the Recommended American Diet, low-calorie regimes also advise that the calories consumed be drawn from meat and dairy products as well as from vegetables of different colors and bread of any color (the four groups). Because the approach is quantitative, they rely heavily on weighing and measuring food portions and counting the calories in them as given by calorie tables.

It should be noted that these values are approximate calculations. The only way to find out the exact number of calories in a food is by oxidizing it until it is reduced to ashes and measuring the amount of heat it gives off, at which point it would be too late to eat it.

THEY CONSIST OF:
Theoretically, any combination of foods that gives the desired number of calories appropriate for the person, even if it's a hot dog and a slice of cake. Current recommendations, however, do stress whole-grain breads and cereals, fresh vegetables and fruits, and lean animal proteins.

Weight Watchers and similar diets allow only specific foods— dairy, fish, lean meats, leafy green and deeply colored vegetables, bread, coffee, fruit. Artificial sweeteners are used extensively, as are canned and frozen foods.

THEY FORBID:
Anything over the allotted daily calorie limit. Generally, high-calorie foods are discouraged: sweets, cream, sauces, eggs, rich pasta dishes, fatty foods, nuts and nut butters, and similar items. Weight Watchers also excludes dried legumes, soups, dried fruit, popcorn, salad dressings, and smoked fish.

THEY IGNORE: Fermented soy products, sea vegetables.

EFFECTS

I'm not aware of any healing effects that this approach to food may have, except for possible weight loss. Slimming down, of course, can by itself automatically bring on an improvement of certain disorders. Unfortunately, when there is no change toward healing at a deeper level, old habits return, and so does the weight. The body will change its shape in a lasting manner only to conform to a change in self-perception, because mind and body are a continuous, individual loop.

Although the concept of calories may be useful as a guide, it is not sufficient in and of itself to help us choose our foods correctly. Classifying foods on the basis of a theoretical number, disregarding not only their qualitative, nonquantifiable values, but even their nutritional composition, has severe drawbacks. It can steer us toward harmful foods that are "low-cal" (diet soda), and away from healthful foods that are supposedly not (split pea soup). Furthermore, calorie counting is not only ineffective in the long run, but also inaccurate. If we were to count all our daily calories, but missed the equivalent of three peanuts daily, we could theoretically gain eight-eight pounds in twenty years—obviously an absurd proposition.*

However, when sensibly applied with good-quality foods, the low-calorie diet can approximate the Recommended American Diet. For these reasons, it is probably the easiest to follow for the majority of weight-conscious people, especially when eating out. It is also the one diet that requires the smallest amount of inner transformation.

THE FORTIFIED NATURAL-FOODS DIET

The approach to nutrition popularized by Adelle Davis (*Let's Eat Right to Keep Fit*), Roger Williams (*Nutrition Against Disease*), J. I. Rodale (*Prevention* Magazine), and their followers consists essentially of eating natural foods plus vitamin and mineral supple-

---

* Roger J. Williams, Ph.D., discoverer of panthotenic acid and former president of the American Cancer Society, notes, "The idea that a piece of pie or a slice of bread or a hamburger contains a specific number of calories, and that these figures can be used to calculate one's calorie consumption is ridiculous." [10]

ments. It is probably the most popular nutritional theory among people who seek to improve their health by improving their diet.

The diet is based on the idea that the cells that make up our bodies need specific nutrients and that the health of the cell determines the health of the body. The best foods to nourish our cells are natural, whole foods, raised with traditional methods of agriculture and animal husbandry, without the use of petrochemicals, synthetic nutrients, or hormones. It also holds that because the soil isn't what it used to be in terms of nutrient content, because we don't always eat as well as we should and therefore might be missing some nutrients unknowingly, we should supplement our diet with vitamins and minerals in concentrated form. These will serve as medicine for current ills, as well as insurance against possible future deficiencies. Whatever nutrients are taken in excess, it is held, will simply be excreted by the body.

IT CONSISTS OF:
- Whole grains, beans, fresh and frozen vegetables, fruit (fresh, frozen, dried), nuts, seeds
- Meat, chicken, fish, eggs, game (all naturally raised and fed)
- Unpasteurized milk, cheeses, yogurt, butter
- Herbs, spices, honey (preferably raw); raw, brown, or turbinado (semibrown) sugar; vegetable salts and sea salt
- Fortifiers: brewer's yeast, blackstrap molasses, wheat germ, bran, protein powders, spirulina, lecithin, desiccated liver, dolomite, and other concentrated foods
- Supplements: vitamins, minerals, digestive enzymes, and so on

IT FORBIDS:
- White sugar, white flour, white rice
- Commercially processed foods, "junk" foods, and those with artificial coloring, flavoring, preservatives, and other additives
- Beef or chicken raised with synthetic feed and hormones
- Coffee, tea, chocolate, regular salt, pepper

IT IGNORES: No major foods.

Tables of opposites and *Balance* are very similar to the R.A.D.

NUTRIENT PROPORTIONS

When natural, whole, unrefined, foods are used, nutrients will be in their natural proportion to each other, and from that standpoint the diet will be balanced. However, if vitamins and supplements are consumed in addition to these foods, an imbalance of nutrients will occur; the excess of concentrated nutrients will cause a relative deficiency of all the nutrients not taken—neglected vitamins, the water, fiber, protein, and carbohydrates left behind.

PROPORTION-OF-NUTRIENTS MODEL

If a balanced diet looks like this:

MINERALS AND VITAMINS	PROTEIN	FATS	CARBOHY-DRATES
▫	◻	◻	◻

a fortified natural-foods diet would look like this:

MINERALS AND VITAMINS	PROTEIN	FATS	CARBOHY-DRATES
◻	◻	◻	◻

(We cannot do a calorie-comparison chart because minerals and vitamins do not provide calories.)

EFFECTS

Literature on the fortified natural-foods diet teems with testimonials to its healing powers. All sorts of conditions are said to have been improved—from white hair darkened by taking two tablespoons of blackstrap molasses daily for six months;[11] to eczema healed with brewers' yeast, desiccated liver, lecithin, and prune juice; to brain-injured children helped by an intense nutritional and supplementational program.[12] The fortified natural-foods diet is certainly a great improvement over the S.A.D, and changing from the latter to the former can indeed be of great benefit. Three aspects of the diet can be credited for the improvements reported:

- Harmful foods are not eaten, thus creating a sort of "negative healing"; that is, you feel better because you don't eat foods that make you sick.
- Healthful foods are consumed, creating "positive healing," or a condition of health via better nourishment.
- Supplementary vitamins and minerals that have a positive effect because THERE IS A DEFINITE DEFICIENCY STATE IN THE BODY.

While the use of supplements as medicine to treat specific conditions is eminently rational, "the shotgun approach"[13] of general nutritional supplementation is not. Taking sixteen or twenty nutrients in pill form "just in case" there aren't enough in the wholesome foods also eaten indicates fear and mistrust of food, and of nature itself. As long as the fear of not having enough motivates our choices, we will always be deficient, and nothing will ever be enough.

A Commentary on Nutritional Supplements

Vitamins are organic compounds (containing carbon and hydrogen) found in all foods, vegetable and animal. Their presence is needed for the smooth metabolism of proteins, fats, and carbohydrates, the formation of body tissues, and cellular energy exchanges. Some vitamins can be obtained by bacterial syntheses in the intestines (mostly the B vitamins) or on the skin in the presence of sunlight, as with vitamin D. On the whole, however, vitamins must be obtained from food.

They are needed in exceedingly small amounts: All together, maybe one-eighth of a teaspoon daily. Yet their absence from the diet can cause serious deficiency diseases (pellagra, beri-beri, scurvy, night blindness), as well as nonspecific disorders such as poor appetite and failure to grow.

Minerals, such as iron, zinc, magnesium, calcium, sodium, potassium, and others, are also needed for proper metabolism. They are found in all plant and animal tissues in minuscule amounts. Current research holds that they cannot be synthesized by the body, but must invariably be obtained from external sources. They play a major role in regulating the acid-alkaline balance, the movement of fluid in and out of cells, electrical activity along the nervous system, oxygen transport, and countless other metabolic activities. A deficiency in minerals can cause such conditions as anemia (too little iron), poor bone resiliency (too little calcium), and increased neuromuscular irritability.[14]

Interest in the molecular and atomic composition of the body has been growing throughout the century as the sophistication of microscopes and research techniques has increased. When vitamins were discovered to be key factors in the biological effects of different foods, the study of nutrition became more and more the study of the effect of these invisible compounds. The scientific, reductionistic approach to nutrition holds that only micro and macro nutrients (vitamins, minerals, proteins, carbohydrates, and fats) need be considered. The intangibles, such as animal or vegetable quality, shape, color, aroma, taste, texture, direction of growth, and climate or season of origin have, it is held, nothing to do with the appropriateness of one food or another.

According to the systems approach, however, *all* the above factors play a role, and we must consider the context in which nutrients appear, as well as their proportion and relationship to one another. When that relationship is altered, the body has to make adjustments that are not always comfortable.

The practice of taking vitamins as "insurance," "just in case we're missing something," ignores this. As an example, let's look at a carrot:

Water
Protein, carbohydrate
Iron, calcium
Phosphorus, sodium
Potassium, B vitamins
Fiber (the chewy part!)
Vitamin A

In its infinite wisdom, nature has designed carrots, and all other plant foods, as systems containing a wide array of nutrients. This is fortunate, because human beings do not always have access to a wide variety of foods. If each food has a range of nutrients, we are then more likely to be assured ample nourishment. Nature has also designed us so that we can chew, swallow, digest, and assimilate the carrot with all its nutrients.

But when we take the vitamin A out of the carrot, put it in a pill with sugars or starches, and swallow that, our body system will be surprised. As it's not used or suited to metabolizing a single element, it soon starts asking, "Where are all the other guys? Where's the chewy part?"

It has been well established that vitamins in the B complex (thiamine, riboflavin, niacin, B_6, B_{12} and so on) are interdependent: Taking one of them increases the need for the others.[15] In other words, taking B_6 tablets can make us relatively deficient in B_1, B_2, B_{12}, and all the others. Why? Because the B-vitamin complex forms a living system of sorts, and breaking up a system always creates a need for that system to rebalance itself. Greater amounts of B_6 must be balanced with greater amounts of B_1, B_2, B_{12}, and so on.

A carrot is also a system. Taking the vitamin A alone will make us relatively deficient in all the elements that usually accompany it in the carrot (or in other natural foods). And how does the body respond when it perceives itself as deficient? It reaches for something to correct the deficiency: In this case, it may go for "the chewy part" and develop a case of the "munchies." Every time I bring up this concept in a class or a counseling session, eyes light up—ahh, is *that* why I'm overeating even when I'm not hungry? Is that why I've been putting on weight since I started a "health regime"? Yes, indeed, yes. In other words, if you take a vitamin A pill in the morning, you may be spending the afternoon looking for the rest of the carrot.

Another way in which the body may try to right an imbalance—other than by adding the missing elements—is to expel the excess. The recommendations to take vitamins are often accompanied with a statement to the effect that if any are taken in excess, the body will simply get rid of them. This is quite true. What we fail to consider, however, is *how* this excretion will be accomplished, or through which organ: kidneys, intestines, lungs, or skin. One young woman who came to see me a few years ago had a rash all over the lower part of her face from ear to ear, like a beard. No dermatologist or nutritionist had been able to help her. I found she was eating quite well, not much fat or nuts or dairy—but she was taking twenty vitamin pills daily. I suggested she stop those and just continue eating good plain food. Two weeks later, I got an ecstatic letter from her telling me that her face had completely cleared up. Obviously, her body had been excreting the excess vitamins through the skin on her face.

As single elements, vitamin and mineral supplements must be considered medicine, whether they're natural or synthetic. They will fill a gap in the metabolism—if there is one. By "gap" I mean a relative vitamin and mineral deficiency created by partial or incomplete foods, such as sugar or white flour because of their unaccompanied carbohydrates (see chapter three, page 63). Thus, even a small amount of sugar in the diet will create gaps that could theoretically be balanced by supplements.

But for a reasonably balanced individual following a regime based on whole foods, extra vitamins will be superfluous and will only create an imbalance where there probably was none.

When supplements are used medicinally, careful attention has to be paid to the dosage. They'll help fill in a deficiency, but once they've done so, their work is over and they should be discontinued. They are of course extremely useful in cases of clinical deficiency or extraordinary individual need. However, in the final instance, single-element substances such as vitamins and minerals cannot truly heal, *because they themselves are not whole*. Furthermore, because they lack the life energy of plants, they cannot stimulate our system to extract what it needs from foods. More often than not, in fact, a nutritional deficiency simply means that the body cannot assimilate or synthesize certain nutrients.[16]

The scientific viewpoint currently adhered to by the medical profession, and by advocates of fortified natural-foods diets, holds that the parts determine the whole, that the cell is the ultimate arbiter and director of the body's nutritional status, and that therefore it is the cellular component of foods—including individual vitamins and minerals—that we must pay attention to. The systems view holds the hierarchy in reverse: The whole determines the parts, health is a condition of the whole body, and a healthy body can overcome a few sick cells here and there.

Let us not completely throw out one viewpoint in favor of another, though, even if we do prefer the systems approach. The concept of cellular nutrition is indeed extraordinarily important and one that helps us get a fuller picture of biological reality. However, my experience has shown me that our health is best served when we nourish the whole body with whole foods, rather than single cells with single nutrients.

THE VEGETARIAN DIET

> Our citizens . . . will prepare wheat-meal or barley-meal for baking
> or kneading. They will serve splendid cakes and loaves on rushes or
> fresh leaves, and will sit down to feast with their children. . . . They
> will have a few luxuries. Salt, of course, and olive oil and cheese, and
> different kinds of vegetables from which to make various country
> dishes. And we must give them some dessert, figs and peas and beans,
> and myrtle berries and acorns to roast at the fire as they sip their wine.
> So they will lead a peaceful and healthy life, and probably die at a ripe
> old age, bequeathing a similar way of life to their children.
>   —Plato, *The Republic*

As young as the Standard American Diet is, so is vegetarianism
old. It goes back at least as far as the sixth century B.C. to the early
Greeks; both Plato and Pythagoras were enthusiastic vegetarians.

Basically, vegetarianism can be defined as a way of eating that
purposely avoids animal flesh foods—meat, fish, chicken, game,
and so on. There are three different approaches to the vegetarian
diet:

- OVO-LACTO vegetarianism, which allows the products of animals obtainable without slaughter, such as milk and eggs
- LACTO vegetarianism, which allows only milk and its derivatives (eggs are unborn chickens)
- VEGANISM, which avoids *all* products of animal origin, including milk, milk products, eggs, all foods containing these,
  and at times even honey. Proponents of veganism may go as
  far as avoiding all products made with wool, leather, bone,
  and fat, including cosmetics, soaps, clothing, and other common items.

There are a number of people today who call themselves vegetarian, but who do eat fish. Technically, that is incorrect, so I
prefer to classify that eating style under the natural-food diets.

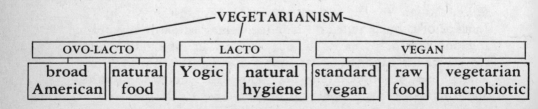

The difference between the Yogic and Natural Hygiene lies in their different basic philosophies: the first is an adjunct to classic Hindu philosophy, which divides foods into *sattvic* (natural, calming, cleansing), *rajasic* (cooked, spiced, gourmet), and *tamasic* (overcooked, spoiled, cured, unwholesome); the second is the brainchild of Herbert Shelton, who emphasized especially right and wrong combinations of food.

A vegetarian way of eating is usually embarked upon as a result of an individual's ideological choice. Throughout history it has had ardent and eloquent proponents, but generally they have been unheeded by society at large.[17] The societies that are close to being exclusively vegetarian are few: The vegetarian Hindus are so for religious reasons; the Indians who live in the Andes at 1,300 feet, and the Mexican Tarahumaras, whose mainstay is parched corn and beans, live at very high altitudes, where a low-protein diet has been proven highly beneficial.[18]

What motivates the choice of vegetarianism is of major importance, as it will determine the type of vegetarian diet followed. There are two kinds of motivation: moral (ethical or religious) and health-oriented. In many cases both play a part, though usually one will predominate. The moral viewpoint holds that it is wrong to kill living creatures in order to eat them, since there is enough nutritious vegetable food to be had. The health-oriented viewpoint holds that eating animal protein causes illness because our bodies are not built to process those foods: Our teeth are designed for grinding and chewing, not tearing; our intestines are too long, and meat putrifies during its slow passage through them, causing body odor, indigestion, and illness.[19] In addition, it is said that the metabolism of animal protein leaves behind toxins and waste matter (such as uric acid), which overwork the kidneys and the digestive system and are detrimental to clear thinking. Animal-protein foods also contain much saturated fat, not found in a vegetarian diet except in palm and coconut oil, and cholesterol, both of which may contribute to cardiovascular disease and obesity.

EFFECTS

In addition to the particular effects of each variation in vegetarian regimes (see the chart on the next page), a few very general observations can be made about the vegetarian way of eating.

A diet based solely on vegetable foods, especially raw vegetables and fruit, has a "cleansing" effect, because vegetables and fruit are

VEGETARIAN VARIATIONS

CATEGORY	CONSISTS OF	FORBIDS	EXPANSIVE	CONTRACTIVE	TABLES OF OPPOSITES WARMING	COOLING	ACID-FORMING	ALKALIZING	EFFECTS
Broad American	Vegetable foods, white flour, dairy products, canned and frozen vegetables, sugar, honey	Meat, fish, chicken, veal, game, lamb, pork	Salad, fruit, yogurt, sugar, soft drinks	Salty cheese, bitter chocolate, eggs	Soup, cheese, eggs	Salad, fruit, yogurt	Bread, sugar, pasta, eggs	Vegetables, fruit, potato, coffee	Unbalanced, fattening
Natural Vegetarian (lacto-ovo)	Fresh fruit, vegetables, whole grains, beans, nuts, dairy, honey	The above, plus frozen and canned foods, white flour and sugar	As above		Grain, beans, hot dishes, eggs	Juices	Beans, grains, flour, eggs	Vegetables, fruit, potato	With enough grain and not too much dairy, or sweets sustainable
Lactarian	As above, minus eggs	The above, plus eggs	Salad, fruit, yogurt	Hard cheese, grain, cooked food	Hard cheese, cooked food	Yogurt, fruit, salad	Flour, grain, beans	Vegetables, fruit, potato	As above, but too much dairy will cause trouble
Fruitarian/ Raw foods (Natural Hygiene)	Fruit, nuts/ Raw vegetables, soaked grain	Everything else	Salad, fruit	Nuts	Nuts	Fruit, raw vegetables	Nuts	Fruit, raw vegetables	Cooling, cleansing, unbalancing in the long run
Standard Vegan	Fruit, nuts, vegetables, grain, beans, sweets, honey, flour products	All products of animal origin	Fruit, salad, sweets	Nuts (grains and beans if used)	Nuts, hot foods	Fruit, salad, vegetables	Flour products, grain, nuts	Fruit, vegetables, potato	With enough grain and beans, minimum sweets sustainable

more supportive of breakdown than of buildup. For this reason, people lose weight when consuming appreciable amounts of these foods. (It is of course possible to lose too much weight: There comes a point when the pendulum swings past the balanced middle, and more buildup foods are required once again.)

A vegetarian diet that includes a high proportion of milk and milk products will have enough buildup foods to keep balance. It may sit well with some people, but in many others it may cause metabolic havoc, especially if the person has allergies or is lactose intolerant. Milk and cheese may in fact aggravate various allergy problems, regardless of what one is "allergic to." Also, as they are very strong buildup foods (milk makes calves grow into cows!), they may cause unwanted weight gain.

There are, incidentally, few eating habits as damaging as strict vegetarianism, or veganism (no animal protein, no milk products), when combined with the frequent use of refined sugar and/or honey. As sugar is a pure carbohydrate and lacks protein, in a vegan diet it will set up a relative protein deficiency, and thereby be weakening. Scientific evidence backs up this contention. In a detailed study conducted by Dr. C. Keith Conners of Children's Hospital in Washington, D.C., it was shown that a combination of a carbohydrate meal and a sugary food was "deadly" in its effects on learning ability and behavior, whereas sugar following a (animal) protein meal did not have such a negative effect.[20]

Well-balanced vegetarian eating, when a person is suited for it, is extremely healthful. Studies done on vegetarian groups such as the Seventh Day Adventists show a much lower incidence of cancer than in meat-eating populations.[21] A diet high in vegetable protein and correspondingly low in saturated fat is also positively correlated with clean coronary arteries.

A raw-foods vegetarian diet, even though it may include nuts and even soaked grains, is strongly tilted toward aiding breakdown because of its low protein and fat content. It's an extremely helpful way of eating when we wish to get rid of excess mucus, fat, or any sort of deposited matter in tissues, blood vessels, or joints. It is also extremely cooling. Most people I know who successfully follow a raw-food regimen live in a warm climate, such as Florida or California. Those who live in New York and other northern cities reported becoming very cold in the winter; they warmed up quickly as soon as they started eating cooked buildup foods, such as grains and beans.

COMMENTS

Vegetarians are often interested in spiritual development, meditation, and the transcendental view of life—that is, the understanding that there is another reality beyond the material world.* It is also popularly believed that vegetarians are peaceful, whereas meat eaters are bloodthirsty and even warlike. According to my observations, this bears out only partially. A well-balanced vegetarian way of eating, when coupled with an altruistic predisposition, can indeed support a peaceful and friendly character. But there are no guarantees: Cain, the tiller of the ground (perhaps a vegetarian?) killed Abel, the keeper of sheep (a meat eater?). Hitler was a committed vegetarian from 1911 until his death thirty-four years later. His case, in fact, is a dramatic illustration of unbalanced vegetarianism: He lived on fruits, vegetables, potatoes, milk, white rice, chocolate, and enormous amounts of sugar and white flour in the form of pastries and cakes.[23] Considering less extreme examples, I have seen many a contentious, cranky vegetarian—myself included at times—and many a kind and patient meat eater. After all, if the "you are what you eat" cliché is true, when you eat beef you become like the cow—not like the butcher.

This point was brought home to me on a five-hour plane trip I took with my children when they were three and six years old, and very lively. I dreaded the confinement and was prepared with healthy snacks, toys, and plenty of crayons. When lunchtime came, the only thing on the menu turned out to be beef bourguignon; the kids were hungry and demanded "airplane food," so with great trepidation and visions of little savages dancing in my head, I let them order it. Much to my surprise, after the meat meal they were quite relaxed and content, played quietly with their books and crayons, and even allowed me a nap! I found out later that one of the amino acids in meat, tryptophan, tends to induce relaxation and sleepiness.

Some people are natural vegetarians, practically since birth, and both the thought and the act of eating animal products is quite repugnant to them; they usually remain in excellent health on a simple vegetarian regime. On the other hand, there are people

---

* Hauschka says that this is because it's harder to convert vegetable protein into human protein, and the extra effort needed is like exercise that develops our inner powers and soul strength. I've noted that the opposite also applies: when people take up meditation, they often find themselves eating less and less animal protein, even if they didn't purposely set out to do so. (However, these observations in no way imply that people who eat meat can't be spiritual.)[22]

who cannot follow a vegetarian way of eating without becoming weak, getting depressed, losing energy, weight, hair, the "creative edge," and feeling generally deprived. Still others go in and out of vegetarian phases.

There are a number of theories that classify the body into various types so as to help us decide what kinds of foods work best for each of us. One theory, which according to some who have tried it is fairly effective, says that body types with strong adrenals do very well on a vegetarian, no-sugar diet, whereas those with strong pituitary-gland activity cannot handle a vegetarian diet too well—they need animal protein.[24] Another theory holds that people with strong, active endocrine systems, a high rate of metabolism, lean bodies, and a liking for exercise do well with large amounts of vegetables and fruits, whereas people with weaker endocrine systems, a slow metabolic rate, and the tendency to put on weight would be uncomfortable on a vegetarian diet and do better with a fair amount of animal protein.[25]

From what I've seen, vegetarianism works best when accompanied by a deeply felt spiritual commitment. When spirit and emotion support a diet devoid of animal products (or with dairy only), our bodies seem perfectly able to extract and transform all the nutrients they need for maintenance and repair from plant products. Vegetarianism does not appear to have equally positive effects when embarked upon solely for "sensible" reasons of health; if passion and emotion are not involved, we seem to be less efficient at processing vegetable matter, and symptoms of insufficiency may result after a number of years. Moreover, if the diet doesn't work, intellectual reasoning or ideology may at times block our awareness of the signals given out by our body indicating distress or discomfort.

To illustrate the weakness of iron-clad logic as a defense of vegetarianism, allow me to present you with two sides of the argument. As I mentioned earlier, moral vegetarianism is based on certain premises regarding the undesirability of killing animals and the unsuitability of our bodies for the consumption of animal protein. Some proponents of vegetarianism also maintain that we should eat nothing that can defend itself or run away from us.

I discovered the other side of these arguments with the help of a young man who once sat next to me on a train going from Philadelphia to New York. When he found out about my interest in food and health, and my own largely vegetarian inclinations, he laughed. "I'm quite the opposite," he said. "I only eat whatever can defend itself or run away; why should I attack helpless plants? So I eat only animals, not even eggs or milk! And you should see my plants! They grow tall and beautiful for me, and perfume my home—they know that I'm not going to eat them." As I sat there too dumbfounded to even wonder if he was kidding me, he went on: "Besides, our teeth are not suited for vegetable consumption. Our incisors are too short—look at the rabbits! And our molars are not wide enough—look at the horse and the cow! And our intestines are too short—the cow's intestines are twenty times their body length, whereas ours are only about four to six times our body length."

Recovering my speech, I started to say that it was quite the opposite, but since I didn't have the exact numbers at my fingertips, I decided that it was better to be quiet and mull over this whole new angle. Eventually I did some research and found that, to my surprise, the young man was right: The dog's intestines are 12 to 15 feet, or about four to five times its body length, if we allow some two to three feet from head to tail. Our intestines are 22 to 26 feet long; if we consider three feet from head to tail (legs don't count), that would make the intestines six to eight times body length. The herbivorous ox, however, has intestines that are 130 feet long; allowing five to six feet from head to tail, that would make them twenty to twenty-two times body length.[26] And where does that leave us in this age-old argument? In the middle! And so, it appears, choices in diet are available to us according to our desire and our comfort.

The young man, however, had not finished: "Not only are our bodies not suited to consume vegetables, but we can be much more spiritual by eating animal protein, which is easier to convert to our own protein and so doesn't use up too much of our energy; we have some left over to put into spiritual matters."

Well. What can I say? As Einstein taught us, everything is indeed relative. We just have to pick the ideas we like and we'll have no trouble finding the arguments and the evidence to support them.

The Question of Vitamin B_{12}

It is widely held that a fully vegetarian diet will be deficient in vitamin B_{12}, causing pernicious anemia and, after ten to twelve years, degeneration of the spinal cord. Studies done early in this century on British vegans, who ate only vegetable foods, no eggs or milk, revealed that many of them did indeed eventually exhibit those symptoms.

B_{12} is thought to originate from bacterial fermentation of vegetable matter in the intestinal tract of herbivorous animals. For this reason, their organs and muscles contain appreciable amounts of the vitamin. However, there is evidence that whole grains such as wheat and oats might in fact also supply the full B complex and deliver from 0.1 to 0.4 micrograms of B_{12} per 100 grams edible portion.[27] The Food and Nutrition Board recommends from 0.3 micrograms for infants to 4.0 for pregnant women. A daily intake of 0.6 to 1.2 micrograms is considered sufficient for the average adult.

A vegetarian diet based on substantial amounts of raw fruit and salads, nuts and seeds, cooked vegetables and potatoes, and only occasional grain, will indeed be deficient in this vitamin; and such was the diet of European vegetarians early in this century. If in addition sugar or honey is consumed, both of which tend to demineralize and weaken the body, the problem is compounded. But when the vegetarian diet is based on whole grains and beans as staple foods, B_{12} is supplied in sufficient amounts: A three-ounce serving of oatmeal will provide the minimum daily requirement for an infant, while as little as three ounces of oatmeal for breakfast and three ounces whole wheat bread during the rest of the day will supply enough B_{12} for the average adult. Sea vegetables contain significant amounts of the vitamin (see chart page 124), and their inclusion in the diet will ensure its availability.

Another factor to consider: Fermentation increases the B_{12} content of foods dramatically. Soybean meal has 0.2 micrograms per 100 grams, while tempeh (a fermented soybean cake that is becoming increasingly available in our natural-foods stores) offers from 1.5 to 6.3 micrograms per 100 grams (3.5 ounces) average serving. The B_{12} increase is due to a bacterium that is present alongside the fermenting mold.[28] It is interesting to note in this context that traditional dietary systems that include a high proportion of complex carbohydrate foods and little, if any, B_{12}-rich organ meats also feature many fermented products.

It seems possible that other fermented foods such as sauerkraut, pickles, miso, sourdough bread, natural beer—in fact, *any* fermentable carbohydrate—could all help our own intestinal bacteria synthesize B_{12}. A pure vegetarian way of eating, then, that also includes whole grains, fermented soy products, pickled or fermented vegetables, and sea vegetables should theoretically provide and/or help synthesize enough B_{12} to meet our needs. It wouldn't be necessary then to resort to injections or supplementation (as many vegetarians do), unless there was a problem of malabsorption.

My own experience corroborates this. Although I have not been a pure vegetarian, since 1964 I've been eating mostly grains, beans, vegetables, miso, natural soy sauce, some seaweed, fruit, nuts, and either fish, eggs, or chicken once or twice a week. No meat, no liver, almost no milk products. My blood was tested extensively at New York's Bellevue Hospital hematology laboratory in 1977, after some thirteen years on this kind of diet—plenty of time for pernicious anemia to develop. The results showed an iron level of 131, well within the normal range of 50 to 160. At this writing in 1984, as I am functioning very comfortably on five or six hours of sleep, with no signs of fatigue or sluggishness, I don't think the picture has changed; and although I eat small amounts of animal protein more often now, I still don't come near the recommended levels of protein or liver.

Not all vegetarians will either consume or absorb all the B_{12} they need. Bill Spear, director of the Macrobiotic Association of Connecticut in Middletown, has been studying B_{12} deficiency symptoms in macrobiotic children. He found that this syndrome appears occasionally in families following a fairly strict vegetarian macrobiotic regime that is also very low in salt and fermented soyfoods such as miso and shoyu (tamari).[29] Pure vegetarians—vegans—may have more difficulty than those who consume even small amounts of animal protein. If you are in doubt, or you are a vegan and often feel tired, have your blood level of B_{12} tested.

VITAMIN B_{12} CONTENT IN FOODS
Micrograms per 100 grams or 3.5 ounces*

Green beans	0–0.2
Kelp	0.5–1.0
Kombu (seaweed)	0.5–1.0
Oats	0.3
Nori (seaweed)	0.7
Soybean meal	0.2
Tempeh	1.5–6.3

* Sources: Benjamin T. Burton, *Human Nutrition*; Sharon Ann Rhoads with Patricia Zunic, *Cooking with Sea Vegetables*.

Wakame	0.6
Wheat	0.1
Whole wheat bread	0.2–0.4
Egg	0.3
Haddock	0.6
Liver, beef	31–120
Milk, whole	0.3–0.5
MDR for adults	0.6–1.2

MACROBIOTICS

The word *macrobiotics* (from the Greek *macro*, "big" or "long"; and *bios*, "life") was first used by the German physician Christoph Wilhelm Hufeland in the early 1800s to denote a European-style vegetarian diet. The Japanese scholar Sakurazawa Nyoiti, later known as George Ohsawa, in the late 1950s applied the term—which he translated as "the art of longevity"—to his Oriental-style natural-foods philosophy and diet. Today, thanks to the work of his two main disciples in the United States, Herman Aihara and Michio Kushi, macrobiotics has considerable popularity as an alternative health regime.

Arising from Oriental philosophy, or, more specifically, from Japanese culture and mores, macrobiotics offers a dietary viewpoint that is certainly different from the Western one. It is in fact a total philosophy of life, with food and diet only a small part of it, albeit the best-known part.*

Briefly, macrobiotics considers that all aspects of our existence must be taken into account in determining a correct eating style: season, climate, location, ancestry, type of activity, agricultural practices, traditional customs, and of course individual condition and constitution. It is also strongly goal-oriented; the goal is not to eat only brown rice, as various nutrition writers and others have misunderstood but to be happy, healthy, free, humble, nonexclusive, grateful for all the bounties of life, and appreciative of our difficulties as our best teachers. To clarify its teachings, here are the Seven Macrobiotic Principles as stated by Aihara:

1. *Ecology:* Eating naturally cultivated, unsprayed, locally grown foods.

* Interestingly, Ronald Kotsch, Ph.D., considers Ohsawa a religious figure, "and while perhaps not a major one, [one] of sufficient importance to warrant our careful consideration." [30]

2. *Economy of Life:* No waste. Eating whole foods, avoiding partial, refined, and processed foodstuffs, which would include such purportedly "wholesome" products as wheat germ, bran, and vitamin pills.

3. *The Yin-Yang Principle:* Discussed in chapter 3 as the theory of opposites.

4. *An Art of Living:* We need to be responsible for our own life and health, which is always changing, so we must always be ready to change and adapt. "No absolute rules exist," Aihara points out, "or can be followed forever." Thus, flexibility is the key.

5. *Appreciation,* or gratitude: Because, says Aihara, it is the root of freedom and happiness.

6. *Faith:* In the wisdom of nature, the balance of opposites, which manifests itself as universal justice, "in the love that embraces everything without exclusions."

7. *Do-O-Raku,* or Tao, the Order of Nature, the enjoyment of life: "Anything we do is a game. It does not matter if we fail or succeed. . . . To live in perpetual ecstatic delight is Do-O-Raku. Those who do so are Do-O-Raku-Mono. If you are a Do-O-Raku-Mono, you are a macrobiotic, whatever you eat . . ."[31]

Michio Kushi, unlike Aihara, does consider food the prime mover: "Without food, man as well as all life does not exist. From food, life has come as well as man." According to his teachings, incorrect dietary practice lies behind virtually every problem we might encounter; a proper macrobiotic diet will help us solve most of life's difficulties, and that means eating grains, beans, vegetables, soy products (miso soup almost daily), no fruit except cooked, and a small amount of white meat fish once or twice a week. In addition to dietary advice, he offers some sensible "way of life suggestions": living happily; keeping active; expressing gratitude; chewing well; "early to bed, early to rise"; avoiding synthetic clothing and opting for natural fibers; avoiding aluminum, Teflon, and microwave ovens; keeping the home in order; and many others.[32]

IT CONSISTS OF:

- Whole grains (50 to 60 percent of total daily food volume) and beans (5 to 10 percent), as the protein base
- Vegetables (25 to 30 percent), especially roots, leafy greens, squashes, cabbage, and fruit (5 percent), in season

- Sea vegetables (2 to 4 percent), nuts, and seeds
- Soy products, such as tofu; and fermented soy products, such as miso, tamari soy sauce or shoyu, and tempeh
- Condiments, mostly salty: gomasio (sesame seeds and sea salt), umeboshi (plums pickled in brine), tekka (a root-vegetable preparation baked with miso), sea salt, as well as unrefined sesame and corn oil
- Fish occasionally, or an egg here or there in the cooking
- Roasted Japanese twig tea—kukicha, or bancha are the preferred beverages
- For special occasions, "anything" goes (barley malt, rice syrup (yinnie), and maple syrup are the preferred sweeteners)

IT FORBIDS:
- Meat, eggs, poultry
- Dairy products
- Tropical or semitropical fruits, juices, soda
- Coffee, commercial tea, and "aromatic stimulant teas," such as mint or chamomile
- Tomatoes, potatoes, eggplant, peppers; sometimes green beans, zucchini, spinach
- Sugar, honey, corn syrup, saccharin
- All artificially colored, preserved, sprayed, or chemically treated foods
- Canned or frozen foods, refined (white) grains and flours
- Hot and aromatic spices, white vinegar, and commercial salt

IT IGNORES: No major foodstuffs.

THE MACROBIOTIC TABLES OF OPPOSITES

EXPANSIVE, COOLING	CONTRACTIVE, WARMING
Salad	Grains
Fruit	Beans
Apple juice	Baked, deep-fried foods
Lightly steamed foods	Salty condiments (miso, tamari,
Oil	gomasio, tekka)
Seaweeds	Broiled, baked fish
Raw, steamed fish	Tempeh
Tofu	

ALKALIZING	ACID-FORMING
Vegetables	Grains, flour
Sea vegetables	Beans
Salt, condiments	Oil

NUTRIENT PROPORTIONS

In this diet, the relative proportions of nutrients can, with some care, be close to the ideal. A major imbalance can occur if there is an excess of carbohydrate foods, namely, a high consumption of sweets—even "natural" sweets, such as whole wheat baked goods with honey, maple syrup, or barley malt—in addition to the grains and beans. This in turn would set up a relative protein and mineral deficiency, and then cause related health problems.

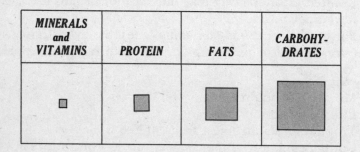

MINERALS and VITAMINS	PROTEIN	FATS	CARBOHY- DRATES
▪	◼	◼	◼

BALANCE

This is fairly easy to achieve on a macrobiotic diet, insofar as the foods consumed are whole foods, and neither overly expansive nor overly contractive food is consumed: Caution must be exercised to avoid an excess of salt, miso, shoyu, tamari, spices, and even of eating too much grain and not enough fish, beans, and vegetables, as this would bring on a condition of over-acidity, perhaps a minor protein deficiency.

EFFECTS

Of all the dietary schools of thought that I've encountered, I find that macrobiotics offers the only truly holistic theoretical approach. In theory, the diet is tailored to the complete set of an individual's circumstances—environment, heredity, present condition, native constitution, and also goals and work activity. Therefore, an Eskimo eating whale meat and a Jamaican eating fried plantains are both "macrobiotic." This need to adapt diet to individual circumstance is one of the core concepts of this book.

In the temperate zone, a broadly applied macrobiotic diet includes whole grains, beans, vegetables of all kinds (except nightshades, see page 176) both cooked and raw, fresh fruit, nuts, sea vegetables, soy products, unrefined oils, a minimum of seasonings, and fish if desired. It is therefore one of the more balanced and healthful ways of eating among all the alternatives we can choose from. In fact, the *Dietary Goals* points in its direction (see page 95, this chapter), as do most other recent official communiqués on the subject of health and diet. With or without nightshades, with or without sea vegetables, it is a way of eating increasingly adopted by many people who may not even have heard of the term *macrobiotics*.

From what I've seen and experienced, one of the first and most unexpected consequences of going on a macrobiotic diet is a feeling of inner balance and centeredness. This is a most elusive and hard-to-define feeling. Those who don't have it know they don't have it, search for it, and complain about the lack of it, whereas those who naturally have it don't know they have it and wonder what the fuss is all about.

This newfound centeredness is the result of the contractive effects of eating whole grains and beans, the nerve-calming action of the full vitamin B complex present in those foods, and the slow metabolizing of their complex carbohydrates. At the same time, avoiding foods that are more expansive and uncentering (sugar, large amounts of fruits, juices, and salads) reduces "spaciness" and unfocused thinking. Calmness sets in, we can say, as craziness dissipates for lack of fuel.

Another effect reported by many is a new, holistic view of life, encouraged, apparently, by eating whole foods, especially whole grains. It is not that the food itself has such a direct effect; but by healing the body, making it whole and well, it leads us to view external reality in similar terms.

A number of people on a macrobiotic diet have reported the remission and/or disappearance of a variety of illnesses and disease conditions, including acne, weight problems, dandruff, depression, hemorrhoids, even cancer. This has been documented in one popular book and many case history reports.[33] Skeptics and scientists may question the value of testimonials, but the fact remains that with this regime, as with some others, many people have experienced remission of disease as an immediate consequence of dietary change, and this cannot be ignored or dismissed. Strictly controlled studies of these claims are unfortunately almost impossible to conduct, as the range of variables in any change of diet is too broad. They include not only food choices and cooking styles, but also expectations, beliefs, subconscious desires to heal or not to heal, native constitution, environment, and many others.

Macrobiotics is no panacea, however, and in fact can be just the opposite. For many people the standard macrobiotic regime is too restrictive, too high in grain, and too alien culturally. Some women gain weight instead of losing it; some people, especially men, lose an excessive amount of weight and are constantly hungry because they don't metabolize the grain protein well and don't absorb enough nutrients.

In some instances the macrobiotic approach has been applied in an extremely restrictive manner, requiring brown rice twice a day, only cooked vegetables (even the salads are briefly boiled!), only salty condiments, no aromatic herbs or spices, a minimum of raw fruit, and fish only sporadically. While this regimen is often of benefit initially, when followed for a length of time it can become too contractive. Reaction-cravings for expansive foods set in, and secret ice-cream and beer binges are not uncommon as the pendulum swings. Overeating is another result of too contractive a diet. A better balance can be obtained by increasing the amount of fish, beans, fruit, and salad, by using grains other than rice more often, by decreasing the overall proportion of grains and salty condiments, and by seasoning foods with herbs and spices.

Because macrobiotics as philosophy deals not only with proper eating, but also sets up general rules of conduct and judgments about the "true" conditions of health and the evils of the world, it often gives rise to arrogance in the teachers, fear and guilt in their followers—the very qualities that it pretends to abolish. It can thus defeat its own purpose, while proving true one of its own maxims: "Everything turns into its opposite." One of the clearest critiques of the macrobiotic movement comes from Leonard Jacobs, publisher of the macrobiotic magazine *East-West Journal*. He writes,

> If someone fails to measure up to our ideal model of health, we may mentally relegate that person to a position of inferiority. It hardly matters to us whether or not they are healthy and enjoying life. We "know" they have fatty deposits around something or other, that they have a heart murmur, that they are constipated, that they have weak kidneys, and no sexual vitality. We "know" these things about others, and we constantly judge and criticize them and ourselves. Of course, we also have the answers, and we either try to make everyone accept these answers, or we consider them too low in judgment to ever attain our widsom.[34]

Food serves us best not as our master, but as our tool and instrument, our helper and facilitator.

The most valuable information I found in macrobiotics is the concept of opposites as applied to food (see chapter three). Not that it is anything new, but no other food philosophy uses it, to my knowledge. It also seems to me that Messrs. Ohsawa, Kushi, Aihara, and many other macrobiotic teachers have been profoundly influential in shaping the emerging modern view of correct nutrition, even if they have not been given official credit for it. Whole grains and beans were not a staple of the European vegetarian/natural-foods approach that I grew up with, nor of the "health food" movement in this country. I'm old enough to remember that there was a time when brown rice was very hard to get, and natural soy products impossible. Only after macrobiotics began to spread, with its concept of grain as a "principal food," and after its followers began to create a demand, did the whole-grain consciousness start taking hold everywhere. Frances Moore Lappé's *Diet for a Small Planet* put the theory of grain and bean complementarity in Western terms and made it understandable to doctors and nutritionists, but I don't think that the AMA would be serving brown rice, as it does at its annual banquet, if George Ohsawa hadn't reminded us of that grain's existence.

Five:
The Health-Supportive Whole-Foods Eating Style

In the preceding chapter I've outlined the various modern dietary practices and their effects. But what is the optimal one? Is there a way of eating about which one can say, unequivocally, that it is the most supportive of health? Is there any incontrovertible evidence?

Popular belief has it, as I mentioned earlier, that we are today much healthier than in the past. This may be true if we compare our life only to life in Europe and America between the fifteenth and nineteenth centuries. But when we compare our health status to that of traditional cultures in other times and other places, it does not show up as an improvement.

In many ways, the health of "primitive" peoples has been and is much better than that of the "civilized" moderns. Explorers in centuries past commented at length on the health and beauty of the natives, both young and old, that they encountered on their trips. L. A. de Bougainville, of France, wrote about the Tahitians he met (he was the first European explorer to arrive on that island): "Their vigor and agility, even in old men, surpass those of our young folk. . . . The contented old age which they attain, without any infirmities, the acuteness of all their senses and the singular beauty of their teeth, which they keep at the most advanced age— what a testimony to the healthiness of the climate and the wholesomeness of the regime followed by the inhabitants!"[1]

Weston Price, a dentist who carried out extensive studies of the dental health of ancient, primitive, and modern people and its relationship to their diet, noted that among 1,276 skulls of ancient Peruvian Indians, he didn't find a single dental-arch deformity. In comparison, as many as 75 percent of contemporary Americans studied exhibit malformation of the jaws and dental arches, with their attendant orthodontic problems. His data on primitive Indians show that close to 100 percent of their teeth are free of caries or faulty position.[2]

Dr. Price's exhaustively documented work, complete with photographs of "before and after" civilization, verifies what both early and modern travelers have reported: People who live, or have lived, a simple existence in accordance with natural cycles and tradition are indeed better off in terms of health than we are. On traditional, local diets devoid of "civilized" foods, such as sugar, canned vegetables, and white flour products, people are longer lived, often handsomer, and generally considerably healthier than their modern counterparts. As soon as processed foods become part of the native diet, problems set in. Tooth decay, tuberculosis, structural defects in children, and difficulties with childbearing are the first symptoms. These health disorders appear even if the lifestyle remains mostly unchanged in other respects. They are clearly not inherited, for they appear in the children, not in the parents.

Interestingly, Dr. Price found that the diet-induced health disorders are often reversible from one generation to the next. When "primitives" who had suffered any of the consequences of "civilized" foods reverted to the native diet, their children once again showed the excellent health and structural strength of their grandparents.

What do native diets consist of? While their effects in terms of good health and longevity may be similar, their content at first glance is noticeably varied. Traditional Maori (New Zealand) food, for example, includes fish, shellfish, kelp, grubs, roots. The ancient Peruvians studied by Dr. Price ate seafood, river plants, potatoes, corn, beans, seeds, and guinea pig meat. Natives of the Outer Hebrides near Scotland ate oat cakes, fish eggs, and fish livers. Early Danes, Swiss, and eastern Europeans lived on raw milk and its products, black bread, fresh vegetables, fruit, and meat once a week. The migratory Indians from the American High Sierras had corn and parched beans as their staples, consuming nothing else during their long journeys. The Sikhs of northern India eat raw-milk products, fruits, root vegetables, porridge from seeds and legumes, and meat every ten days. The Masai in Africa live almost exclusively on meat, milk, and blood, while other African peoples consume sorghum, millet, fresh vegetables, and game. The Tasadays, last of the Stone Age cave men, discovered some years ago in the Philippines, feast on wild yams, grubs, frogs, bananas, and fruit. The early Greeks lived on bread, barley meal porridge, lentils, flaxseed, greens, turnips, figs, olives, goat cheese, fruit, wine; meat was for holiday feasting and for war. (The effects of this spartan fare were admirable. Besides laying the foundations for the next 2,500 years of Western thought and culture, the Greek writers and philosophers were quite long-lived. Plato lived to eighty-seven, Sophocles to ninety-one, Hippocrates to eighty-three, Euripides to seventy-eight, Democritus to ninety; and Socrates' life was taken when he was three score and ten.)

In recent years, nutritional studies have been made of those traditional peoples who have been found to be generally healthy and long-lived. What do their diets have in common? Laboratory tests show that despite the seeming diversity, their diets are all low in calories, protein, and fat, and high in complex carbohydrates. In addition, by examining these traditional diets we notice that they consist of foods that are:

- Fresh or preserved with natural means (dried, pickled, smoked)
- Locally grown or obtained
- Seasonal
- Naturally grown (no chemical fertilizers or pesticides)
- Cooked according to traditional methods
- Appropriate to the food consumer's special condition; that is, different foods are given to infants, pregnant or nursing women, sick people, warriors
- Agreeable to the prevailing standards of taste

An interesting detail is the fact that almost no traditional tribe or society is totally vegetarian. (Even primates, which we always visualize with a banana in their hand, will munch on small animals if given the chance.[3]) One exception is the Hindus, who became vegetarian for two main reasons: (a) the Buddhist and Jainist religious belief in the transmigration of souls, according to which killing and eating an animal that may be housing a human soul is tantamount to killing and eating a human being; and (b) the economic priority of keeping cows for their milk rather than killing them for their meat.[4]

Most inhabitants of the temperate zones, however, consume a higher proportion of vegetable foods than of animal foods. For example, prehistoric American Indians subsisted on yams, potatoes, manioc, squashes, and small amounts of meat. In Europe, the traditional family diet for centuries consisted of cabbages, turnips, onions, radishes, willow and birch shoots, young nettles, ferns, mushrooms, and small game. Vegetable foods, such as beans, lentils, and chick-peas, were staples in the Near East, Central America, and parts of Europe as well and were supplemented by game and small animals, such as snails, shellfish, and river crabs.

Similar dietary practices can be found today among isolated groups that still live on native foods and remain in excellent health. Dr. Alexander Leaf's study of the inhabitants of Hunza (Pakistan), Vilcabamba (Ecuador), and Abkhazia (USSR) is a classic in the field.[5] People in those remote regions live well past a hundred, even over a hundred-and-thirty. Invariably, they are married, work hard, keep very active, lead useful lives within their communities, are greatly respected, and eat very simple, locally produced foods. The Abkhazians of central Georgia, in the USSR, consumed only 70 percent of their calories in the form of vegetable foods at the time of the study, yet this had apparently not always been so. When they were young, according to one of the aged Abkhazians, "we had only beans and rice to eat, but now we have meat and wine every day." It is a well-documented fact that a low-calorie diet during early life extends the total life span.[6]

By today's standards, it would appear that the dietary regimes that have kept many peoples healthy throughout history are paltry and inadequate. A diet of mostly leaves, roots, parched corn, and beans is probably not one your doctor or nutritionist would recommend. Yet I strongly suspect that such a regime might have some surprisingly positive effects on health.

My own way of eating, which for lack of a catchier term I call the health-supportive whole-foods eating style, is strongly anchored in these dietary practices of the past. It is certainly less spartan, more varied fare than that of ancient and/or primitive peoples. But the principles are the same. The most significant difference, perhaps, is that in earlier times people living at one with the earth and nature followed healthful eating patterns automatically, intuitively. It has taken me twenty years of testing and reworking to formulate the dietary principles that inform this book.

The health-supportive way of eating is what I teach and live by, and what I have raised my children on. I feel strongly that it is the way of eating that best supports our health, on all levels. It certainly has done so for us.

It is, in one sense, a mixture of all the diets I've described in the preceding chapter, and draws on all of them. In general, it stresses a greater use of fresh vegetables, fruits, nuts, seeds; and a return to the consumption of unrefined cereals, beans, and other complex carbohydrates. The effect of food on the health of both body and mind is considered from a much broader perspective than is usual today: you need to know a lot more about food than just its nutrient content. Rather than quantity of nutrients, what is stressed is the "wholeness" of the foodstuffs. Other concerns are freshness, avoiding chemical additives, eating foods grown naturally, without petrochemical fertilizers and pesticides, and the appropriateness of the food to the health of the person eating it. It also favors the consumption of fewer animal protein foods and more protein from vegetable sources than is common in our society, although it recognizes that most people need modest but regular amounts of animal protein.

One of the diet's key principles is flexibility. Its limits and allowances vary for each person, so that it can range from total vegetarianism to the inclusion of even some red meat; from a high proportion of raw foods to a total avoidance of them; from 45 to 50 percent whole grain to maybe 5 to 10 percent. A health-supportive way of eating will support for one person the ability to do a lot of strenuous exercise; for another, long hours of mental concentration; for a third, stamina enough to work fourteen hours a day without undue stress and strain; and for all, as close an approximation to the Conditions of Health (see chapter eleven, page 239) as possible.

The philosophy underlying the health-supportive way of eating is expressed throughout this book. In addition, one of its major components is the rejection of guilt and fear in connection with food selection. We can approach food as our ally, our teacher, and our rudder. It will nourish us well if well chosen; if incorrectly chosen, it will teach us some lessons about our body that we may, or may not, heed. If we make mistakes in food selection, either perversely or in ignorance, we will have to pay for it, so why feel guilty on top of that? The results of our eating choices, if negative, should be considered information, not punishment.

IT CONSISTS OF:
- Whole grains, beans, fresh vegetables and fruits in season, nuts, seeds, sea vegetables, all organically grown whenever possible
- Fermented or pickled vegetables or beans (pickles, sauerkraut, tempeh, and so on)
- Fish, organic eggs, or naturally raised fowl when desired, and, for some people, an occasional small amount of red meat, naturally raised if possible
- Herbs, spices, sea salt, natural soy sauce, unpasteurized miso (fermented, salted soybean paste), and other natural condiments in moderate amounts
- Unrefined sesame oil, extra-virgin olive oil, or, for occasional frying, cold-pressed safflower oil; unpasteurized butter, tahini, sesame butter (the total daily fat intake from all sources ideally should not exceed two tablespoons, plus or minus)
- For sweeteners, fruit juices, maple syrup, rice syrup, or barley malt in very modest amounts
- Spring water for all cooking and drinking
- Popular herb teas, such as peppermint and chamomile, roasted green tea (bancha) or twig tea (kukicha), grain coffees (made from dark-roasted chicory, barley, and so on)
- Dairy products, unpasteurized if possible, as an occasional treat (if they cause no clear problem)
- Guilt-free meals out with friends or family when the occasion arises

IT AVOIDS (IF POSSIBLE, MOST OF THE TIME):
- Sugar (white, brown, raw) and honey
- Pasteurized, homogenized, vitamin D–fortified milk; cheeses, ice cream, sour and heavy cream, yogurt
- White flour, white rice (except in ethnic restaurants on occasion)
- Canned and frozen foods
- Steak, nitrate- and nitrite-cured meats and fish, commercial eggs
- Iodized salt, commercial soy sauce, highly seasoned foods
- Lard, shortening, commercial oils, fried foods, nut and peanut butters (except in small amounts on occasion)
- Fluorinated, chlorinated tap water (except in restaurants); distilled water

- Coffee, hot chocolate, "maté" herb tea, and other caffeinated or medicinal beverages, except as needed
- Grim meals that are "good for you"
- Hedonistic meals that mess up the body's balance for longer than a day or two

TABLES OF OPPOSITES

CONTRACTIVE	EXPANSIVE
Grains	Herbs and spices
Beans	Teas
Pickled foods	Juices
Fish	Vegetable oils
Fowl	Fruits
Eggs	Salads
Sea salt and salted condiments	Vegetables, including potatoes

WARMING	COOLING
Hot soups, stews, casseroles	Cool cooked vegetables, grains, beans
Fish	Salads
Fowl	Fruit
Eggs	Herbs, spices
Vegetable oils	Teas, juices

ACID-FORMING	ALKALIZING
Vegetable oils	Fruits
Whole grains and cereals	Vegetables
Dry beans and peas	Sea vegetables
Fish	Fermented or pickled vegetables
Fowl	Sea salt and salted condiments
Eggs	

NUTRIENT PROPORTIONS

In a healthful way of eating all nutrients should be present in sufficient amounts for optimal physiological function, but not to excess; they should also appear in a natural relationship to one another—comfortable proportions (by percentage of calories provided) to my taste, are approximately:

20–25% fats
10–12% protein
70–75% carbohydrates (65% complex or starches, 5% fruit sugars)

Though most vegetable foods except nuts and seeds generally

contain little fat (0.1 to 4 percent), the extra fat shown above would come from the use of cooking oils, nuts, and seeds, and the occasional use of butter and animal-protein foods.

PERCENTAGE OF CALORIES PROVIDED BY VARIOUS NUTRIENTS IN THE HEALTH-SUPPORTIVE WHOLE-FOODS DIET

PROTEIN	FATS	COMPLEX CARBOHY- DRATES	SIMPLE CARBOHY- DRATES
■	■	■	■

BALANCE

It is achieved in this approach to food by making sure there is no excessive reliance on any one side of the tables of opposites, that is, by using as the focus of the meal beans and whole grains, which are at once expansive (being vegetable foods growing upward) and contractive (because of their shape and energy), and so in and of themselves fairly balanced. There are three easy ways by which to plan a well-balanced meal:

1. By color: It should include foods that are green, red, orange or yellow, white, and brown.
2. By flavor: There should be something sour, bitter, sweet, spicy, and salty in each meal; it will then be satisfying.
3. By texture and shape: The meal should include hearty starches (grains or tubers), protein (beans or animal food), roots, leaves, and fruits. Among the vegetables, there should be something that grows upward (leafy greens, celery, broccoli), something that grows downward (roots such as carrots or parsnips), something that grows sideways (squashes), and perhaps something that hangs (green beans, fruit).

The concept of food groups (discussed in chapter three) can be adapted to a health-supportive way of eating as well. I'd like to propose the following classification as a variation on the traditional four food groups:

HEALTH-SUPPORTIVE FOOD GROUPS

1. The Complex-Carbohydrate Group:
   a. Whole-grain cereals (two or three servings daily): brown rice, whole wheat, barley, oats, millet, buckwheat, rye, corn, bulgur, popcorn, kasha, whole-grain bread
   b. Starchy tubers (two or three servings per week—optional): yams, manioc, yautias, and other similar foods

2. The Protein Group:
   a. Dry beans and peas (one or two servings daily): split peas, lentils, chick-peas, kidney beans, aduki beans, and so on
   b. Animal-protein foods (one to five servings per week—optional): fish, fowl, eggs, meat

3. The Vitamin/Mineral Group:
   a. The leafy green vegetables (one or two servings daily): kale, collards, mustard greens, dandelion, chard, turnip tops (all cooked), lettuce, parsley, dill, escarole, chicory, watercress (all raw)
   b. The roots and squashes (one or two servings daily): turnips, parsnips, carrots, rutabaga, butternut squash, acorn squash, radishes, and similar foods
   c. General vegetables (one or two servings daily): celery, broccoli, green beans, cauliflower, onions, leeks, scallions
   d. The sea vegetables (two to five servings per week): dulse, irish moss, agar, kelp, hiziki, and similar foods
   e. The nightshades (two to three servings per week if diet includes some dairy): potatoes, tomatoes, eggplant, peppers
   f. Fresh or cooked fruits (one or two servings daily according to season—between meals for raw fruit)

4. The Lactobacillus Group (three to five servings per week): fermented foods, such as pickles, sauerkraut, miso, tempeh, fermented-milk products (optional)

5. The Fun-Foods Group (weekends, parties, special occasions): milk, cheese, alcohol, chocolate, sugar, paté, fried foods, and such

Note: It is especially important to remember that in a dietary system that includes a considerable proportion of complex carbohydrates, good and thorough chewing is essential. Digestion of carbohydrates begins with the enzyme ptyalin (or salivary amylase) in the saliva. If the food is not in the mouth long enough for the salivary amylase to do its job, the burden falls on the *pancreatic* amylase in the duodenum. Most people's pancreases—and especially those of sugar-eaters—are simply not up to this task. The result will be sensations of bloating and gas, general discomfort, and of course disillusionment with the "healthy" diet. So please remember: CHEW EVERY BITE UNTIL IT IS THOROUGHLY INSALIVATED—thirty-five to forty times.

The health-supportive way of eating, by definition, is goal-oriented and therefore would inevitably be somewhat different for each of us. The guidelines given here and in chapter eight, "Changing the Way We Eat," are, I think, broad enough to cover most individual needs and conditions. They provide the general principles by which you can orient yourself. The details, however—whether, for example, you should eat a bowl of beans or a piece of meat today—must be worked out individually by each person. They will also change continuously over time as our bodies—and our minds—change. The goal must be kept in mind at all times: What are we watching our diet *for?* Are we becoming the kind of person we want to be? *Is it working?* I cannot stress enough the importance of flexibility and adaptability to change. A rigid dictum, strict rules to follow, and a list of "allowed" and "forbidden" foods have no place in the health-supportive diet.

Following such an eating style demands self-determination, free will, and accepting responsibility for our choices. It engages our creativity and our intelligence. It allows for growth, change, discovery, and continuous learning, all of which make it not easy, but very interesting and even exciting.

Caution: The comments on the effects of food on our health, as delineated in this and the next chapter, do not take into account the possibility that you might be taking medications. Everything changes if that is the case, in ways unpredictable and devastating. Many prescription or over-the-counter medications increase excretion or decrease absorption of nutrients, and natural, healthy food might not have much of a medicinal effect. To read more on this subject, please refer to the *Handbook: Interactions of Selected Drugs with Nutritional Status in Man*, from the American Dietetic Association.

Eating Out: How to Manage

Eating a healthy diet can be a challenge for those of us who are always on the run.

"I work all day long," you're probably thinking, "I don't have time to cook! Not only that, I *like* to eat out four or five times a week, maybe more. How can I find whole grains in the coffee shop?"

Another problem is that our human lifestyle is very complicated. Something as basic as eating has taken on a myriad of subtle nuances and become, thereby, a mode of communication. In our society, if we order sushi, our meal companions will have a totally different sense of us than if we order pot roast. Russell Baker, whose satirical essays regularly appear in the *New York Times*, once wrote a delightfully wry yet oddly truthful piece entitled "Power Lunching," in which ordering raw alligator steak and turnips was seen as an expression of power! How would it look in a business lunch if you just had soup, salad, and mineral water?

Let's deal with both these problems—matter and mind—one at a time. On the question of *what* to eat, try these simple rules:

- Never eat dessert containing white sugar. Get your carbohydrates from whole grain if available, or from bread, pasta, and starchy vegetables.
- Keep it simple, choosing dishes with fewer ingredients over more complicated mixtures.
- Go for soups, especially lentil, split pea, and other bean and vegetable soups; fish, salad, potatoes, vegetables; fowl on occasion; rye toast, turkey sandwiches if you wish. Take it easy with tuna and egg salads and the like, which generally contain a lot of commercial mayonnaise.
- Whenever possible, eat in natural-foods restaurants and have some whole grain, such as brown rice, kasha, or millet. Even there, keep it simple: There is a lack of classical techniques in natural-foods cooking that allows chefs a tremendous freedom in creating new dishes. Some of those are delicious. Others can turn out to be very peculiar concoctions; when in doubt, you're better off with the simpler selections.
- In ethnic restaurants, you have a variety of choices. From a Japanese menu, choose sushi if you like it; also the spinach (*oshitashi*); rice-cucumber rolls (*kappamaki*); cold or hot tofu appetizers; miso soup; casseroles, such as the *yosenabe* (fish and vegetables in broth); soba (buckwheat) noodles with or without the deep-fried *tempura* (avoid the latter if you are concerned about fat intake). Teriyaki dishes are usually very

salty; take it easy also with the soy sauce as a general condiment.

- In Chinese restaurants, mixed vegetables, noodles, scallops, fresh fish (shrimp are almost always frozen in this country), chicken with broccoli, and similar dishes are among your better choices. You may want to request reduced salt, soy sauce, and oil in the cooking and no MSG. (You can have your request honored because Chinese dishes are generally cooked to order, with the exception of soup, dumplings, egg rolls, and similar preparations.) If possible, avoid the egg foo young, probably one of the oiliest dishes ever invented—your liver will be grateful. You can get a fair number of vegetarian dishes in both Chinese and Japanese restaurants; however, they all use polished white rice, so the nutrient content is off balance and lower than desirable. For that reason, these meals are really better balanced if you have a small amount of animal protein with them; that is also the traditional dietary system, and heeding it is a good idea. If you can find an Oriental restaurant that serves unpolished brown rice, then of course a vegetarian meal would be an excellent nutritional choice.

- Make sure to order dal in Indian restaurants; it will complement the abundance of vegetarian dishes and white rice with important vegetable protein from the beans. The Hindu cuisine is probably one of the best balanced for vegetarians, even though it does use polished rice; when brown rice is used, you will be fully satisfied with an Indian meal. You may just want to be a bit cautious with overly pungent (hot) dishes and also with the fried breads, although perhaps the light and crisp pappadum is a treat worth sinning with.

- Mexican, Brazilian, and other Latin American (except Argentine) restaurants generally offer delicious rice (white) or corn and bean dishes; they may be a bit overspiced sometimes. With some vegetable soup and salad, you can put together a reasonably satisfying meal.

- Italian restaurants have great soups, such as minestrone, *pasta e fagioli*, and *escarole in brodo*. One of the more interesting Italian dishes is *bolito misto*, a huge plate of blanched or steamed fresh vegetables with a piece of boiled chicken on top; unfortunately, not many restaurants serve it. The pastas are usually made from white semolina flour; some enlightened restaurants are now offering whole wheat pasta, but that needs longer cooking, and sometimes doesn't get it. Go for pasta primavera, a fine dish if it isn't smothered in cheese. On the whole, pasta dishes with white clam sauce or pesto are easier on your system than canned tomato sauce and melted cheeses. You may also find sautéed fresh zucchini, broccoli, or escarole, but these are often drowned in oil. (Curiously enough, I find overly oily dishes much more troublesome to digest than those with an excess of butter, even though that flies in the face of conventional nutritional wisdom. You can test it out for yourself too—and listen to your body's feedback rather than anyone's theories.)

- Speaking of butter, in French restaurants you can guiltlessly go for poached fish, potatoes, vegetables, and salad. If you're being super-cautious you can ask them to hold the butter sauce, and if you're hedonistic, you can have it served on the side and enjoy it in moderation.

Many good restaurants will, upon request, prepare a steamed or sautéed vegetable platter; the better the restaurant, the more wonderful such a platter will be, so don't hesitate to ask. In fact, not only restaurants will do that, as I found a good four years ago, when I went to a wedding in a church in New Jersey; the meal was catered and took place in the church dining room. The entrée was a sixteen-ounce T-bone steak with potatoes and carrots. I asked the waiter to bring me two servings of vegetables and give my steak to someone else, thinking it would be a fairly simple thing to do. Well, everybody got served except me, and I was beginning to feel ostracized and disdained by the meat-eating world . . . and then the waiter showed up with a cornucopia of gorgeous, lightly steamed carrots, zucchini, green beans, cauliflower, and broccoli, placing it in front of me. The kitchen had actually gone to the trouble of preparing them without advance notice, even in the midst of serving over a hundred dinners. My table companions were amazed, and also a little envious—I certainly had the most beautiful plate! Fortunately there was enough to share among us, so we all enjoyed it together.

I think it's safe to say that health consciousness is now so prevalent in our society that hardly anyone will look askance if you order vegetables and low-fat dishes and avoid the steak and martinis.

In fact, when dining is a social occasion, it's a good idea to avoid talking about food, unless it is to comment on its delights. Neither defend nor apologize for your dietary choices, whatever they are; if you do, you will only be expressing unnecessary guilt feelings. You have a right to eat whatever you please, be it vegetarian, standard American, "nouvelle cuisine," macrobiotic, junk food, or last night's leftovers. Whatever choices you make will have an effect, and if the effect is what you want, fine; if it is not, you have the freedom to change your choices. Guilt usually arises when transgressions go unpunished; in the case of food choices, it is unnecessary because if you make mistakes, you will inevitably get caught. If you must be very strict about what you eat, you'll be happier staying home. Eating out is usually a social event, a means of exchanging energy with the world around us. Do the best you can to make sensible food choices, but don't agonize too much, neither feel put upon if the food isn't perfect; just chew it well, enjoy the occasion, and be grateful for what you've got.

For the Dietitian and the Health Professional: Nutrition in Numbers

The nutrition guidelines of various official agencies invariably tell us *how much of each nutrient* we should consume per day: so many grams or miligrams per pound of body weight, taking into account age, sex, and special conditions such as pregnancy or lactation. The "Dietary Goals Report," together with its critics and amenders, as well as the Pritikin Program, all speak of the *percentage of calories provided by the various nutrients* in the diet. The macrobiotic approach suggests consuming various foods according to their percentage *by volume* in the daily diet.

For the cook, these extensive charts of numbers are extremely confusing to translate into edible meals. It has occurred to me, as I was wrestling with the numbers, that the two scientific models could very easily be integrated with my own "proportion of nutrients" charts, so as to offer an ideal model against which to compare the nutritive adequacy of each meal. To that effect, I worked out seven guidelines for menu planning which I hope will be useful to those who plan menus in hospitals, institutions, and restaurants. These guidelines are based on the premise that the principal goal of a well-balanced menu is to provide optimum nutrition, minimum waste, no foods that deplete nutrients nor provide empty calories, and to leave the food consumer with a sense of balanced satisfaction, comfortable energy, and no cravings. Meals that meet these criteria will be cost effective; they will also attract repeat business to the commercial establishments that offer them, because they will make people feel good.

SEVEN GUIDELINES FOR MENU PLANNING

1. Plan the following *percentages of calories* to be provided by
   Protein: 10–12%
   Fat: 20–25%
   Starch (complex carbohydrates): 60–70%
2. Consequently, plan the following *proportions of nutrients* by weight:
   - FAT should be *double* the calories of PROTEIN, therefore there should be equal amounts by weight (1:1)
   - STARCH should be about *five times* the calories of PROTEIN, thus five times the weight (5:1)
3. Plan the following maximum amount of
   - FATS: 2–3 teaspoons per meal per person (25–30 gr.)
   - SALT: ¼ teaspoon per meal per person (1 g.)
   - SUGAR (refined): ¼ teaspoon per meal per person (1 g.)
4. Use whole grains as your preferred source of starches, or complex carbohydrates. Second best are starchy vegetables; third best are potatoes. Only as a last resort choose refined grains such as pasta or white rice.
5. Use mostly fresh or dried foods. Avoid foods that have undergone extensive technological processing as much as possible. Avoid the use of chemical preservatives, such as sulphites, on raw foods and salads.
6. Offer ingredients and cooking styles in season; that is, raw and tropical produce in hot weather, steaming soups and stews in the winter.
7. Offer at least one dairy free, unsweetened cooked fruit dessert for those who want it or those who refrain from eating wheat and/or dairy and/or sugar.

The above guidelines will ensure a satisfying meal with little incentive for binging or "cheating," provided of course that all the ingredients are whole, natural foods, without chemicals or sugar.

REMEMBER THESE SIMPLE NOTIONS: For *low sodium meals*, instead of focusing all the fear on the salt, watch for hidden sodium in little suspect food: dairy products, especially cheese; baked goods

with sodium bicarbonate in the baking powder; and commercial
foods containing various preservatives, additives, and stabilizers
with sodium compounds (sodium citrate, sodium silico aluminate,
and the like).

For *low-fat meals*, simply eliminate dairy products altogether,
avoid fried foods, fatty meats, heavy dressings, and you're on your
way.

Six:
The Effects of Different Foods

Before you go about changing your diet in any way, you must understand in more detail how specific foods can affect you. Body, mind, emotions, activity, spirit—all are influenced in some way by the food we eat.[1] Most foods can have both negative and positive influences, depending on the quantity in which they are consumed: Too much of a "good" food can be as detrimental to your well-being as the "unhealthy" kind, and occasional moderate amounts of the latter may in fact have little if any negative effects. Although I have my opinions, of course, on what foods are "better"—opinions based on many years of study, observation, and experience—I will try to show you both the positive and the negative aspects of each food stuff. It will be up to you to decide how each will fit into your life. My commentary on the spiritual effects of foods is based on traditional viewpoints, such as Hindu and Chinese philosophy, as well as Western anthroposophy; however, I pass on only those theoretical considerations that match my personal observations.

The food categories we'll examine are *milk and dairy products, meat, fish, fowl, eggs, grain, beans, roots, leaves, sea vegetables, fruit, nuts, nightshades, herbs and spices,* and *sugar, salt and fats.*

MILK AND DAIRY PRODUCTS

- Expansive: milk, butter, yogurt, soft cheeses
- Contractive: hard, salty cheeses

- Buffers: either acid-forming or alkalizing
- Mostly cooling: except butter and high-fat cheeses
- Buildup food

A newborn who drinks its mother's milk receives the perfect food, custom-made to fulfill its needs, until such time as the youngster can begin to partake of the same food as adults. Milk is richly nourishing, soothing to the soul, and carries the warmth of life that will help a child develop its own ability for warmth and love. Because of this, milk in general—not only human mother's milk—has come to be associated with good nourishment, and with the ease, bliss, and innocence of childhood. According to Hauschka, "Milk prepares the body for habitation by the soul and spirit. It brings a person down to earth and gives him a feeling for the oneness of the human race."[2]

But what happens when human beings drink the milk of another animal? And when that milk, moreover, is subjected to various processes that alter its natural state? Fresh, raw milk from cows, goats, sheep, camels, yaks, and similar animals may have a number of nourishing qualities and nutrient elements; but, it has a different chemical composition from human milk, and it lacks the human energy field, the human quality. When this milk is, in turn, pasteurized and homogenized, and when synthetic vitamins are added to it, we can be certain that it is a totally different substance from the one that goes directly from the human mother's nipple to her child's mouth (without even coming in contact with air). As such, it must also have a totally different effect.

According to modern nutritional thinking, milk (and today that means pasteurized, homogenized, vitamin A and D fortified cow's milk) is an "excellent food" beause of its high volume of component elements such as protein and calcium. The fat content of milk has recently come under criticism, so that it is now considered desirable to consume "skim" or "low-fat" milk (although the American Academy of Pediatrics does not recommend low-fat milk for infants). As we have seen in chapter two (see page 55), human mother's milk has somewhat more fat than cow's milk. I would argue, therefore, that perhaps it is not the fat but the protein, calcium, and sodium concentration in cow's milk—considered so healthful—that we should be concerned about.

Compare the nutrient composition of cow's milk and mother's milk:

COMPARISON OF NUTRIENTS IN HUMAN
AND COW'S MILK

Macronutrients in grams per 100 grams

	PROTEIN	FAT	CARBO-HYDRATE
HUMAN MILK	1.1	4	9
COW'S MILK	4	3.5	4.9

Micronutrients in milligrams per 100 grams

	CALCIUM	PHOS-PHORUS	SODIUM
HUMAN MILK	33	18	16
COW'S MILK	118	97	50

Note the following:

- Cow's milk has three times more protein and almost four times more calcium (both buildup elements) than human milk. It is, indeed, perfectly suited to the developmental needs of a calf, which, when grown, will weigh three or four times as much as a human adult.
- The ratio of calcium to phosphorus in human milk is 2.35:1 but it is only 1.27:1 in cow's milk. According to Dr. Frank

Oski, chairman of the Department of Pediatrics at Upstate Medical Center, State University of New York, in Syracuse, "only foods with a calcium-to-phosphorus ratio of two to one or better should be used as a primary source of calcium."[3] That is because phosphorus can combine with calcium in the digestive tract and actually prevent the absorption of calcium. Paradoxically, then, human beings absorb less calcium from the high-calcium cow's milk than from the lower-calcium human milk. To put it another way, regarding the optimum amount of nutrients that we need, it's not quantity that counts, but context.

- Human milk has a bit *more fat* than cow's milk—4.0 grams as opposed to 3.5 grams. This indicates to me that pointing to the fat in cow's milk as detrimental could be barking up the wrong tree. In fact, fat is the *only* nutrient with similar values in both kinds of milk; values for all the other nutrients are dramatically disparate, as the charts show.

- Human milk has almost double the carbohydrate found in cow's milk—9 grams as opposed to 4.9 grams. Consequently, cow's milk is relatively "deficient" in this nutrient. This may explain the observable custom of sweetening cow's milk or including sugar in a dairy-based dietary system. In other words, consuming cow's milk (or its products) provokes a craving for sweets. Milk and cookies, for this reason among others, do belong together.

- Human milk contains only 16 milligrams of sodium, as opposed to the 50 milligrams in cow's milk. Moreover, salt is added to almost all cheeses to give them flavor. Therefore it seems that cow's milk, with its naturally occurring excess, along with salted cheese, could be among the most common sources of excessive sodium in our Standard American Diet.

According to our systems model, more is not always better, and too much of something can create as many problems as too little, throwing the system out of balance. If we put human milk into the system of a human being, the result is smooth growth, correct energy level, and no excess because all the elements are fully utilized. This eminently human food matches the human metabolism. But if we put in cow's milk, say 100 grams, the foregoing charts clearly indicate that we will have 2.4 grams of protein and 85 milligrams of calcium *in excess* of human needs.

Protein and calcium are building blocks; they are, and help create, solid matter. It is inevitable that, when out of proportion, these elements will create some waste matter of excess in the body by their presence.[4] What are the effects of that excess?

Nutritionists say that whatever nutrients we take in excess of need are excreted. This is perfectly true, and when our organs of elimination are unblocked, excretion proceeds smoothly. But in our current collective condition, are they? I think not. And if they're not, what happens?

From infancy on we partake of dense, heavy foods: cheese, baked goods, meats, fried potatoes, ice cream. Push a thick, dense substance through a strainer, and soon enough the small openings get clogged, rendering the strainer less and less effective. The same thing happens with our organs, such as the liver, the intestines, the lungs, and especially the kidneys. Faced with a daily load of waste matter far in excess of what the body is prepared to handle, our organs soon become less and less efficient in excreting the excess through normal channels. Other avenues to the exterior are then formed, via the skin and the mucous membranes of all our body's orifices. The excess matter that cannot be excreted remains inside the body. Unused matter in the body, according to Ayurvedic and Chinese medicine, turns into mucus or pus— the perfect culture medium for bacteria. Dairy products, then, are a ripe breeding ground for infections.

The host of common problems of buildup and excretion that plague us today—asthma, allergies, strep throat, tonsillitis, ear infections, pimples, acne, overweight—can be taken as proof that our organs of elimination are *not* in fine working order. The fact that these conditions and many others tend to clear up when dairy products are removed from the diet indicates that cow's milk and its derivatives—because of their high content of buildup elements of protein and calcium—may be closely associated with them.

The addition of synthetic vitamin D to cow's milk appears to cause a great deal of trouble as well. Introduced with the best of intentions, to forestall rickets in children, this vitamin encourages the deposit of calcium in the body. Artifically encouraged, calcium is often deposited in the wrong places. For that reason, added vitamin D has been identified as a causative factor in extensive injury of the cardiovascular system, calcification of the kidneys, and mental retardation.[5]

In many cases, the excess calcium of fortified cow's milk is excreted by the kidneys. When it can't go through because the holes in the strainer, as it were, are already blocked, it can remain in them and form kidney stones. It may also form deposits in various areas of the female reporoductive organs, at times hardening into cysts. There may be some relationship between dairy food intake, vitamin D fortification, and the tendency in some women to develop calcium deposits on the strings of their IUDs. The most dramatic example I found of the presence of excess calcium in the human system was in the case of a young woman who consulted me regarding her diet. She had had an operation on her kidneys during which an external tube was inserted temporarily between kidney and bladder, bypassing the ureter. Within a month, the tube was totally blocked by hardened calcium deposits that impeded the flow of urine, much to the surprise of her doctor. She was drinking two or three glasses of milk daily at the time. When I met her, she was well recuperated from her operation, although her kidneys still gave her trouble, and she had skin problems and allergies. After she eliminated milk and milk products from her diet, all those problems gradually disappeared, and she reported that her energy increased markedly.

Many people, in fact, report a noticeable rise in energy once they stop using dairy products as a main food. "I used to feel so lethargic," said a handsome middle-aged woman after taking my cooking classes for ten months. "Now I feel fantastic!"

Women suffer more from the buildup and blocking effects of milk products than men do, and the problems take longer to heal. From a natural, systems viewpoint, this makes perfect sense: Milk is supposed to go out of the woman, not into her. When the flow is reversed, the energy system backs up—and everything gets stuck. One woman came to see me complaining of painful premenstrual swelling of the breasts; all I suggested was that she stop consuming her daily quart of milk—after all, where does milk come from? A month later she called me and asked, "Is this for real? Could it make such a difference so soon?" I spoke to her five months later and found that the breast soreness only recurred mildly the month she ate some cheese or ice cream.

The consumption of dairy products, including milk, cheese, yogurt, and ice cream, appears to be strongly linked to various disorders of the female reproductive system, including ovarian tumors and cysts, vaginal discharges, and infections. I see this link confirmed time and again by the countless women I know who report those problems diminishing or disappearing altogether after they've stopped consuming dairy foods. I hear of fibroid tumors being passed or dissolved, cervical cancer arrested, menstrual irregularities straightened out. "Dairy products seem very much associated with menstrual cramps and heavy flow," noted Christiane Northrup, M.D., an obstetrician and gynecologist from Portland, Maine. Dr. Northrup also reported in a telephone interview with me that the women with the most severe cases of endometriosis or fibroids were heavy consumers of cheese, ice cream, butter, or milk. Several of her patients had their fibroids shrink after they eliminated those foods.

Even fertility appears to have been reversed with this approach in several instances—not so strange when you consider that in some cases infertility results from the fallopian tubes being blocked by mucus. When the mucus caused by dairy foods clears up, conception is more likely to occur. In addition to its macronutrients, milk, being a product of the reproductive glands, also contains an appreciable amount of hormones, including gonadotropins, thyroid-releasing hormones, ovarian steroids, and an epidermal growth factor.[6] What role the growth factor may have in the development of gross overweight or cancer has not yet been investigated, but I suspect we may be hearing more on the subject in the near future.

Although the pasteurization of milk eliminated many infectious diseases, it is not without its drawbacks. In tests with animals, calves given their own mother's milk that had first been pasteurized didn't live more than six weeks. An increased incidence of problems, including a reduced ability to reproduce, was noted in laboratory animals fed pasteurized milk for several generations. Also, the vitamin C content of milk is reduced by 50 percent during pasteurization,[7] a factor that may lie behind our continued concern about getting enough vitamin C.

The homogenization process has come under fire as well. Kurt Oster, M.D., of Bridgeport, Connecticut, has advanced the theory that homogenization, by breaking up milk molecules into smaller pieces, allows some substances to pass through the intestinal wall unchanged by the digestive process. One of these substances is an enzyme called xanthine oxydase, or XO, normally found in milk fat, which helps in the breakdown of protein. After passing through the intestinal wall and being picked up by the lymphatic system, says Dr. Oster, the XO ends up in the bloodstream. As it courses through the arteries, it scratches and corrodes the inside of the arterial walls, causing small primary lesions. As a defense against this, the body deposits fibrin and cholesterol over the lesions to avoid further damage.[8] (The Federation of American Societies for Experimental Biology prepared a critique of the Oster theory for the FDA, called "A Review of the Significance of Bovine Milk Xanthine Oxydase in the Etiology of Atherosclerosis," in 1975; some merit was found in the theory, but as usual, the results were deemed inconclusive.)

The American practice of homogenizing milk, and then fortifying it with synthetic vitamin D, which encourages calcium deposits, may be among the reasons why very young children in this country already have hardening of the arteries. It may also explain why milk products seem to cause so many more health problems here than elsewhere: In other countries the milk is used raw, or at most is pasteurized. A 1960 study of ulcer patients in the United States found that those on a high milk diet (the Sippy diet) had more than twice as many heart attacks as patients who did not follow a milk-diet therapy. At the time of the study, milk in the United States had been homogenized for about ten years. A similar study conducted in Great Britain (reported in the same paper), showed that British ulcer patients on the high milk diet had 50 percent fewer heart attacks than their American counterparts. (They still showed up with almost twice as many attacks as patients who were not on the milk diet.)[9] The paper was written in 1960; as late as 1967, only 7 percent of the milk in Great Britain was homogenized, as compared with 95 percent in the U.S.

According to systems theory, a system is disturbed by the addition or subtraction of a single element; this allows other elements within the system, suddenly unbalanced, to cause trouble they normally would not. With that in mind, we can be suspicious of the removal of fat from milk. What is worse: A whole food that is an excess, or a partial food—low-fat milk—that is a relative excess? Both will cause trouble, but there is always a good reason for the natural proportion of elements within a food system. Butterfat may help in the assimilation of calcium from milk;[10] hence, low-fat milk could create a relative calcium deficiency, even in the face of the apparent calcium excess in cow's milk. Also, because, as Oster pointed out, butterfat contains a protein-splitting enzyme (XO), by removing that fat we could be making digestion of milk protein more difficult. In addition, removing the fat from milk results in a 20 percent relative increase of protein, which makes the kidneys work harder. One mother I know found that her baby developed diaper rash after she started giving him skim milk and powdered milk. As diaper rash is often the result of excess ammonia in the urine, and ammonia is a by-product of incomplete protein metabolism, I thought there might be a connection. When she eliminated the skim milk and increased breast feeding and fresh vegetables, the rash disappeared.

Lactose—the carbohydrate in milk—has come under scrutiny lately. The healing professions have finally noticed that many people have acute reactions to milk, including cramps, bloating, intestinal gas, and diarrhea. These symptoms are caused by a lack of lactase, the enzyme needed to digest lactose, a condition called lactose intolerance. It sounds like a disease, and people who are diagnosed as lactose intolerant think there is something wrong with them.

There isn't. All normal mammals stop producing the enzymes needed to digest their baby food once they're weaned. A few human populations have had to rely on the milk of their herds for food in difficult or inhospitable conditions: northern Europeans during the winter nights that last for months, Berbers crossing the Sahara with their camels, vegetarian Hindus. These populations developed the genetic ability to continue producing the lactase enzymes, and thereby remained able to digest milk throughout their adult years. Almost everyone else, including 70 to 90 percent of blacks, Chinese, Japanese, Ashkenazi Jews, and Mediterraneans, has lost that ability.[11] In the United States, up to 25 percent of the Caucasian population is lactose intolerant. There also seems to be a relationship between colic in breast-fed infants and the cow's milk drunk by their mothers.

As with all other things, dairy products do have their positive aspects. Fresh, raw, unpasteurized milk from healthy cows or goats used in small amounts is a fine food for young children. In fact, when breast-feeding is not possible, raw goat's milk is the next best choice. Although its nutrient values are similar to those of cow's milk, it appears to cause fewer allergic reactions and has not been homogenized or fortified. Good-quality unpasteurized, aged cheeses are a pleasant party food; they encourage friendly feelings and good conversations.[12] Yogurt and fermented milks, such as kefir and buttermilk, are easy to assimilate (the lactose has been broken down by the fermentation process), and can be an occasional tasty, cooling treat in the summer.

I find that on the spiritual level, milk reunites us with the Mother energy, and supports all the feelings associated with childhood: emotions close to the surface, easy laughter, easy tears, contentedness, dependency. It keeps us in innocent bliss and lacking in conscious awareness. In effect, as long as we consume milk or milk products regularly, we have not been fully weaned—thus, regardless of chronological age, we remain unable to attain our full potential as adults. It's interesting to me that religious cults that encourage dependency on a father figure or guru encourage also the regular consumption of sweets and milk products, both childhood foods par excellence. There may be a profound truth in what Saint Paul wrote to the Hebrews 5:13: "For every one that useth milk is unskillful in the work of righteousness: for he is a babe."

The Question of Calcium

Whenever it is suggested that milk and milk products be avoided, there is always the inevitable question: "And where will I get my calcium?" Although calcium is found in innumerable foodstuffs, we have been brainwashed to believe it is only in milk. But how do cows and elephants maintain their bone structure and their size? It is certainly not by drinking some other animal's milk. They do so by eating their natural foods, that is, leaves, grass, and other vegetable matter.

How much calcium is needed in the diet has been much argued over. The World Health Organization suggests 400 milligrams daily; the Recommended Daily Allowance in America has been 800 milligrams, until recently, when it was raised to 1200 milligrams. This interest in adequate calcium intake has been sparked by concern about the bone-thinning condition known as osteoporosis, which for reasons not yet clearly understood seems to hit particularly hard in our society at women past the menopause.

There are many foods that contain calcium in a natural, easy-to-assimilate form and are a sound alternative to dairy. They are:

- Beans and nuts
- Greens, especially broccoli, collards, kale, mustard and turnip tops, parsley, watercress, dandelion
- Sea vegetables
- Sesame seeds and tahini
- Canned salmon and sardines with bones
- Soup made with one or more bones (fish, fowl, or beef) and one tablespoon of wine vinegar (which draws out the calcium and makes it available in the broth)

The chart on the following page shows the exact amount of calcium available in nondairy foods.

NONDAIRY SOURCES OF CALCIUM*

Food	Milligrams Calcium per 100 Grams (3½ Ounces)
VEGETABLES	
Beet greens, cooked	118
Broccoli cooked or raw	130
Chard, cooked	73
Collards, boiled, drained†	188
Dandelion greens, boiled, drained	187
Kale, boiled, drained	187
Kidney beans, cooked	40
Mustard greens, boiled, drained	138
Okra, cooked	82
Parsley	203
Parsnips, cooked	57
Rutabaga, cooked	55
Turnip greens, boiled, drained	184
Turnips, cooked	40
Watercress	151
SEEDS	
Almonds	254
Brazil nuts	186
Peanuts, roasted	74
Raisins	62
Sesame seeds	1,160
Walnuts, roasted	83
SEAWEEDS	
Agar	567
Dulse	296
Hiziki	1,400
Kelp	1,093
Kombu	800
Wakame	1,300

* Sources: Benjamin T. Barton, *Human Nutrition*; USDA Handbook No. 8; and Michio Kushi, *The Book of Macrobiotics*.

† Spinach also has appreciable calcium values, but is high in oxalic acid, which binds the calcium and makes it hard to assimilate. Note that most popular spinach dishes are served with cheese, eggs, or at least bacon—these help counteract the oxalic acid. Sunflower seeds also serve that purpose.

FOR COMPARISON

Canned salmon, with bones	200–250
Canned sardines, with bones	300–437
Carrots, cooked	33
Cheddar cheese	750
Cottage cheese	94
Milk, cow's	118
Milk, human	33
Swiss cheese	925

Let us now look at the calcium question from another angle. Instead of seeing osteoporosis as a condition of *lack*, let's consider it as a condition of *drain*. In other words, the question will be not "What is the way to add more calcium to the system?" but rather, "What is draining or keeping calcium away?" If we can find an answer to this, we can also find a different solution to the calcium shortage. That is, instead of increasing input, we can simply change conditions so that there is no unwanted output, no drain.

The list of foodstuffs that in one way or another affect our body's calcium balance is surprisingly long, even if we ignore the simple, nourishing foods of the foregoing list. Some will add calcium in an unbalanced context; some are counterbalancers to these; some will drain calcium from the system, which is fine if there is an excess, but detrimental if there isn't. Still others will cause calcium to be deposited in soft tissues or other inappropriate locations. It is important to understand that it is not enough that a food be high in calcium. The body has to be able to assimilate and utilize the calcium properly.

FOODS THAT AFFECT CALCIUM BALANCE IN SOME WAY

DAIRY PRODUCTS
Milk
Cheeses
Yogurt
Ice Cream

CONCENTRATED SUGARS
Sugar
Honey

HIGH-PROTEIN FOODS
Meat
Fowl
Fish

NIGHTSHADES
Potatoes
Tomatoes
Eggplant
Peppers (red, hot, green, cayenne, paprika, Tabasco, and so on)
Tobacco

WINE   CITRUS
                              Lemon (especially in tea)
VINEGAR   Orange
COFFEE   Grapefruit
                              Other juices, in some cases
ALCOHOL

SALT

Let's look at these group by group.

DAIRY PRODUCTS

As we saw, the calcium in dairy foods comes in an unbalanced
relationship with phosphorus, so a fair amount of it will be incompletely absorbed or incorrectly assimilated.*

CONCENTRATED SUGARS

These create an acid reaction in the body, and acidity deminer-
alizes the system; this occurs because when sugar is metabolized,
it creates various organic acids.[14] Sugar intake also alters the cal-
cium-phosphorus ratio in the blood by causing the phosphorus
level to drop,. When not enough of the latter is present, calcium
cannot be absorbed by the body.[15]

HIGH-PROTEIN FOODS

According to research done at the University of Wisconsin by Dr.
Helen Linkswiler and Dr. Josephine Lutz, a diet with a high-protein content acidifies the blood (much as sugar does), and acidified
blood will dissolve calcium from the bones. In one study conducted by Dr. Lutz, people on a diet that included 102 grams of
protein (which is average) excreted almost twice as much calcium
as those consuming only the RDA of 44 grams. Because the calcium intake of both groups was the same, the excreted calcium
had apparently been removed from the bones. The researchers
suggested lowering the intake of protein to prevent calcium loss.[16]

---

* Current nutritional thinking also postulates that the cavities found in the teeth
of children who go to sleep with a bottle of milk occur because the lactose (milk
sugar) is concentrated in the mouth, harboring tooth-attacking bacteria. However, research presented to the International Association for Dental Research
shows that bacteria will not attack healthy teeth in a well-nourished individual.[13]

In another study it was found that vegetarians do indeed have a much lower incidence of osteoporosis than do meat eaters.[17]

NIGHTSHADES

This botanical group includes tomatoes, potatoes, eggplant, peppers, and tobacco. (For a fuller discussion of nightshades see this chapter, pages 176–80.) The alkaloids in these plants seem to affect the calcium balance in some way. One researcher has reported that cattle that graze on one variety of nightshades develop malformed skeletons and become unable to walk, grazing on their knees.[18] Dietary systems that include these foods invariably contain considerable quantities of milk and milk products: pizza, eggplant parmigiana, potatoes with sour cream, and so on. My theory is that the high amounts of calcium in the milk products are held in check by the nightshades, perhaps destroyed or used up, and so balance is maintained. In my own experience and that of some of my students, consuming nightshades on a dairy-free diet has resulted in a loss of calcium, evidenced by brittle nails, painful gums, and dental caries. Eliminating the nightshades, rather than increasing the dairy, solved the problem. It is also interesting to note here the results of one study of osteoporosis sufferers: It was found that three-quarters of them smoked between one and two packs of cigarettes daily.[19] Tobacco, of course, is a nightshade.

WINE, VINEGAR, AND CITRUS

These foodstuffs, because of their natural acidity, require the buffering action of calcium during metabolism and will find it either in a high-dairy diet or by removing it from the teeth and bones. In other words, it's wise to have wine accompanied by cheese, or vinaigrette on the salad only if there's cream or cheese in the rest of the meal, or orange juice only if one also has milk or cream cheese for breakfast. In a diet low in or devoid of milk products, such foods as wine, vinaigrette dressing, or orange juice will decalcify the system. Tea with lemon is a particularly corrosive drink; if it's served in a Styrofoam cup, it will eventually eat holes in it. My own nails began to grow normally once I stopped drinking that beverage completely, and several of my students found that getting off orange juice had a similar effect. People with low calcium reserves may develop brittle nails when consuming other juices as well.

COFFEE, ALCOHOL, AND SALT

Caffeine, alcohol, and salt all bring about calcium losses. The effect of coffee is minor, it would take eight or more cups of coffee per day for the calcium loss to be significant. Several studies show that alcohol consumption interferes with the absorption of calcium and can be toxic to bone cells. Social drinkers run two and a half times the risk of contracting osteoporosis than nondrinkers do, and alcoholics are known to lose bone mass. As far as salt is concerned, in one study Dutch students excreted 20 percent more calcium when they consumed 6,000 milligrams of sodium than when they ingested only 3,000 milligrams daily.[20]

On the whole, it seems quite likely that any acid-forming foodstuffs in appreciable quantities demineralize the system. These include, besides sugar and high-protein foods, flour, bread, legumes, and grain, either whole or refined. Any time such foods are consumed, it is important that they be balanced by alkalinizing ones, preferably vegetables and seaweed. (See page 73, "Acid and Alkaline" for more details.) Otherwise, buffering minerals, including calcium, will be removed from the body's storage places, such as teeth and bones.

MEAT

- Contractive
- Acid-forming
- Warming
- Buildup food

Thousands of words have been written both praising and decrying the use of meat.* I can think of no other food that has excited the passions of food theorists as much as meat—a fitting metaphor, perhaps, for meat in the diet has a reputation for exciting our passions.† Meat has traditionally been associated with strength and the male principle of action and expansion. Warriors and rulers were fed meat, while monks and scholars, especially in the Orient, ate simple vegetarian fare.

---

* "Strong meat belongeth to them that are of full age, even those who by reason of use have their senses exercised to discern both good and evil."[21] Pythagoras, on the other hand, felt that meat clouded the reasoning powers and warned judges against eating meat for at least twelve hours before a trial.

† "[Meat] weighs us down with earthly heaviness, and stirs up instinctive will forces which express themselves in passion and emotion."[22]

Because of its high protein content, meat is a building food. Its fat content makes it especially warming as well. In amounts appropriate to a given organism, it energizes and helps build strength. An excess of meat, on the other hand, quickly causes problems of accumulation of matter: clogged vessels and organs, putrefaction, infection. Eventually, it makes the muscles slack and the joints stiff. Daily consumption of meat, together with dairy products, is at the core of our excessive protein intake, which has been associated with dehydration and heatstroke in athletes, fatal exacerbation of kidney and liver malfunctions, increased acidity of body fluids, infant deaths, premature aging, heart disease, and cancer.[23] A high-protein diet creates toxic by-products in the form of unused nitrogen; excreting these can seriously overtax the kidneys, unless large amounts of water are taken to flush them out.

In our modern times, one of the greatest problems with meat, as with almost all other foods, is the degeneration of its intrinsic quality. There is a vast difference in effect between eating the meat of a recently caught wild deer and eating that of a steer that has been penned up for months at a time and was suffering from tuberculosis and cancer. Antibiotics and steroid hormones in the feed, added to prevent infections and increase weight quickly, are passed on to the consumer at dinnertime. The antibiotics so consumed are associated with a decreased responsiveness to antibiotic therapy when it is medically necessary.

In 1977 Richard P. Novick, M.D., director of the Public Health Research Institute of the City of New York, wrote that "Recent years have witnessed massive increases in the use of antibiotics for livestock as well as for human medicine. These practices have caused the development of vast populations of disease-breeding bacteria that are simultaneously resistant to many different antibiotics and are becoming a greater and greater threat to human as well as animal health."[24]

The problem of sex hormones added to the feed or implanted in cattle is of a magnitude we haven't begun to grasp. I suspect it will take another generation before we can begin to discern what is going on. For the past thirty years, natural and synthetic sex hormones have been used both in cattle and in poultry to promote faster growth and more efficient assimilation of the nutrients in feed. The hormones include androgens (male hormones such as testosterone), progestogens, and estrogens (both female hormones including progesterone and estradiol). Hormonal imbalances—which can be created by the introduction of hormones from the outside—can lead to such disorders as obesity, infertility, diabetes, dwarfism, gigantism, kidney disease, hypertension, precocious puberty, hypoglycemia, masculinization of females, feminization of males and even cancer.[25] In Puerto Rico between 1973 and 1981 there was a dramatic incidence of premature puberty, breast growth (in boys and girls), and ovarian cysts in children, some as young as eight months; when the children were taken off fresh milk and meat from local sources, the symptoms, in all but 8 percent of the cases, regressed.

Sex hormones are used not only to fatten cattle. They are used to bring a pen of cows into heat so they can all be bred at the same time; to bring about abortions in heifers who are destined for the feedlot and eventually, slaughter; or to increase milk production. Significantly, technical instructions accompanying animal-diet supplement-hormone products invariably warn women of child-bearing age to be extremely cautious when handling them. They can apparently cause abortions and menstrual cycle changes simply by absorption through the skin.[26]

According to obstetrician-gynecologist Christiane Northrup, there may be a strong link between the hormones in meat and milk and the excessive breast and uterus tenderness experienced by some women. It may not be unreasonable to suspect that just as the hormones fatten the cows, so they would also fatten susceptible human beings that consume the milk and meat of cows so treated.

In addition to the medications and additives they are dosed with, grazing animals condense in their body tissues many of the pesticides, herbicides, and other toxic substances used in raising their feed crops. As these substances accumulate in high concentrations in their fat, liver, and kidneys, they present obvious hazards to the meat consumer as well. The problem with meat today, then, is perhaps not that it is meat, but that it is very tainted, chemicalized, adulterated meat, from sick and overmedicated animals. In any case, my comments about the effects of animal protein apply generally to reasonably healthy, naturally raised animals. We simply do not have enough information to determine how many of the physiological effects of meat are due to the chemicals or to the meat's intrinsic quality.

Meat has certain effects that are not directly related to its physical composition. According to my observations meat eating supports assertiveness, competitiveness, drive. In appropriate amounts, it can keep the senses sharp, reasoning powers keen, and generate excitement and high energy for physical work. On the other hand it can also cause lethargy and sluggishness, a dulling of the senses, as well as aggressiveness, anger, impatience, and a quarrelsome temper.

From a spiritual point of view, meat keeps us tied to physical reality and material considerations, prompting us to manipulate matter and expand our territory, sometimes to the point of war. Eating meat to excess inhibits a feeling of oneness with the universe. It can foster self-righteousness, intolerance, and the noisy kind of arrogance that demands center stage and looks for enemies.

FISH AND FOWL

- Contractive
- Acid-forming
- Moderately warming
- Buildup food

Fish and fowl have some of the same effects as meat, although to a considerably lesser degree.

They are buildup foods, high in protein; their lower fat content makes them less warming than meat, a helpful situation in warm climates. Lower fat consumption is also associated, as practically everybody now knows, with a lower risk of cardiovascular disease. As with meat, however, it is not unreasonable to wonder whether the manner in which the animals are fed and raised may have both physiological and psychological effects on the consumer.

Commercially raised chicken and turkey, the most popular among the fowl, are at present thoroughly contaminated with artificial growth hormones and feed chemicals. Our sense of taste is at times a fine indicator of the quality of a natural food, and there is a surprising difference in the taste of a commercially raised chicken and that of a chicken raised on natural feed and allowed to run free and peck; the latter tastes noticeably better.

Fish are suspect if they come from rivers that may be polluted with industrial wastes. Even saltwater fish are questionable, as they may have been sprayed or irradiated to preserve freshness during the trip from deep sea to market. There is no way in which the average consumer can tell how the fish in the store has been treated, for no warning labels are required by law. Ideally they should be, so that we can exercise our informed consent. Meanwhile, the only choice we have is either eating what's available or not.

On the whole, fish and poultry, like meat, are energizing, warming foods. Fish may be slightly more stimulating, while turkey may have a more calming effect, because it contains the amino acid tryptophan.[27] When consumed in correct amounts according to individual need, these foods support assertiveness, the ability to work hard and follow through. In excess, or when not needed, they may create all the problems associated with excess protein consumption, including sluggishness, lethargy, overworked kidneys, impatience, aggressiveness, and shortsightedness.

*E*GGS

- Contractive
- Acid-forming
- Warming
- Buildup food

Most animal-protein foods consumed in our culture are pieces of a whole—except for smelts, sardines, whitebait, soft-shell crabs, and eggs.

Are eggs as healthful as we think? Or as dangerous? Controversy rages. As usual, each side is right about half the time. What is certain is that eggs are easily digested, and their protein almost fully utilized by the body. Perhaps this is because they are a whole food—there is no element in excess, or out of balance with the others, and hence no part is left behind (except the inedible shell).

Eggs can, of course, be consumed in excess, especially when the diet already contains much other animal protein and fat. I was deeply impressed as a child when my mother pointed out that an egg is, in fact, a potential chicken. "It's a very powerful food," she said. "It has a lot of outward-going energy, even though it seems so mild. Be cautious with it." The Chinese consider one egg sufficient for six people (as it is when mixed into eggdrop soup or fried rice).

Because they are a product of the female hormone system (manufactured by the hen's ovaries), eggs may stress the human female reproductive system in some way. It is possible that they may overactivate it, and, on the reverse swing, weaken it. Women who have problems related to the ovaries may want to consider very carefully whether they need to eat eggs or not.

Splitting the egg and eating only the white—mostly protein—and discarding the yolk—high in fats—may be reasonable practice from a mechanistic nutritional viewpoint that holds protein in high esteem and disparages fat. It is absurd, however, from our systems approach. The white and the yolk form a whole and balance each other, the fats in the yolk helping in the assimilation of protein. In fact, eating only the egg white would be tantamount to eating only white flour on the grounds that the wheat germ has too much oil in it.

Eggs suffer the indignities of commercial production as much as chickens do. Egg-laying chickens, whose feed is laced with antibiotics and hormones, are kept in tiny cages under lights that never go out, and their hormone systems are overworked so that they lay eggs at a much higher rate than is natural. Perhaps the appearance and protein content of the eggs they produce is the same as that of eggs laid by healthy chickens fed natural food and allowed to play with the roosters. However, if we stick to systems thinking, we'll have to admit that the chicken's feed and environment will make a difference in the eggs. Just because this difference cannot be analyzed through a microscope does not mean that it is therefore invalid or one to be dismissed. To what degree the difference is significant can be debated and disagreed about, but a difference it is nonetheless. I personally declare my strong preference for "organic" eggs produced under natural conditions, obtainable in most health food stores. Not only do such eggs taste cleaner, less "eggy," than commercial ones, but I simply feel safer eating as close to the natural order as possible. In all probability it is less stressful for our organism to consume fresh foods raised with natural methods.

What are the psychospiritual effects of consuming eggs? From my observation of people whose major source of animal protein is eggs, I would say that too many eggs encourage a tough and brusque attitude, perhaps overwhelming gentler feelings of kindness and patience. On the other hand, modest amounts of eggs—just as with meat, fish, and fowl— support aggressiveness, drive, and the ability to run a business and to actualize potential energy.

GRAIN

- Contractive
- Acid-forming

- Moderately warming
- Buildup food

Cereal grains are associated with the rise of civilization the world over. Mythologies consistently credit supernatural beings with having brought and taught their use to humans. Grain foods—rice, bread, corn—are part of religious ritual and ceremony and revered as essential to life everywhere. They are the first solid foods given to infants, and when prisoners in times past were given bread—whole-grain bread—and water, it was because they could live on that. Jonathan Swift's Gulliver found this out in one of his travels:

> Oats . . . These I heated before the fire as well as I could, and rubbed them till the husks came off . . . I ground and beat them between two stones, then took water and made them into a paste or cake, which I toasted at the fire, and eat warm with milk. . . . And I cannot but observe that I never had one hour's sickness while I staid in this island . . .

There are good reasons for the popularity of grains. They are, together with beans, the only foods that contain all the major nutrient groups needed by the body: carbohydrates, protein, fats, vitamins, minerals, and fiber. Animal foods contain protein but no carbohydrates (with the exception of milk and its products); sugar is pure carbohydrate without protein; and fruits and vegetables are high in vitamins and minerals but too low in protein and fats. That is why grain "comes closer than any other plant product to providing an adequate diet."[28]

Their protein content makes grains body builders, while their complex-carbohydrate content ensures a steady blood sugar level supportive of intense mental activity. The right amount of whole grains in the diet will support resistance to stress (thanks to the vitamin B complex), endurance, steadfastness, and the capacity for steady work.

Too much grain can make the body acidic, as meat would, unless it is accompanied by appropriate quantities of vegetables, seaweeds, or fruits. If it is not well chewed, grain can also cause flatulence and overweight. The saliva contains an enzyme called ptyalin, which initiates the breakdown of starches, and if that enzyme doesn't get a chance to act, the rest of the digestive process becomes much more laborious.

Grain consumption also has certain nonphysical, psychological or spiritual effects. Eaten to excess, grain may cause a certain rigidity, self-righteousness, and the kind of quiet arrogance that admits no correction. In the right amount, whole grains—not cracked, or ground, but unbroken—can foster a holistic world-view. Ancient Central American Indian lore has it that grains facilitate socialization and social intercourse; and in the West, breaking bread with one's neighbor is the ultimate symbol of a spiritually strong social connection. Time and again I hear from my students that a change of diet toward one that includes a significant proportion of brown rice, millet, barley, kasha, and wheatberries has helped dramatically in changing their perception of life—from a fragmented, alienated, self-centered view to one of connection, integration, and oneness.

BEANS

- Contractive
- Acid-forming
- Warming
- Buildup food

Grain and beans have traditionally formed a pair in dietary systems world wide. We can name the classic combinations almost as if they were one word: rice-and-beans, lentils-and-barley, cous-cous-and-chick-peas. In the Americas, we find cornbread and black-eyed peas as native staples. Aduki beans, soybeans, rice, and millet are the basic foods of China and Japan. Kidney beans, split peas, lentils, and white beans are all popular in Europe as complements to wheat, barley, and rye. Lentils, green and yellow split peas, mung beans, and many other legumes are used daily with rice in Indian households. Chick-peas and fava beans are favored in Africa and the Middle East, accompanying millet, couscous, and bulgur wheat.

In her well-known and aptly titled book *Diet for a Small Planet,* Frances Moore Lappé conferred scientific understanding upon these traditional pairings. The concept of "complementary proteins" is currently well established among all those even marginally interested in nutrition. This concept holds that it is the combination of certain plant foods (grain with beans, or beans with seeds) that provides a higher amount of usable protein than would be expected by just considering the protein content of the individual foodstuffs. For example, if you were to eat enough wheat to get 30 grams of usable protein, and enough beans to get 70 grams, when you eat them together you would actually get 133 grams, not 100.

Although all plant foods contain all eight essential amino acids (the ones that cannot be manufactured by the body), these appear in patterns that apparently make them less usable than the protein in eggs, milk, and meat. However, when people are raised on low-protein diets, as they are in most of the world, they are much more efficient at extracting the full nutritional value of plant foods than people raised on high-protein diets. When people switch from an animal-protein diet to a vegetarian diet, then, it is particularly important that they consume complemented vegetable proteins, because their body system is conditioned to expect protein that is fully utilizable. Unfortunately, many people who have added whole grains to their diet and eliminated or greatly diminished their consumption of animal protein still neglect the use of beans, to their nutritional detriment.

All legumes are very high in protein. When raw, in fact, they have the highest protein content of all natural foods (some aged cheeses may contain a bit more, but cheese is a concentrated "partial" food insofar as it is made from milk by discarding the whey):

GRAMS OF PROTEIN IN 100 GRAMS RAW*

Red Beans	Brown Rice	Milk	Hard Cheese	Meat
22.5	7.5	3.5	21–26	20–22

In cooked legumes—which is how we eat them—the protein content is lower, whereas in cooked meat it is higher:

GRAMS OF PROTEIN IN 100 GRAMS COOKED*

Red Beans	Brown Rice	Meat
7.8	2.5	28–30

The discrepancy occurs because beans and grains are cooked in water and thus diluted; meat, on the other hand, loses water during cooking, and its nutrient elements thus become more concentrated. But before we jump to our conditioned belief that "more

* Source: USDA Handbook No. 8.

is better," let's remember, mother's milk contains only 1.1 grams of protein per 100 grams. As daily fare, therefore, it might be more appropriate for us to choose foods with a lower protein content.

Because of their protein content, beans are body-building, warming foods. They provide us with the protein needed for body repair without saddling us with the cholesterol, fat, and toxic nitrogen by-products of meats. The warming effects of beans manifest themselves especially in such dishes as soups, stews, and casseroles—classic standbys for cold winter evenings before the advent of central heating. The one exception is soybeans, which have been classified as cooling.[29]

Soybeans are quite different from other legumes. Extensively used in the Orient in various fermented and aged forms (miso, natto, shoyu, tempeh, tofu), the soybean has been called "the vegetable cow" due to its nutritional versatility. It is the highest in protein among all beans; its proportion of essential amino acids is close to that of animal products, and therefore it is considered to be a "complete protein." As a result, the nutrition-conscious movement that has been developing over the past ten to fifteen years has elevated soybeans to a lofty status, and soy products such as tofu, miso, and tempeh have been enthusiastically adopted by natural cooks (among whom I count myself).

Yet the enthusiasm can go too far. I once had as a student a man who always looked profoundly pale. When I inquired about his diet, it turned out that he was eating five or six cakes of tofu daily. He reasoned, as many people do, that because it is a "good source of protein," the more he ate of it, the better. His meals, even his snacks, consisted of a slab of tofu, a piece of bread, some lettuce and sprouts, and dressing. When he cut down on tofu and began to consume regular cooked beans, whole grains, and a variety of vegetables, his color improved vastly, as did his energy and general health. Although tofu is "high in protein," it is not a whole food. It contains 28 percent less iron, only 10 percent of the fiber and B vitamins, and none of the vitamins A and C found in cooked whole soybeans (the "whole food").

The traditional Japanese diet that includes tofu and other soybean products uses these in small amounts; rice, not tofu, is the staple food. Interestingly, the Japanese also use seaweed as a daily food: Miso soup with tofu is made with seaweed stock, sushi is rolled in nori seaweed, and other sea vegetables such as agar, hiziki, and wakame are consumed regularly. This custom begins to make sense when we find out that soybeans contain a thyroid-depressing element;[30] seaweeds, being rich in iodine, a mineral needed for proper thyroid function, counterbalance that effect.

Folklore has it that appreciable quantities of soybeans and their products, especially tofu, can lower, or cool, sexual energy. Research done at the universities of Illinois and of Kansas has shown that soybeans may interfere with the absorption of zinc.[31] As zinc is one of the minerals most strongly associated with the healthy functioning of the sex glands, this bit of folk wisdom appears realistic. It is therefore possible that a meal consisting of soyburgers, tofu fries, soymilk shake, and a slice of tofu cream pie may cause as many, though different, problems as the original fast-food meal it tries to replace.

Traditional diets use beans of all kinds with grains in a proportion of roughly one part beans to two parts grain.[32] The macrobiotic diet suggests one part beans to five or six parts grain.[33] Our taste and desire may suggest still different proportions, ranging from very little beans to only beans. In any switch from a diet plentiful in meat to one plentiful in beans, however, it is a good idea to take it slowly. The intestines may need six months to a year before they can digest beans comfortably.

As a protein food, beans are weighty and keep us tied to the material world. In excess, they could cause the tissues to become hard and dense, much as meat does.[34] It was perhaps for that reason that Pythagoras, the Greek mathematician and philosopher, who was also one of the earliest known vegetarians, encouraged his followers to abstain from beans.

Yet all things have two sides, and the weightiness of beans has its distinct advantages: In a vegetarian diet that may have a tendency to carry us upward, causing us to feel light and expanded, beans provide the material anchor of protein and thereby keep us plugged into the reality around us.

ROOTS

- Contractive
- Alkalizing
- Warming (when cooked)
- Moderate breakdown food

Sprouting downward from the seed, the root turns away from the light, burrowing deeper and deeper into the cool, moist earth.

It anchors the upward-growing shoot, drawing nourishment from the soil and sending it toward the sky. It represents stability and strength. Some roots are so powerful that they can crack rocks that stand in the way of their growth.

We humans mirror the plant structure, but in reverse: While plants grow from the seed up, we grow from the head down. Although I'm reasoning more in poetic than strictly scientific terms, some correspondence can be established between root and head. When we stand at ease, our head, the seat of identity, points upward, while our trunk and extremities point downward. In plants the root, which gives strength and stability, reaches down for the center of the earth, the trunk and branches grow upward. The root system is usually much smaller than the rest of the plant; our head, too, is much smaller than the rest of our body, in a proportion ranging roughly from 1:6 to 1:8. Another bit of South American folk wisdom—that consuming roots helps to establish our identity—begins to make sense. Note in this connection, the popularity of carrots among children, who unconsciously might be involved in sorting out their private identities. Because roots are contractive, grow in darkness and quiet, are connected to the earth, and draw in and distribute nourishment, they may also stimulate those same qualities in us when we eat them: contractiveness, steadiness, earthiness, and the ability to nourish.

There are two very different kinds of roots: those that are used as vegetables and those that are used as condiments. The most popular roots that are eaten as vegetables are sweet ones, such as carrots, parsnips, turnips, celery root, and rutabaga. Burdock, a wild root, is very thin, long, and extremely hard to dig up. Its resilience, hardiness, and resistance to cold weather are reputedly transferred to those who consume it.

Roots that are commonly used as condiments or as side dishes include radishes, onions, garlic, daikon, ginger, and horseradish. They are contractive, but have a sharp, expansive flavor—a particularly striking union of opposites. Because of this they promote "making whole" (uniting opposites) or healing. And in fact these pungent roots are often prized for their medicinal qualities. They are considered especially helpful in clearing up congestion and excess mucus: The contractive accumulation of matter is dispersed by the penetrating sharpness of the root.

In traditional ethnic cuisines horseradish, ginger, and the common radish also serve as aids in the digestion of fatty, oily, or fried foods. Horseradish in particular, often used as a seasoning for roasted meats, is said to stimulate the liver and the secretion of gall.

I have not seen many people who eat an excess of roots, so I cannot offer a firsthand comment on the effect such an excess would have. What I have noticed, however, is that the contractiveness and stability of roots, when added to the contractiveness and solidity of grains and beans in some vegetarian diets can encourage a certain inner hardening, a self-righteousness if you will, an emotional rigidity and a lack of physical motion. On the whole, people who eat a high proportion of roots, grains, and beans tend to sit and think, rather than run or dance. This tendency can be counterbalanced if desired by the uplifting, expansive energy of fruit, herbs, and spices.

LEAVES

- Expansive: lettuce, parsley
  Contractive: cooked bitter greens
- Alkalizing
- Cooling
- Breakdown food

When a seed sprouts underground, a shoot grows upward in the direction opposite to that of the roots. This shoot turns into stalk and leaves, which reach for the sky. Leaves absorb light and transform it into matter; they are the seat of trapped sunlight that has materialized into chlorophyll and carbohydrate. We, coarse creatures that we are, need plants and leaves as intermediaries for our energy exchange with the cosmos, for we are unable to engage in that exchange directly.

Leaves move in the wind, and perhaps for that reason they are thought to be, in South American folk wisdom, best suited to support motion. It is interesting to note that people who start jogging or running find they tend to eat more salads than before.

As with roots, we can distinguish two kinds of leafy vegetables: those that taste light and bland, such as the various lettuces, and those that taste sharp or bitter, such as watercress, chicory, dandelion, mustard greens, and so on. While bitter cooked greens are contractive, light-tasting raw ones—lettuce, parsley, dill—are expansive. In general, they support a lightening and an opening up. Raw salads in a regimen that also includes a reasonable amount of contractive foods will ensure a needed lightness and airiness.

A lack of fresh leaves may result in pallor and a sallow look. An excess of raw greens, on the other hand, can result in intestinal distress in susceptible people, and perhaps a craving for sweets.

FRUITS

- Expansive
- Alkalizing
- Cooling
- Breakdown food

Fruit is the final stage of the unfolding of a plant. With its fruit, the plant in a sense reaches its fullest self-development, attains its ultimate goal. The rest is up to the birds, the bees, the wind, and the rain. Strife has ended, peace reigns, and there's nowhere left to go but back: After maturing, the fruit decays. Only then will the seed that it carries have a chance to sprout into new life.

Fruits are usually expansive, cooling, relaxing, and generally alkalizing (with the exception of plums, prunes, and cranberries, which can be acid-forming). Because their energy goes upward and outward, most fruits will support openness, lightness, even cheerfulness, and an expansive behavior. In excess, they may cause us to become overexpanded, "spaced-out." Metaphorically speaking, if we move away too far from the contracted center, we lose our concentration and our focus. (Other plant derivatives such as sugar, alcohol, and drugs will make the condition even more pronounced.[35])

In some cases excess fruit or fruit juices, because of too much expansiveness, can weaken the intestines. Laxatives and enemas are then needed to keep this organ system working. Very fluffy, frizzy hair, perhaps split at the ends, is sometimes the symptom indicating such a condition.

Most fruits, as products of warmth and sunlight, are well digested at room temperatures. Cooking tropical fruit may push their energy just over the brink of expansion into contracted limpness. Accordingly, cooler-climate fruits such as apples and pears take to cooking much better than papayas and pineapples; countless variations on baked apples, apple pies, and pear tarts are witness to that fact.

Chilling fruit, on the other hand, will increase its ability to cool the body; this may be desirable in the sweltering summer heat, but less so in winter. In fact, because fruit is so cooling to begin with, people who go on all-fruit diets during the cold weather find themselves chilled to the bone.

According to my own observations, a fully fruitarian diet seems to support contentment, gentleness, lack of competitiveness, as well as a certain detachment and perhaps even celibacy. It is obviously a diet ideally suited for the pursuit of inner peace, or for nourishing those who have already attained it. Fruits are not tissue-builders, but help the body and spirit work harmoniously together.[36] Fruit eating also supports artistic expression, which in a broad sense could be to a human as a blossom is to a plant. It does not, however, encourage creativity in more mundane areas, such as business or urban planning.

NIGHTSHADES

- Expansive
- Alkalizing
- Mostly cooling, except long-cooked tomato sauce
- Breakdown foods (except potatoes, which are buildup foods)

The classification of plants that we've followed so far has been a simple one, based more on sense perception than on rigorous biology. There is one group of plant foods, however, that must be considered under its botanical classification because sense perception alone would not be sufficient to help us understand its effects and meaning.

The nightshade family, or *Solanaceae*, comprises some ninety-two genera with over two thousand species; its members include many stimulating, poisonous, or medicinal plants, such as tobacco, henbane, mandrake, and belladonna (deadly nightshade); ornamental plants, such as petunia, chalice vine, and angel's-trumpet; and some of our most widely used food plants—potatoes, tomatoes, eggplant, and peppers of all kinds (green, red, chili, paprika, cayenne, hot, sweet, and so on, except for black and white pepper).

Potatoes, tomatoes, and peppers were used as food by the Incas; at that time, potatoes were apparently much smaller than they are today, ranging in size from that of peanuts to that of prunes. Unknown in Europe before the Spaniards brought them over in the sixteenth century, tomatoes were first used as ornamental plants; the leaves and shoots had been found to be poisonous, and the fruit was thought to be equally unwholesome. Eventually, due to the ease of its cultivation, the potato became a major starch food, especially in northern Europe, replacing the more traditional barley and oats; in southern Europe tomatoes began to be used in soups and sauces. The eggplant may have been cultivated in the Old World as long as five thousand years ago; it has been a staple of Greek and Middle Eastern meals for centuries.

Nightshades are high in alkaloids, chemical substances that are products of plant metabolism and have a strong physiological effect. Alkaloids share with protein a high nitrogen content, but are in fact "denatured proteins," the other side of the coin; that is, rather than being tissue builders, they are stimulants, hallucinogens, medicines, and poisons. The presence of nitrogen also makes them alkaline; therefore, they neutralize acidity. Among the better known alkaloids are caffeine (in coffee), theobromine (in chocolate), opium, morphine, heroin, strychnine, quinine, and in the nightshades, nicotine, atropine, belladonna, and scopolamine.

Alkaloids are found in all parts of the food nightshades; some of the mature fruit, such as eggplants, peppers, and tomatoes, contain only faint traces. The potato contains the alkaloid solanine, which is found most abundantly in and under the skin. Storage conditions that include light and heat may, over time, increase the solanine content after harvest up to toxic levels. Improperly stored old potatoes have been known to cause gastrointestinal inflammation, nausea, diarrhea, dizziness, and other symptoms that can be severe enough to require hospitalization.[37]

Cattle grazing on the nightshade *Solanum malacoxylon* grow sick and deformed from an excess of vitamin D, which causes an increase of calcium and phosphate in the blood, a condition that leads to calcification of the aorta, kidneys, lungs, and the back of the neck.[38] It may be relevant to note here that calcification of soft tissue—that is, the deposition of calcium (bone matter) in inappropriate places within the body—is possibly the most prevalent physical symptom in modern industrial cultures. Hans Selye has called it "the calciphylactic syndrome," and it is involved in arthritis, arteriosclerosis, coronary disease, cerebral sclerosis (senility), kidney stones, rheumatoid arthritis, chronic bronchitis, osteoporosis, lupus erythmatosis, hypertension, and even certain forms of cancer.[39]

Nightshade foods may subtly remove calcium from the bones and deposit it in joints, kidneys, arteries, and other areas of the body where it does not belong.[40] We can make sense out of this through the balance-of-opposites theory, in this case of the acid and the alkaline. In a meat-and-dairy diet, the acid-forming meat protein must be alkalized with minerals; the alkaloids in such nightshades as potatoes and tomatoes may be instrumental in keeping the alkalizing calcium from dairy foods in solution, or pulling it out of blood or bones. If the process overshoots and too much calcium is liberated, the excess could indeed be redeposited in soft tissues as spurs, plaques, stones, or other calcifications. Vitamin D_3 in the *Solanum* nightshades has been found to be involved in promoting calcification of body tissues. Additional vitamin D in the diet, such as in fortified milk and other dairy products, breakfast cereals, and margarine, may then intensify this process.

Arthritics have been advised by one researcher to follow a "nonightshades diet" and avoid not just the obvious foods but also processed ones that have even the slightest traces of potato flour, paprika, cayenne, tabasco, hot peppers, and any condiments containing these. The consumption of foods with vitamin D added is also discouraged, as we normally get enough of this vitamin from the sun. People who have followed these suggestions report good results, including remissions of arthritic pains, rheumatoid arthritis, osteoarthritis, bursitis, tennis elbow, gout, lower-back pain, headaches, high blood pressure, and a host of related conditions.[41]

I have personally encountered a number of cases where joint pains have disappeared entirely after several months on a strict no-nightshades diet and no smoking (tobacco is a nightshade also). In other cases, muscle pains and charley horse (which have been associated with lack of calcium) followed a meal high in sweet peppers or spiced with hot peppers.

It's interesting to note that over thirty years ago, well before nightshades had fallen under any kind of suspicion, the macrobiotic regimen proposed by George Ohsawa recommended a total avoidance of these plant foods, deeming them too expansive: quick to grow, high in potassium and water, sharp of flavor in some cases. The stricture against nightshades in the macrobiotic regimen is coupled with the stricture against meat and milk products: Perhaps avoiding these foodstuffs, while increasing fresh vegetables, grains, and beans, might allow a disturbed calcium metabolism to calm down, and could lie behind the apparent success of macrobiotics in restoring joint flexibility and in shrinking spurs, plaques, and stones. One of the nightshades, tobacco, is known to be involved in causing cancer. There's another question to consider: Potatoes and tomatoes reproduce quickly, growing easily and fast—could there be a connection between them and fast-growing cancers, farfetched as it may seem?

Macrobiotic recommendations aside, there does seem to exist a relationship between our widespread use of potatoes and tomatoes and our high intake of milk and milk products. They are often almost irrevocably paired: tomato sauce and cheese, potatoes and cream. Which came first, the dairy or the nightshades? If the nightshades affect our calcium metabolism, then the milk products could be needed to provide us with extra calcium; or, conversely, our excessive calcium intake from milk products may create a demand for a food such as tomatoes, to break up the accumulation. To keep us balanced, then, do tomatoes need cheese, or does cheese need tomatoes? The answer is yes, to both. You will find it easier to give up nightshades and dairy both, than either one or the other. Conversely, a dairy-free diet that does use nightshades to an appreciable extent could result in calcium loss, as happened to one of my students who had that condition clinically diagnosed. When she eliminated the nightshades, the calcium loss was reversed.

Let's take the question of nightshades a step further. Why have potatoes and tomatoes, once regarded as poisonous, taken up such a large space in the Western diet? I'm thinking now not in nutritional, scientific, or economic terms, but in "cosmic holistic" ones. I believe in a rational universe, one in which things happen not by chance, but for a good reason, whether we can discern that reason immediately or not; I also believe that societies often act like whole organisms, with a collective consciousness and a collective unconscious. Thus, for an answer that satisfies my belief in the interconnectedness of all things, I'll turn once again to my favorite food philosopher, anthroposophist Rudolf Hauschka. He says that the potato and tomato are "gifts of the Western Hemisphere" and appeared at the beginning of a new phase in the development of consciousness, namely, the Age of Reason. They may be viewed, Hauschka contends, as foods that stimulate intellectual activity, abstract thinking, and materialism. They also "bolster up a certain egoistic self-satisfaction." Such an attitude lies behind the rise of the double-edged sword of Western science and technology; the price we had to pay for our giant strides in knowledge and in our ability to influence our environment was "a temporary side-tracking into a materialistic point of view." This phase may now be coming to an end. The nightshades, Hauschka writes, "have helped us on our way through a materialistic phase that now leaves us a heritage of capacities which, if we lay hold on them, can be the foundation of a new scientific outlook."[42]

And indeed many people are replacing potatoes with whole grains even as they move from a materialistic worldview toward a more holistic and spiritual one, while at the same time retaining the information and skills attained during the "materialistic" phase.

SEA VEGETABLES

- Contractive
- Alkalizing
- Cooling
- Promoting both buildup and breakdown

Many societies living near the sea have used sea plants as an important food source, as well as for their medicinal properties. They were in use in China, Japan, and Korea as early as 3,000 B.C.; Pythagoras referred to edible species in his dietary treatises, and they have been a staple in the diets of Aztecs, Vikings, Irish, Scots, Maori, and many islanders in the South Pacific.

In our society, sea vegetables have long had a great many industrial uses—in fodder and fertilizers, as thickeners and emulsifiers, in ice cream and other processed foods, in beauty aids such as creams and lotions, in paints, paper, and many other products. But it is only in the last twenty years or so that they have been used in any appreciable quantities *as food*. This increase in consumption is probably due to the increased popularity of the macrobiotic dietary system, which in turn is based on traditional Japanese cooking. The most popular sea vegetables available, usually in health food stores or Oriental markets, are kombu or kelp, wakame, hiziki, nori (used in sushi making), and kanten or agar, a seaweed that acts like gelatin. Irish moss and dulse, extensively used in the British Isles, are also increasingly available, as are some seaweeds like alaria and kelp, harvested off the coasts of Maine and Massachusetts.

Sea vegetables are extremely concentrated sources of nutrients. Dried dulse and nori are 20 to 34 percent protein, and all seaweeds are rich in calcium, iron, phosphorus, potassium, manganese, sodium, zinc, and of course iodine because they grow in sea water. They also contain appreciable amounts of vitamins A, C, and the B complex, including B_{12}. Because of this, sea vegetables are especially valuable in diets low in or devoid of animal protein and dairy. Small amounts, maybe a maximum of a tablespoon or two daily, are an excellent addition to a dairy-free vegetarian regimen. Seaweeds are known to aid the healthy growth of nails, hair, bones, and teeth; ensure proper metabolism; reduce blood cholesterol; stimulate the reproductive organs; act as antiseptics; help digestion; and keep the endocrine glands, especially the thyroid, functioning well.[43]

An additional bonus in our nuclear times is that the sodium alginate in sea vegetables appears to neutralize radioactive substances in the body, such as strontium 90, by chelating—or binding—and then harmlessly excreting them. I have found it particularly comforting to have a bowl of miso soup with seaweed after having had X rays for something or other.

It is of course possible to eat too much seaweed. This leads to an excess of minerals in the body, which can negatively affect certain organs, especially the skin and the thyroid gland. In one case I observed kelp tablets caused a series of welts on the arms and face; apparently the body couldn't handle the excess concentrated minerals and simply pushed them out through the skin. (The problem disappeared when the kelp was discontinued.) Thyroid problems can arise from an excess of iodine as much as from a deficiency. Considering that we are already ingesting large quantities of this mineral because of its presence in fertilizers and table salt, the situation definitely bears watching. Early warning symptoms of an excess of iodine might include underweight, hyperactivity, rough skin, acne, mental and emotional imbalances, and a "spaced-out" feeling. (It is interesting, I think, that a fast-food "junk" meal of hamburger, french fries, and chocolate shake provides 200 percent of the RDA of iodine. Bad news, perhaps, for acne sufferers.)

HERBS AND SPICES

- Usually expansive
- Usually alkalizing
- Either warming or cooling
- Stimulating general metabolism

Herbs and spices are unusual because they belong to two worlds: that of cooking, by virtue of their being flavor enhancers; and that of medicine, by virtue of their healing properties. In fact, a moderate amount of aromatic herbs and flavorful spices can be quite healthful: They can aid in digestion, prevent flatulence, help in fat breakdown, tonify, stimulate, relax, and generally please our soul with their aromas.

Because herbs and spices are used in such minute quantities, their nutritional significance, in terms of nutrient density, is negligible. In traditional dietary systems, however, they are viewed as important mediators of metabolic processes. Ayurveda, the ancient Hindu art of medicine and life prolongation, holds that the presence of a condiment can completely change and greatly enhance the physiological effect of a foodstuff. As a result, Indian cooking is redolent with aromatic spices such as ginger, coriander, cumin, anise, and cloves, all of which are said to promote digestion and help assimilation, especially of starchy vegetables, beans, and grains. (The use of the fiery chili pepper, a nightshade, is not truly traditional in India, for it is only a few hundred years old, and the peppers were originally imported from the Americas. They are now used with great abandon by insensitive or overzealous cooks, a practice that has led to much gastric inflammation and irritation. I myself have found that if I eat an abundance of cayenne and chili-spiced foods, the result is muscle trouble, such as spasms in my back and charley horse in my calves.)

Green herbs, such as dill, chervil, parsley, the mints, summer savory, marjoram, and thyme, lighten and lift otherwise heavy dishes. They calm and harmonize, and aid in the assimilation of nutrient substances by the blood. Aromatic seeds, such as coriander, caraway, fennel, and anise, aid in carbohydrate metabolism; interestingly enough, they are often used in breads and other baked goods.[44]

Their aromatic quality marks most herbs and spices as "expansive." The "contractive" ones are few and have bitter, acrid, or dry flavors: asafetida (Hing), juniper berries, and perhaps cinnamon, turmeric, and coriander seed if we go by their flavor rather than by their aroma. (Many of the healing herbs, as opposed to herbs that are used mostly in cooking, have these strong, "contractive" flavors; for a more thorough discussion of these than the present book can provide, please consult one of the many fine herbology texts now available.[45])

Taking a position opposite to the Ayurvedic, macrobiotics recommends avoiding all aromatic herbs and spices because of their "expansiveness."[46] In truth, such abstinence is at times quite appropriate for people who are trying to correct an overexpansive condition, either mental or physical. The most dramatic example I encountered of such a situation was that of one of my students. She had signed up for a year of classes, so I saw her weekly and watched her change. She started out as a puffy, ungainly, mentally scattered person and then decided to go on a contractive diet. She became very strict in her eating habits: only whole grains, beans, cooked vegetables, and seaweeds. She touched nothing expansive: no fruit, no juices, no sweets, no condiments. For a time she became so sensitive that even a pinch of oregano in a dish made her high. This phase lasted about eight months, at the end of which she slowly returned to a more varied eating pattern, adding salads, fruit, and more seasonings to her meals. After another year she also added some animal protein again. Over a period of two years, she transformed herself into a slim, elegant, well-focused woman—one of the more dramatic cases of personal alchemy I have witnessed.

From what I have experienced and observed, however, an insufficiency of aromatic condiments may give rise to difficulties with assimilation, excess mucus, a certain dullness of mood, a grave demeanor, and an overearnest, even plodding approach to life. In other words, no fun, no lightness.

An excess of stimulating condiments and highly spiced foods, on the other hand, may create digestive distress, muscular weakness, a "spaced-out," hyperactive condition, and a lack of concentration and focus. As with all things, "the right measure" is what works: The proper amount of herbs and spices is the one that keeps our digestive processes running smoothly and our soul content.

SINGLE-NUTRIENT FOODSTUFFS: CRYSTALS AND FATS

The three most unfoodlike substances that we consume are salt, white sugar, and oil. They are, respectively, a pure mineral, a pure carbohydrate, and a pure fat. Let's begin by looking at the first two, without cultural, nutritional, or gustatory biases—as if we were examining them for the very first time.

Both salt and sugar are crystals. They precipitate out of liquids (seawater, cane juice) and form themselves into evenly ordered molecules with smooth planar surfaces. They have, therefore, a most distinct characteristic: They are form created out of formlessness. And it is a highly ordered form at that: crystalline substances are composed of row after row of similar, clearly shaped molecules.

Crystals are fascinating phenomena. Though they are minerals, and thereby lifeless, they can nevertheless grow. In fact, they are regularly "grown" in laboratories for various scientific purposes. An entire science, crystallography, is dedicated to the study of the properties of crystals. Without crystals, the field of electronics, semiconductors, and transistors could not exist.

How do crystals grow? They emerge, as Aphrodite from the sea, out of a highly saturated solution. As the liquid cools or evaporates, the substance dissolved in it precipitates into a solid form of smooth surfaces. If the crystallization process in nature is slow and steady, the resulting crystals will be large and beautiful—gemstones, diamonds, quartz. If the process is hastened and has to endure abrupt changes in temperature, the crystals will be smaller, sometimes even impossible to discern with the naked eye. Yet, regardless of size, there will still be a precise order and a repetitiveness to the molecular arrangement of a crystalline substance.

Sugar and salt, the edible crystals, have both at one time been considered precious luxuries. Salt cakes were used as money in early Rome, where soldiers earned a "salary."* In Persia around A.D. 600 sugar was considered "a rare and precious miracle drug," a sedative dispensed with great caution.[47] Both substances have been intimately involved in the development of European trade and commerce with faraway lands—as, in fact, have been the spices of India.

Today both sugar and salt, precious substances though they once were, have swung from their original exalted place to the opposite. They are cheap and plentiful, available to all, and during this century they have been consumed in ever-increasing quantities. As we know that quantity changes the quality of things, it comes as no surprise that the erstwhile magic medicines have of late turned to poison.

Let us now look at the differences between our crystalline seasonings. Salt first, as it is older.

Salt

- Contractive
- Alkalizing

* From *salarium*, "money given to Roman soldiers to buy salt."

- Holds heat
- Promotes metabolism

Salt stands alone among all traditional foods and condiments: It does not grow originally in a garden or run through the fields, but is obtained from the evaporation of seawater or, today more commonly, mined from the land. It gives the sea its character, and our tears their peculiar flavor. Scientists say that all life emerged from the ocean's saline depths. Although not "live" itself, salt acts as a base for and a supporter of life. "Life began in salinity, and cannot free itself therefrom," wrote trace-mineral expert Henry Schroeder.[48]

In terms of opposites, salt is contractive and tightening. Its main element, sodium, is a major alkaline component of the fluid that bathes the cells of our body; it is closely associated with the transmission of electrical impulses and the maintenance of the acid-alkaline balance. Prolonged perspiration, vomiting, diarrhea, and extensive use of diuretics can cause a depletion of sodium; this condition then causes muscular cramps, weakness, headache, and the collapse of blood vessels.[49] Without sodium, our nervous system couldn't function, and we'd be, quite possibly, vegetables.

Although salt is thought of mainly in terms of its sodium content, the chloride in it is also significant. Chlorine, in fact, is a component of our powerful digestive juice, hydrochloric acid. This could be the reason why in Ayurvedic medicine salt is considered a digestive aid, especially helpful in the assimilation of cooked foods.

But it is not just sodium or chlorine that our bodies need. We are drawn to the whole, to the sodium chloride (NaCl) system, which is what nature offers us in salt crystals. Battles were fought, trade routes developed, lands explored because of salt. Why?

Perhaps it is its crystalline nature that we crave. Just as salt supports life processes on the physical level, it may do so on the nonphysical as well. Hauschka says that we add salt to foods "not only to give them flavor but to make us think."[50] It helps to *crystallize* our thoughts. Historically, the idea has some indirect support: Primitive, intuitive societies rarely use salt, but the Greeks, an intellectual, thinking society if there ever was one, used it with great respect. An example closer to home: I noticed that my children invariably began to demand a saltier taste in their foods, refusing the unseasoned baby pap, at about the age at which they started to speak, and therefore also to think abstractly.

Our nutritional need for salt has been established at ½ gram daily for the average adult. Three grams (⅗ of a teaspoon) is still considered a reasonable intake. But the average American consumes twelve grams daily, maybe even eighteen—three or more teaspoons! This amount includes not only the salt added to the cooking pot or sprinkled at the table but the NaCl used as preservative or flavoring in cheeses, processed meats, canned vegetables, ketchup, snacks such as salted nuts and potato chips, and so on. Additional sources of sodium are baked goods—because of the sodium bicarbonate in the leavening—preservatives based on sodium compounds, and even club soda.

If a little bit of mineral matter in the form of salt is essential to our lives, stimulating digestion, strengthening and activating us on all levels, an excess of salt, as we're finding out, can cause much trouble. Not only does it promote tightness and hardening, but it acts like a rein or a dam, holding in the fats. A high sodium intake, it has been found, interferes with the body's ability to clear fats from the bloodstream.[51] Excess sodium is involved in kidney trouble, water retention, hypertension, cardiovascular disease, and possibly stomach cancer and migraine headaches.

But before we place all the blame on salt generally, let us not overlook the fact that the commercial land salt generally available today is higher in sodium than traditional sea salt, both because it is land-mined and because of the various sodium compounds that are added to it. The presence of these additives must have an effect on the body, perhaps deleterious. The salt that is obtained by evaporation of seawater contains about 78 percent sodium chloride (NaCl) plus 11 percent magnesium chloride and smaller amounts of magnesium and calcium sulfates, potassium chloride, magnesium bromide, and calcium carbonate. Land-mined salt from Utah, on the other hand, contains 98 percent NaCl (plus 0.2 percent iron, 0.31 percent calcium, and smaller amounts of sulfur, aluminum, and strontium).

USDA standards for "table salt" or "food-grade salt" are set at no less than 97.5 percent NaCl, no more than 2 percent calcium and magnesium, and up to 2 percent of "approved additives." The latter include potassium iodide to supplement the iodine-deficient diets of people who have no access to fish, seafood, or sea vegetables; dextrose, a type of sugar, added to keep the iodide from oxidizing; sodium bicarbonate, to keep the salt from turning purple after the addition of the first two ingredients; and either sodium silico aluminate, calcium carbonate, sodium ferrocyanide, green ferric ammonium cytrate, yellow prussiate of soda, or magnesium carbonate as anticaking or crystal-modifying agents. Food-grade sea salt processed in France and obtainable in this country in health food and specialty stores has a high NaCl content (99.94 percent) but no additives;[52] that in itself makes it a more desirable item in my opinion.

Certainly there has not been enough research to determine what effect long-time use of, say, yellow prussiate of soda may have in the presence of sodium bicarbonate and iodide. (Sufficient iodine for healthy thyroid function can be obtained by a modest consumption of fish or sea vegetables. Remember just one fast-food meal provides 200 percent of the R.D.A.!)

If we return for a moment, to our earlier model of nutrient proportions (see chapter three, page 52), we will see that a high intake of salt must be accompanied by a correspondingly high level of protein and carbohydrate intake. Therefore, salty natural food substances such as miso, tamari, shoyu, pickles, and condiments can cause a condition of chronic hunger, which can be alleviated by decreasing the salt intake and increasing the protein somewhat by using more beans and fish.

On the spiritual level, a lack of salt, if we are not ill, "eventually takes the ground out from under the spirit in each one of us."[53] Without grounding we cannot build, and thus our personal evolution comes to a halt. Excess salt, on the other hand, may cause either a shriveling and hardening or a bloating and holding as the soul rigidifies, holding on to the past, and turns into a hardened pillar.

Between the two extremes, Folk wisdom acknowledges a connection between salt and a delightful spiritedness; witness the expressions "old salt" and "salt of the earth." There is no substitute for the salty flavor.

Sugar

- Expansive
- Acid-forming
- Holds cold
- Promotes both buildup and breakdown to excess

In terms of opposites, sugar is expansive and loosening; because it is a carbohydrate, it is acid-forming (the carbohydrate metabolizes into water and carbonic acid, which then turns into CO_2, carbon dioxide). Sugar and salt, then, though both crystals, have opposite effects.

The word *sugar* has two meanings, an unfortunate situation that has caused a great deal of confusion in the lay public. One meaning is the popular one: Sugar is the sweet white or brown stuff spooned into coffee, sprinkled over grapefruit, used by the cupful to make cookies and cakes. The other meaning is chemical: Sugars are sweet-tasting, crystalline carbohydrates that are part of foodstuffs. They are often named according to the foodstuff with which they are associated. These are lactose (milk), maltose (malt, grain), fructose (fruit), as well as glucose (the form of sugar found in the blood), sucrose (refined sugar), and others.

The carbohydrates (both sugars and starches) are found in natural foods such as grains, beans, vegetables, and fruits. Sugars are called simple carbohydrates, and starches complex carbohydrates. In natural foods they come with a team of co-worker nutrients that help the body metabolize them; they are then called natural carbohydrates. White sugar, white rice, and white flour—separated from the minerals, vitamins, protein, and fiber that originally assisted them—are known as refined carbohydrates.

Crystalline table sugar, a simple refined carbohydrate, is obtained by first extracting the juice from sugar cane, leaving the bulk and fiber behind. The juice is then purified, filtered, concentrated, and boiled down until sugar crystallizes out of the syrup.* In this industrial refining process, substances such as sulfur dioxide, milk of lime, carbon dioxide, charcoal (from charred beef bones), and calcium carbonate are used as purifying agents at various stages. Also a purified substance, sugar is a "naked carbohydrate": It has been separated from all its natural teammates (water, minerals, proteins, vitamins, fiber). What happens in our body when we ingest it?

Our bodily system is designed to interact with other systems; in the case of food, these systems are natural, whole foods, as provided by the earth. When we ingest a single part of a system, mechanisms of adjustment and compensation must be activated

---

* When the cane juice is simply boiled down by natural means, as during the making of maple syrup, the result is a heavy, sticky brown sugar with a fair amount of molasses left in it. This natural sugar is not as deleterious as the refined white stuff; however, it is often contaminated with sand, earth, mold, and bacteria. It is also hard to buy in the United States. The "brown" sugars sold in this country are simply white sugar with some molasses added back in.

to keep homeostatic balance. The more complex an organic system, the more varied will be its range of responses. Our body is highly resourceful: To metabolize refined sugar, it draws the missing companion nutrients (needed as catalysts in the digestive process) from other sources. These sources can be either other foods present in the same meal or the body's own tissues. For that reason, when we consume straight white sugar (as well as white flour), we lose B vitamins, calcium, phosphorus, iron, and other nutrients directly from our own reserves. This is the other reason for dental caries: Not only do bacteria touch our teeth, but our teeth—storing places for calcium—become weakened as calcium is withdrawn from them internally and thereby become more susceptible to bacterial attack. This "siphoning" effect of sugar is also what lies behind the gnawing hunger it can produce in some people; since the hunger is for the missing elements—fiber, vitamins, minerals, protein, water—it can provoke great binges as the sugar eater searches to satisfy it. The best nutritional balance would be a fair amount of extra animal protein, but only if the sugar binge is not a result of high protein consumption to begin with.

What do I mean by that?

We saw earlier (chapter three) that there is a certain balance between meat consumption and white-sugar intake. The naked carbohydrate of white sugar dovetails perfectly with the carbohydrate-free protein of meat. In other words, if you eat meat, you need sugar, and vice versa. This relationship may explain the apparently healthy condition of some people who eat both foodstuffs in moderation—they remain in a balance of sorts. Serious trouble ensues when the sugar intake exceeds the amount necessary to balance the meat. This can happen—and does happen—easily, because sugar is physically addictive, much like a drug. "The difference between sugar addiction and narcotic addiction," wrote William Dufty in *Sugar Blues*, "is largely one of degree."[54]

Two responses in the sugar "user" qualify it as an addictive substance: (a) Eating even a small amount—one piece of candy, one bite of cake—creates a desire for more sugar; some people can't stop once they start; (b) quitting sugar cold-turkey brings on withdrawal symptoms that can last from three days to three weeks: strong cravings, fatigue, depression, lassitude, mood swings, maybe headaches.

Excessive sugar consumption is believed to be involved in a host of very common problems: hypoglycemia or hyperinsulinism, diabetes, heart disease, dental caries, high cholesterol, obesity, indigestion, myopia, seborrheic dermatitis, gout;[55] genetic narrowing of pelvic and jaw structures, crowding and malformation of teeth;[56] hyperactivity, lack of concentration, depression, anxiety;[57] psychological disorder, insanity;[58] and even violent criminal behavior.[59] A study of one hundred women published in the July 1984 issue of the *Journal of Reproductive Medicine* found that the intake of sugar, dairy, and artificial sweeteners correlated positively with the incidence of *Candida vulvovaginitis*; after being put on a diet restricted in those elements, more than 90 percent of the patients were found to be free of yeast infections for over a year.[60] Probably the major drawback of sugar is that by raising the insulin level, it inhibits the release of growth hormones, a situation that in turn depresses the immune system.

I stress that these problems result when the sugar intake provides more "naked carbohydrates" than are needed to balance the animal-protein intake. When we consider that white flour supplies additional "naked carbohydrates," it is possible that only a small amount of sugar will create an excess. This is corroborated in a recent study that showed that the combination of a carbohydrate meal and a sugary food was "deadly" in its effects on learning ability and behavior, whereas sugar following an animal-protein meal did not have such a negative effect.[61] In a vegetarian diet, sugar will very quickly create a relative nutrient deficiency; therefore, vegetarians who eat sugar will get sicker faster than meat eaters who do the same.

There are, of course, many people who are not conscious vegetarians, but who simply happen to eat little animal protein and large quantities of sweets and who thus experience many of the problems of excess sugar consumption. Such is the case not only with careless eaters, but also with many poor and underprivileged people, who obtain a very high proportion of their daily calories from cheap sugared foods and drinks. It is possible that a considerable share of the social problems in the inner cities, including crime, is directly related to the malnourished and demineralized condition of individuals who live largely on those foods. In times past, poor people at least ate bread and beans and other people's leftovers; now they get doughnuts and candy bars, which can make them unstable and ineffective, lessening their ability to learn, advance and grow. They feel cheated, and rightly so; they are cheated—of normal nourishment, among other things. Amelioration of many serious social problems could lie as close as a banished sugar bowl: Programs for imprisoned criminals that institute dietary changes and eliminate sugar have been remarkably successful in preventing repeat criminal activity.[62]

Considering all the damage done by sugar, why does almost everyone like it so much? Native people who've never tasted it before eagerly adopt it; children can't keep away from it, even if they've been raised on "healthy" foods. The only people who seem able to avoid sugar are those who have consciously stopped eating it in order to improve their health. Having once gone through the withdrawal symptoms, they realize that they do not want to suffer again the physical and mental consequences of eating sugar. But almost everybody else loves the stuff. Why?

If, as we've been assuming, the whole earth is a system, and living systems tend to keep themselves balanced as they evolve toward forms of higher complexity, sugar eating must fit somewhere in the earth's balancing act. What is the "cosmic" reason that makes refined sugar so attractive to the great majority of people? The answer that has come closest to satisfying me comes once again from food philospher Rudolf Hauschka.

He points out that sugar's crystalline nature makes it similar to salt, but rather than crystallizing thought, sugar strengthens ego awareness and enhances personality. Geographically, its consumption does correlate with societies of strongly developed individuals: Much more sugar is consumed in the individualistically oriented Western countries than in the socially oriented Eastern ones. (However, the latter are doing their best to catch up!) Sugar has done its job, says Hauschka, when people develop a full consciousness of themselves as individuals and of their place in the universal order. After that stage of development is reached, even small quantities of sugar become superfluous, and eliminating it from the diet quite easy.

As a minerallike crystal, sugar must be dealt with respectfully. It is powerful stuff. If one is to use it at all, it would probably be more effective (in terms of strengthening the personality), and least harmful, if consumed in the same way as salt: a teaspoon a day, hidden in various foods so that we don't taste it directly.

From a spiritual standpoint, with too much sugar we become excessively individualistic, perhaps to the point of alienation and even criminality, as we feel our separateness too keenly and painfully. If individual consciousness is not awakened, the pendulum will swing, and the opposite effect becomes manifest: The sugar eater becomes a sleepwalker and lives each day in an unconscious fog. The right amount of sugar (which could be none!) will support our self-awareness and our strength of personality. It seems to me, from interacting with people who have stopped using sugar, that once we become clear and comfortable with ourselves, we don't need sugared sweets anymore.

Fats and Oils:

- Expansive
- Acid-forming
- Warming
- Buildup food

Like sugar, fat appears in the diet in two forms: (a) as a single element in the form of oil, butter, or lard; or (b) coupled with protein as part of natural foodstuffs (meat, cheese, avocados, nuts, whole grains). Like all other foodstuffs, it, too, has its positive and negative effects.

On the positive side, fat carries flavor and is what makes foods delicious. Truly low-fat food can be palatable, refreshing, even tasty—but never deeply yummy. Biologically, fat is the carrier for the fat-soluble vitamins A, D, E, and K, as well as a source of essential fatty acids necessary for proper cell function and for the development of the whole organism. The metabolism of fats creates body heat, and since they pack twice as many calories per gram as protein or carbohydrate, a high-fat diet helps maintain normal body temperatures in cold weather better than a high-protein or a high-starch diet could.[63] (Traditional dietary customs support this observation: Healthy, rugged Eskimos consume a high proportion of animal fats, especially seal oil, whereas the long-lived peasants from tropical Ecuador attain their advanced age on a diet that derives no more than 12 percent of its calories from fats.) Furthermore, fat is a source of energy, and its presence frees up protein for tissue-repair. (Carbohydrates also have this "protein-sparing" effect, but fat is twice as efficient.)

Much has been said and written about saturated and unsaturated fats, conventional wisdom being that saturated (mostly animal) fats may encourage heart disease, whereas unsaturated (vegetable) fats may discourage, perhaps even reverse it. However, more recent research shows a possible link between processed polyunsaturated vegetable fats and cancer.[64] In our choice of cooking oils and fats, then, we are caught between a rock and a hard place. A high total fat intake appears to be positively linked with both cardiovascular disease and breast and colon cancer. Various institutions such as the U.S. government, the American Institute for Cancer Research, the New York Hospital–Cornell Medical Center, and Memorial Sloan-Kettering Cancer Center now strongly recommend a reduction of dietary fat intake from 45 to 35 percent of total calories. Other health researchers, beginning with the late Nathan Pritikin, feel that it is safe to go down as low as 10 percent of total calories.

In practical terms, I have found that in a healthy, mostly vegetarian diet, one to two tablespoons of cooking oil per person per day is quite enough and allows the addition of perhaps the equivalent of ¼ to ⅓ cup nuts or seeds or other naturally high-fat food. This can come to about 20–25 percent of total calorie intake.

Fat and *oil* are generic terms, and it's important that we identify what exactly we are dealing with. Cancer is associated with *processed* vegetable fats, including hydrogenated vegetable fats, such as shortening and margarine (there appears to be no increased cancer risk among Africans, Japanese, and Eskimos, whose dietary fats consist mostly of polyunsaturated fish and vegetable oils). Margarine is an unsaturated oil through which hydrogen has been forced; this process converts it into a saturated fat so that it remains solid at room temperatures. This technology is in fact a molecular manipulation, which could cause problems as yet undetected. Hydrogenation, as well as extremes of heat, can change the form of unsaturated fat by rotating the carbon-hydrogen groups at their bonds, thereby changing the actual shape of the fat molecule.[65]

This detail may seem unimportant, but it isn't. Research has shown that the *shape* of molecules has great bearing on their function as well as on their effect;[66] a change in shape could thus in fact alter function, perhaps adversely. Studies on the effect of hydrogenation found that it can alter cell-membrane function, making the membranes more permeable to carcinogenic substances.[67]

The best quality fats to use, in my experience, are extra-virgin olive oil, unrefined sesame oil, and ghee (sweet, preferably raw, clarified butter). I generally use only the first two, because I'm too lazy to clarify the butter; however, I found that using a small amount of unsalted natural butter for my family is very satisfying and has not brought us any noticeable ill effects. I prefer these cooking fats because they have been used in traditional settings for thousands of years. They need low technology for their extraction and remain free of rancidity for a long time without refrigeration (ghee does, not butter). Once in a great while I use some "cold-pressed" sesame or safflower oil for frying; but those oils have been bleached and deodorized and tend to become rancid faster than the unrefined ones.

Oils become rancid by aging and from being heated and cooled either through cooking or because of the method of their manufacture. Rancidity involves oxidation of the polyunsaturated fatty acids, which then results in the formation of free radicals (substances with an extra electron that have magnetic properties, are strongly reactive, and have been implicated in the development of cancer, arthritis, cardiovascular disease, stroke, and in the aging process).

For occasional baking, I have found that the best fat is sweet raw butter. Desserts baked with whole-grain flours, natural sweeteners, and oil often have an oily, heavy feeling; their digestibility and taste are vastly improved when the same recipe is made with sweet butter. (Considering that I use no dairy in my cooking, this recommendation may seem like heresy; yet I feel that taste tells a lot. Baking is a technique developed in wheat and dairy cultures, and some consideration must be given to the fact that whole wheat cookies made with oil taste heavy, whereas the same cookies made with butter taste light.)

From our systems viewpoint, we can assume that extracted fat, whether animal or vegetable, has more potential for causing trouble than the fat naturally present in whole foods, where it occurs in a context that includes other balancing nutrients, such as proteins. A high intake of oils and/or butter could indeed seriously overwork the body, especially if coupled with much salt and a sedentary lifestyle. If the fat metabolism becomes deranged through abuse, it is conceivable that we could develop an intolerance to natural fats as well. In that case, a low-fat diet would be extremely helpful, as it would give the body a chance to repair the situation.

According to our model, the body can deal with excess fat input in either of two ways: by excreting it or by accumulating it. Excretion can be effected through normal channels, or through the skin, scalp, or mucous membranes. Pimples, for example, are a common reaction to the high fat content of cheese, butter, nuts, and nut butter. Accumulation can cause obesity, fatty deposits in the arteries and around the internal organs, and a high lipid content in the blood.

A deficiency of fats can create a sensation of inner cold; body functions slow down for lack of warmth, and the tissues grow brittle. An excess of fats causes inner body heat, and can also slow the circulation and clog the capillaries, thereby causing cold extremities. When too much fat accumulates around the organs, body functions slow down due to a blockage of the flow of fluids and energy. Opposite conditions, then—either too much or too little fat—result in the same effect, a slowing down of the metabolism.

Curiously enough, excess fat can also be associated with dry skin. When it accumulates subcutaneously, fat prevents moisture from within the body from passing through to the upper layers of the epidermis. Dandruff, fissures, and scaling, therefore, can be the result not of too little but of too much fat.[68]

On the psychospiritual level, too little fat tends to make us joyless and cool. An excessive fat intake, on the other hand, will depress psychic and spiritual activity, dull the senses and reflexes, and generally slow down all our functions, especially when it is coupled with much sleep. The right amount, and the right quality, of fats will keep our skin smooth, our eyes bright, our body temperature comfortable, and our general disposition warm and friendly.

Seven:
The Effects of
Food Preparation

Raw foods are nature undiluted. They offer us their pure being, without distractions. A raw carrot is a pure carrot; raw wheat or potatoes are unmistakable; raw meat is just that. Yet we do not always accept nature's bounty unadorned. All cultures *modify* their foodstuffs, either by the application of heat (cooking) or by engaging the services of microorganisms (fermenting or pickling). Preservation is not the only reason for using these transformative techniques. They have both metabolic and psychospiritual effects on the human organism. It is important to consider these effects when making food choices.

Cooking

All cultures cook. Perhaps not all of their foods, but certainly some. Why this strange and laborious activity? Why not eat everything as we find it, pure and natural, as the animals do?

Anthropologist Peter Farb, author of *Consuming Passions—The Anthropology of Eating,* believes that the curiosities of human behavior always have a rational explanation. Thus, there must be a sound reason for the universality of cooking, or else it wouldn't have lasted this long. And indeed there is: Cooking softens the cellulose and fiber in starchy foods and thereby makes their nutrients more available to digestion. In the case of animal-protein foods, though heat in fact toughens the proteins, it helps inactivate bacteria and microorganisms that could cause putrefaction and disease. Although cooking alters the energy field of foods, this need not be construed as negative, even though some nutrients may appear to be lost. We obviously do better with cooked meat or chicken, boiled rice, beans in soup or casserole, rather than any of these foods raw.

Warmth, moisture, darkness, time—those are the elements of cooking. They are also the elements of digestion. Thus, as Farb points out, cooking is a sort of predigestion.[1] It takes over some of the work done by the stomach, pancreas, and liver, so that it's *easier* for the body to absorb the nutrients that it needs. But why do we need this extra help?

The digestive system is intimately connected with the nervous system. A stomachache from emotional turmoil, a mental block from constipation—both illustrate that two-way connection. When a lot of energy is spent on digestion, there is little left for thinking. After a heavy meal we need a nap, a walk, a few turns on the dance floor; we'd be hard put to write a doctoral thesis. Conversely, when less energy is used up in digestion, more of it is available for the brain to use. Therefore, when cooking or fermenting simplify the digestive processes, we do have that extra bit of energy needed for specifically human activities, such as writing, building bridges, designing clothes.*

Because cooking makes digestion less stressful, people with digestive problems have found relief when they avoid all raw foods. The purported "loss" of nutrients in cooking is negligible if we take into account the fact that those nutrients that are present will be better assimilated. The higher amount of nutrients in raw foods is useless when these nutrients are not absorbed. If the raw foods cause digestive disorders, as they do for some people, they can even be harmful.

Cooking contracts vegetable foods, reducing their volume; thus we get more nutrients with less bulk. This reduction in bulk also means that the food is more *concentrated*. For most people cooking will therefore support mental concentration—better than, say, expansive salads with many different ingredients. The application of

---

* Anthropologist Carleton Coon speculated that "the introduction of cooking may well have been the decisive factor in leading man from a primarily animal existence into one that was more fully human."[2] The most primitive tribe discovered in our time, the Tasaday in the Philippines, had no wheel and no weapons—but they did have fire, which they started with wooden sticks, and over which they roasted wild yams and other foods.

fire to food may have resulted in the development of civilization by creating mental focus and concentration.[3] (Of course it could have been the other way around: First we became mentally focused, then we found the way to eat to support that state.)

There are seven major cooking techniques, with variations according to each ethnic cuisine. They are, from the most expansive to the most contractive:

- Boiling
- Steaming
- Sautéeing or stir-frying
- Broiling (under heat)
- Baking
- Deep-frying
- Pickling

Boiling and pickling are opposite methods: The first one adds water and removes minerals, thereby expanding the food; the second adds minerals and removes water, thus contracting it. Let us also note, at this point, that boiling has undeservedly gotten a very bad name in the past thirty or forty years. "Boiled to death" is a commentary often made about overcooked food. The fact is that boiling will sometimes make inedible food edible, even though it may be at the expense of some apparently "lost" nutrients. A case in point is that of bitter greens such as kale, collards, mustard greens, even carrot, radish, and turnip tops.

Up until perhaps twenty or thirty years ago, it was customary to boil leafy greens and throw away the water. With the discovery of vitamins, and of the fact that these substances are drawn into the water during boiling and thus discarded along with it, this practice came under attack. Today we are encouraged to steam greens in small amounts of water until they are bright green and still crunchy, and preferably to keep the water for other uses so as to avoid losing the nutrients.

Folk practices, however, are not often irrational or mistaken. It may be that boiling greens and discarding the water gets rid of certain medicinal and perhaps undesirable elements, which have a strong and bitter taste. The fact that mustard greens, turnip tops, collards, and similar vegetables, once staples of the hearty peasant cuisine, are not consumed much today, may be because the light steaming now recommended as the ideal cooking method leaves these vegetables tasting too strong and unpleasant.[4] Cooking greens also eliminates oxalic acid, which interferes with calcium absorption, and makes the calcium in these foods more assimilable.[5]

I brought up this comment in a cooking class, and some students decided to test whether it was true. We found that boiling kale, uncovered, for ten minutes, made it sweet and delicious; curiously enough, the color remained a brighter green than when the kale was steamed. Steaming it left it hard, bitter, and dull—not a culinary success. Steaming most bitter greens, we found, doesn't make them tasty enough to be eaten regularly, whereas boiling makes them quite pleasant. Sautéeing the chopped boiled greens in some olive oil with garlic or mushrooms further enhances their flavor.

Contrary to what we might expect, boiling does not leave greens totally devoid of nutrients, because they are so astonishingly high in vitamins and minerals to begin with.

NUTRIENTS IN 100 GRAMS*
(3½ oz or 1 cup cooked, drained vegetable)

VEGETABLE	VITAMIN A	VITAMIN C	IRON	CALCIUM
Collards (raw)	9,300 IU	152 mg	1.5 mg	250 mg
Collards (cooked)	7,800 IU	75 mg	.8 mg	188 mg
Kale (raw)	10,000 IU	186 mg	2.7 mg	249 mg
Kale (cooked)	8,300 IU	93 mg	1.6 mg	187 mg
RDA—adults	5,000 IU	45 mg	18.0 mg	1,000 mg

As the foregoing table shows, a cup of cooked, drained kale or collards will fulfill our total daily requirements for vitamins A and C and give us 5, 10 percent or more of our calcium and iron for the day. Not a bad showing for a single serving of a lowly boiled vegetable!

In light of all this, we might do well to go back to the old-fashioned methods of cooking leafy greens. By doing so, we may bring back one of the most nutritious staple foods of our ancestors and get, in a natural—and cheaper—form, those nutrients that many of us now ingest via pills.

Steaming is a very popular way of preparing vegetables nowadays, as it adds only a little water and does not leach the nutrients. It is a substitute for blanching, which consists of boiling firm vegetables only briefly but thereby draws nutrients out into the water.

* Source: USDA Agriculture Handbook #8.

The disadvantage of steamed vegetables is that is hard to add any interesting flavors to them except by means of a sauce; thus they can eventually become quite boring, in spite of their healthfulness.

Sautéeing and stir-frying are done on a hot surface with a small amount of oil and will quickly seal in nutrients while softening the cellulose of vegetable foods. These techniques lend themselves well to incorporating herbs, spices, and seasonings into the food. In French cooking, sautéeing is often used as a preliminary for further cooking, as with soups and casseroles. Chinese-style stir-fried dishes are cooked quickly on high heat and served immediately.

Broiling, done under high heat to sear and brown foods, is moderately contractive, as it draws water out. It is a technique used most often in modern households with gas or electric ranges, which keep fire contained while allowing a space underneath. In traditional technologies, such as open fires and brick ovens, this particular cooking method is difficult to implement.

Shorter cooking times are generally more appropriate for warm weather, as they do not contract the food overmuch nor add too much heat. Long, hot cooking, as in baking and deep-frying, works best in the cold. Deep-frying, though an old and very popular cooking technique, is one not generally recommended in light of our current nutritional information. In spite of that, deep-fried food remains highly favored by many and is served unabashedly by scores of restaurants. I find that it is only edible when crisp and dry and served with a sharp side dish, such as horseradish, mustard, ginger, or grated Japanese radish (daikon) to aid in the digestion of the fats.

Many of my students ask me about microwave cooking. They often have an intuitive feeling that it must affect food, yet they don't know how. Fire heats food by friction, as it causes the molecules to move around and rub against one another. Microwaves heat food by alternating the magnetic polarity of the atoms; that is, the positive pole is made negative and back again, thousands of times per second. In other words, the electromagnetic field is altered. Very little research has been done on the health effects of microwave cooking; however, food tastes peculiar when prepared that way, and I share my students' intuitive feeling that something is not quite right. If the electromagnetic field is altered, the shape of various components of the food must change somewhat, that is, vitamins are undoubtedly affected adversely; the food's energy field is probably weakened. I also wonder if a steady diet of microwaved foods wouldn't affect our thinking ability in some way. Time will tell.

Cooking makes animal foods tasty and safer to eat. The other side of the coin is that too much cooked animal protein causes indigestion, intestinal putrefaction, body odor, bad breath, and stresses kidney and liver function. Raw animal protein may be more digestible,[6] but on a spiritual level it brings us too close to the animal being, so we instinctively shrink away from it. In the few cases in which we do eat it, such as in sushi (raw fish) or steak tartare, it is invariably accompanied by strong seasonings—ginger, mustard paste, capers, black pepper—as well as elaborate visuals, so as to distract us from its rawness.

Too many cooked vegetable foods, and an absence of raw ones, often brings on sluggishness and pallor; I have seen young children with rickets who were brought up on all cooked vegetable foods, and I suspect there may be a correlation there; this theory remains largely speculative.

On a spiritual level, too much cooked food deprives us of light, and blocks feelings of inner joyfulness and fun. Too little, on the other hand, deprives us of warmth and of that wonderful feeling of community that can only be found around a fire and a steaming pot.

FERMENTING

It is widely assumed that the discovery of the fermentation process occurred by accident: a mash of fruits or berries, left in the sun for a while, eventually provided a startling aroma, a not unpleasant taste, an unexpected physical effect. Fermented alcoholic beverages may have been around for some ten thousand years already; but there are many other fermented products that we consume.

Bread, wine, cheese, and beer are the best known of these in the Western Hemisphere, together with pickles and sauerkraut. Milk and its products are fermented regularly by many cultures, especially in warm climates where refrigeration is scarce. Yogurt, kefir, koumiss, and cheeses of all kinds, made with the milk of cows, goats, sheep, yaks, camels, mares, buffalo, and probably some other animals, were staple foods of early Asian nomads, Hindus, North Africans, and Europeans.[7]

In the Far East, fermented grain and vegetable products are used often, sometimes daily. Among the best known are: tempeh in Indonesia, miso and shoyu (fermented soy products) in Japan, a fermented fish sauce called nampla or moc man in Thailand, Vietnam, and Cambodia, fermented black beans in China, kimchi in Korea, and many others.

Much as cooking demands an external agent in the form of heat, fermentation cannot proceed without the aid of external yeasts and bacteria. These microscopic living organisms begin by breaking down the carbohydrates and proteins in a food into carbon dioxide, constituent amino acids, and alcohol. When salt is added during this process, it prevents the formation of toxin-producing microorganisms. Originally, fermentation was left to the chance presence of airborne, invisible yeasts or bacteria, but that gave no assurance that each batch of fermented food would be of similar quality. Eventually, the fermentation organisms were found and tamed, and consistent quality became attainable through the application of specific spores or yeasts, such as lactobacillus bulgaricus for yogurt, koji for miso, rhizopus oligosporus for tempeh, generations of sourdough starter for bread.

Fermentation completely changes the character of a food. It makes bland foods tastier, richer, and stronger. It improves their keeping qualities, so that in areas where no refrigeration is available food can still be wholesome. Most important, fermentation increases nutritional richness: The bacteria synthesize additional enzymes and vitamins and create a more digestible amino acid balance.[8] They are especially helpful in the synthesis of vitamin B_{12}.

In addition, fermented foods improve the intestinal flora, thereby aiding in the digestion of dense protein and carbohydrate foods. Probably for this reason corned beef and pastrami are always served with pickles or sauerkraut, and the Japanese surround rice with miso soup and rice-bran pickles.

Too much fermented food—wine, beer, pickles, sauerkraut, miso, tempeh—will cause some problems, though the nature of the problems will vary greatly according to the particular foodstuff involved. The effects of too much alcohol are well known. An excess of miso may result in backaches, water retention, and a short temper, as its high salt content stresses the kidneys. Other salt-based fermented foods can cause similar problems in susceptible persons. In addition, fermented foods, as well as yeasted breads or cakes, are not recommended for those with either systemic or localized yeast infections.

The right amount of fermented foods, on the other hand, will aid in the digestion of the rest of the meal, especially when it is high in protein, fats, or grain.

Eight:
Changing the Way
We Eat

Food is selected according to a harmonic order to give a body to
your thoughts, and your thoughts determine your choice of foods.
So your choice of foods perfectly embodies your view of reality at
any given moment. —Richard France, *Healing Naturally*

HOW DO YOU FEEL?

Throughout most of history, human beings have eaten what the earth and their immediate environment provided. Natural, seasonal foods—found, grown, or caught—were the norm everywhere on the planet. They were prepared simply, according to traditional methods: eaten fresh, or roasted over a fire, sometimes fermented, perhaps dried or smoked to preserve them for lean times. And special foods for special occasions and conditions were part of each group's cultural heredity. On the whole, one was grateful for what one got.

All this has changed dramatically in our times. In the most sophisticated towns and cities, as well as in the simplest country stores, exotic and plain fare from all corners of the globe can be found, as modern transportation has brought the bounties of the whole world to our doorstep. Food has gone, in some ways, from being nourishment and sustenance to being art and plaything. No longer bound by any long-standing dietary tradition, we must, every day, make conscious food choices, choices based most often on our taste buds, and sometimes on our notions of what is healthy or not. "Changing our diet" for health reasons bespeaks our affluence. We would not—could not—change our diet during a famine. Being faced with so many choices demands of us greater responsibility, a clearer vision.

With all the recent emphasis on "healthy" eating, it is important to remember one thing: Food does not *make* us healthy. The right kind of food will allow us to reach our maximum health potential, to become as healthy as our genes and constitution may permit. It will support what we are at our best. It will not interfere with our development, but it will also not make us more than what we can be. In short, good food is effective because it is passive. The wrong kind of food will act like a block or a dam, deflecting our growth and thwarting our unfolding. In other words, it will actively create trouble, and *make* us unhealthy.

We should be clear about this whenever we decide to change our diet. No particular food, or way of eating, is a panacea, regardless of appearances. I'm sure each of us has heard stories of people who healed themselves of lifelong conditions by a change in diet. But although the diet seems to be what has brought on the cure, like a magic wand, I prefer to look at it differently. I feel that it's not the brewer's yeast, or the fruit salad, or the black-strap molasses, or the brown rice, or the miso soup, or the yogurt. Good food will nourish us without causing stress, and thus allow our immune system to spend its energy in healing. Thus many different diets will have healing effects. Often it is not just what we eat, but also *what we don't eat,* that helps us become healthy again.

Although I believe that rigid theories of what is right and wrong to eat are misguided, reality being fluid and changeable, certain principles *do* apply. I have outlined them in chapter five, "The Health-Supportive Whole-Foods Eating Style."

The details of health-supportive eating, however, depend on you, and it is up to you to adjust your particular food choices continually. To do this, *keep in mind the effects of different foods,* as outlined in chapter six. And, equally important, *listen to your body.*

Listening, however, is not enough; you also need to be able to interpret what you hear. As an example of the way you can use the foregoing models, here is a quick overview of some telling discomforts and the general change in dietary choices that would help to set them straight:

1. Do you feel spacy, unable to concentrate, scattered, "can't get it together"? Are you dropping things, bumping into things, starting lots of projects but not finishing them? YOU MAY BE TOO "EXPANDED": Increase contractive foods and diminish the expansive ones.

2. Do you feel tight, tense, on a narrow path? Do you get feedback from your environment that you are unyielding and rigid? Are you prone to tension headaches and do you have trouble changing or starting new projects? YOU MAY BE TOO "CONTRACTED" OR "TIGHT": Eat fewer contractive foods, more expansive ones.

3. Do you have a sour taste in your mouth, unrelated to lemon or vinegar, when you wake up in the morning and at other times? YOUR DIET MAY BE TOO "ACID": Eat more alkalizing foods.

4. Do you go on binges of sweets after eating a vegetarian meal with much fruit and salad? YOUR DIET MAY BE TOO "ALKALINE," OR TOO LOW IN PROTEIN: Add some beans, grain, fish, or fowl to your diet.

5. Are you tired or depressed often? Any of the above may apply, or else you're eating sugar or honey. Avoid these foods as your first measure; if that doesn't help, see number 4.

Let's now get into some more specific details about how to make your eating system work for you.

WHEN TO CHANGE YOUR DIET

If you are contemplating a change in diet, there are several questions that you must ask yourself: What do you want your diet to do for you? When should you change your diet? How should you go about it? How do you know if you've made the right choices? What do you do if you haven't? What can you expect from a major change? I will provide you with some answers, but by no means all. First, in broad terms, your diet should

- Support your general health, your activity, your chosen work, and your spiritual aspirations
- Feel comfortable and right, tasty and satisfying
- Help you feel *centered* and *clean*
- Keep your weight and energy at a comfortable level
- Help restore your health if you've lost it

Your diet should not

- Block your health, your activity, or your work
- Make you depressed, bloated, overanxious, irritable, tired, overweight, underweight, or cause pain anywhere along the digestive tract
- Cause you guilt, worry, or confusion

Change is the real secret of a successful life—the ability to adapt to new circumstances, new forms, new events that arise out of the old. Continuous change is also what keeps our bodies healthy: sloughing off old cells, getting rid of metabolic waste matter, blood and lymph flowing easily, their pH balance constantly monitored and adjusted. Whenever we are stuck, when change and movement are blocked, stagnation and illness set in.

It is time to change your diet when

- It's not doing what you feel it should do (see above)
- You *feel* you're ready for a change

In addition, you may have various complaints or discomforts that you feel are associated with the way you eat. Often, your family doctor will tell you "it's all in your head," or "food has nothing to do with it"—but deep down in your bones you *know* that things would vastly improve if you ate better, and most of the time you'll be right.

There is another time to change your diet, and that is the most difficult time of all: when you've already changed to a strongly recommended, clearly stated, apparently sensible health regime—and it's not working, or not working anymore. You don't feel right, your energy's down, your spirits are down, perhaps you're losing too much weight, or gaining too much—and you're feeling vaguely guilty because it seems that it's you who is wrong, not the regime, with its great backup and testimonials to its effectiveness. (For more on this, see "Can Health Food Make Us Sick?" page 221, in the following chapter.)

It is a difficult moment, because you have already made a change, a new commitment. If you have invested considerable time and energy into putting the new approach into practice, it's even harder. Yet sticking to a regime that doesn't work for *you* is point-less, regardless of its objective validity, scientific basis, or philosophical justness; regardless, too, of the conviction, clarity, credentials, or rhetoric of its proponents. This caveat applies to *all* diets, from the most "sensible" Recommended American Diet (RAD) to the most "outlandish" raw-foods regime.

You should always take into account where *you* are at this point in time: If you have been eating raw foods for five years, you may well need a changeover to macrobiotics or a hearty R.A.D.; or, if you have been doing the Standard American Diet (S.A.D.), you may need a raw-foods regime to alkalize and clean yourself out.

The time that is most highly indicated for a change in diet is when you are feeling stuck and need out.

How to Change Your Diet

Tuning in to Your Body Signals

If you have decided that you do need to change the way you're eating, you must then decide *how* to go about it. The first thing to do is to *pay attention* to everything you eat and to how you feel right afterward and up to twenty-four hours later. "There is a wisdom in [the body] beyond the rules of physic," wrote Francis Bacon. "A man's own observations, what he finds good of and what he finds hurt of, is the best physic to preserve health."

We each know much more about ourselves than we realize. The problem is that the knowledge is nonverbal; that is, it is not intellectual or rational. Our deepest self-knowledge resides in the body, which a great deal of the time does not speak the same language as the mind. Our senses are directed outward, and no sensory nerves are connected to the major organs that support life. Therefore the only "body information" we get are vague sensations and generalized signals. We are usually not consciously aware of that vast filing system of useful information about our general and specific condition, and have to go to a professional healer or physician who has made it his or her life's work to read other people's signals. If our code can be cracked, and the healer tells us what we already know about ourselves, we think the professional is right, and go home happy, believing we gained some new information.

Because our subconscious signals are nonverbal, our highly verbal society often ignores them or pronounces them insignificant, not real. "I feel" is not a medically acceptable statement about our physical condition if it is not supported by clinical findings. And yet, as one doctor once said to me, "You *are* sick when you *feel* sick." The reverse may also be true.

What I find significant is not that I may feel tired, for example, but that I feel that it's "not OK" to feel tired *in this particular way*. There are certainly times when it's perfectly fine to feel tired, as after a vigorous hike or a football game. But when the feeling is "*this* is not OK," it's time to investigate. And that is the clue to accessing our body's information system.

We can actually approach our body as if it were a computer, which works on a 0-1, on-off, or yes-no binary response range. And we can begin by using the responses we most easily identify, namely, "ok" and "not ok." Very often we cannot tell what we feel, or describe it in words; but we can almost invariably tell whether it feels good or bad, pleasant or unpleasant, right or wrong. Those sets of yes/no feelings are an excellent compass by which to chart our course of action, not only with regard to food but in all areas of our lives.

You can get in touch with these feelings most easily in the following manner: Relax for afew minutes with eyes closed; send a question down to your solar plexus, just as if you were beaming a sonar wave to the bottom of the ocean. The question should demand only a yes/no or an OK/not-OK answer. For example, ask yourself, "Is this food (or diet) good for me?" not "*What* should I eat?" A distinct feeling will well up: "Yes, mmm, it's OK," or "No, wrong, no good, danger." Regardless of how "good" the food you want to change to is, how sensible the theory behind it, or how desperate you are, *heed your gut feelings*. If it doesn't feel right, look elsewhere, try something else. To paraphrase Pascal, the body has its reasons that reason knows nothing of. (Watch out, however: If most foods feel "not OK," you may be anorexic. In that case, please seek help until you find a well-rounded variety of foods that you can eat.)

There is another crucial detail to keep in mind here: "OK" feelings about food are not to be confused with "delicious." Ice cream may be delicious but will not necessarily evoke an "OK" feeling. If you're starting on a new healing regime, you may balk at some new foods, such as seaweed or beans, yet your inner guide will probably whisper, "OK."*

* The technique for accessing feelings and subconscious information via body sensations has been explored in depth by Eugene Gendlin, Ph.D. He found that

Besides the yes/no response, you may of course draw a blank: The sonar wave does not bounce back, or you cannot interpret what it means. In that case, first rephrase the question, putting some thought into it. Or ask for help, consult the experts, get a second opinion. The answers and recommendations that you get you can then subject to the same treatment: "Is this approach OK for me?"

In our quest for healing ourselves with food, only individually can each of us decide what makes us feel better and what not, and when. Listening to your inner guide, then, simply means heeding yes/no signals from your body. With just a little practice, it's a skill available to you and will guide you not only in what to do but also in whose advice to follow.

How Fast?

Next, there are two obvious ways in which to go about changing your diet: slowly or suddenly.

A slow change is easy, but undramatic. You finish the old foods you still have in the cupboard or fridge and replace them with the new foods little by little. You change items in your meals one by one, stop using old favorites, add some new and strange things. Slowly, you move into a new eating style; if it's the right one, you *love* it. And because the change was gradual, there's a good chance that you'll stay with it, because you've had the opportunity to adjust to the food, as well as to adapt the food to your needs.

In a gradual change, health improvements are often not clearly noticed; at times they are attributed to something other than the food. Therefore, it may be handy to have an evaluation of your health and your diet both before and six months after the change. It's often surprising how much we can forget.

A sudden, drastic change can be just what is needed in cases of extreme stuckness, so as to initiate motion. It's also the style that may suit some personalities best. If you are one of these, you will throw out all your old groceries in one afternoon and bring in the new ones, become very strict very quickly, and admonish all your friends and relatives to do the same. You will probably feel dra-

---

people who respond most successfully to therapy invariably tuned in to their body feelings in some way and used the feedback to chart and correct their course of action. He emphasized that this skill is for "everybody in all of life's situations." See his book *Focusing* for a clear and cogent discussion of this technique.

matic improvements very clearly related to the change in your food habits.

The drawback here is the pendulum effect: The drastic change is a strong swing out and could easily be followed by a strong swing in. It also could be brought back gently, thereby keeping a comfortable balance; this takes some work, however. If the swing back flies free with no constraints, we have the possibility of eventual mad binges on "forbidden" foods. The swing back could occur anywhere from a few days to a few years after the original change. The more rigid and regimented the new diet was, the more violent the swing back could be—so please be cautious.

Which Way?

There are many combinations and changeovers possible among the diets delineated in chapters Four and Five. Let's look at those switchovers that are most common and helpful.

IF YOU'VE BEEN EATING	IT'S GOOD TO SWITCH TO
S.A.D.	Vegetarian Raw food (for a while)
	Fortified Natural Foods Diet (if needed)
Raw foods	Macrobiotic Health-Supportive
Vegetarian with dairy	Macrobiotic
Vegan	Health-Supportive
Fortified Natural Food	Health-Supportive
Macrobiotic	Health-Supportive with raw foods
Health-Supportive	Eat as you please

The progression that people seem to follow most often, from what I've seen, is as follows: from the S.A.D. to Fortified Natural Foods to Vegetarian/Raw food/with dairy to Macrobiotic and eventually to Health-Supportive. Sometimes it goes S.A.D. → High-Protein → Fortified vegetarian w/dairy → Macrobiotic. And of course there are many variations in between. If you need more specific details, or if your diet is too eclectic to fit into any of the above categories, here (on the following page) are some basic, simple rules to get you unstuck, fast.

If you've been too tight (high-protein, salt, fats, strict macrobiotic)	Loosen up (with salad, raw fruit, juices)
If you've been too expanded (from raw foods, juices)	Contract (with beans, grains, cooked foods)
If you've eaten too much sugar	Eat plenty of vegetables, some grain, beans, protein
If you've eaten too much meat	Go vegetarian
If you've been a strict vegetarian	Add some fish or organic fowl, with gratitude
If you've been fortifying your diet	Simplify it
If you've been eating very austerely and are beginning to feel empty	Open it up, amplify, enrich, binge
If you've been binging	Fast

In addition to balancing yourself in this way, keep in mind the following suggestions:

FOOD CHOICES IN CONTEXT

SITUATION	AVOID	DO EAT
In hot weather	Large proportion contractive food Fats High protein Hot, hearty cooked foods Root vegetables in large amounts	More expansive foods Low-fat animal protein (moderate) Salad, fruit Leafy green vegetables
In cold weather	Large proportion expansive food: Raw fruits and juices Salads Cold foods	More contractive foods Root vegetables, winter squashes Stews, casseroles, bean soup Some fats and animal protein Pickles or fermented foods
To support mental concentration	Sugar and sweets Alcohol Overeating Large salads Canned and frozen foods	Grains and beans Nuts and seeds (moderate) Small portions Casseroles and soups Cooked vegetables

FOOD CHOICES IN CONTEXT

SITUATION	AVOID	DO EAT
To support physical activity	Fats Heavy meats Over 40 percent grains and beans Excess salt, miso, tamari	Salads, leafy greens Fruits Moderate animal protein Grains and beans in salads
To support artistic expression	Large proportion contractive food Excess salt Fatty foods Any overly strict regimen	More expansive food Sweet vegetables (squash, yams, parsnips) Sweet fruits (bananas, dates)
For losing weight	High protein Dairy Fats Heavy, hearty foods Refined carbohydrates Salty foods	Moderate protein (beans, fish) Vegetables Whole grains Light, refreshing dishes Complex carbohydrates Fermented foods Fruits, some juices
For working with machinery, electronics, fluorescent lights, computers, word processors	Strict vegetarianism (vegan or macrobiotic) Sugar Lots of juices	Cooked vegetables Whole grains, beans Some animal protein daily In some cases, coffee Fermented foods Some fats
To support meditating, spiritual disciplines (yoga, t'ai chi)	Animal protein, red meat Processed foods Sugar Dairy	Whole grains Beans Vegetables Fruit and nuts

Most important, DON'T BE AFRAID OF FOOD. Food is a friend and ally—we cannot do without it. But we can abuse it, misunderstand it, not listen to what our body tells us after we eat it. Only thereby do we turn it into an adversary.

Now let's see how we can expect our body to react to a change in diet.

Nine:
What to Expect from a Change in Diet

WITHDRAWAL SYMPTOMS

It goes without saying that a positive change in diet should make us feel better. Perhaps not one hundred percent, but there should be a discernible change toward healing. The healing process itself often becomes manifest in certain general physical withdrawal symptoms. Because these can sometimes be mistaken for symptoms of illness, it is important to know of them in advance. The information that follows is based on the systems model of the body we've been working with, on my experiences and observations over the past twenty-five years, and on the concepts of healing advanced by most natural-health theorists regardless of the details of their respective dietary proposals, including, among others Michio Kushi, Samuel Hahnemann, Paavo Airola, and Herbert Shelton. (It is unfortunate that the irritating rhetoric and ill-chosen expressions of several authors of natural-healing theories have prevented their ideas from reaching a wider audience, for many of the ideas are indeed valuable.)

Let's keep in mind our model of the body as a system where, between the input and the output, a lot of activity takes place. This activity consists of building up, breaking down, transforming, transporting, synthesizing, holding, expelling, and otherwise manipulating matter and energy.

It often happens that the output cannot keep up with the input:

The organs of elimination (bowels, kidneys, lungs, skin) may be sluggish, inefficient, or blocked. As a result there is a backup of matter, and the body starts accumulating debris in the form of fat and calcium deposits, plaque (in arteries, on teeth), mucus, hardened stool, tumors, cysts, stones, even water. Most of us, perhaps all, walk around with some kind of old accumulation somewhere in the body. (It is important to note that even so we function amazingly well, all things considered.)

It is impossible to have a totally clean body at all times. Even if we were able to rid ourselves of every scrap of metabolic waste, we would stay that way only a few minutes. New waste material would be formed almost immediately by the normal activities of our cells. Some natural-healing philosophies are overridingly concerned with continuous "cleansing." This kind of obsession can be paralyzing and destructive.* What we can hope for, however, is a well-functioning body that moves waste matter along smoothly and disposes of it promptly and efficiently, before it has had time to harden, putrefy, or turn toxic.

Nature does most of the work for us. In the world outside our bodies, whenever there is a pileup of garbage, insects and scavengers come to break it down and convert it into something useful, such as humus (black soil) or compost. So it is inside our bodies: If there is a pileup of waste matter accumulating, the immune system decides it's time to clean up. It then provokes, say, a cold, or some other mucous discharge to flush out the obstruction, calling in an army of bacteria to help dispose of the stuff. It is unfortunate that we have come to misread these minor cleanup reactions as illnesses and thus undesirable. According to the medical model, the infection (or disease) is *caused* by the bacteria. The immune system is charged with the task of clearing up the infection, and antibiotics are used to kill the bacteria. This model offers no cogent explanation for either natural or acquired immunities. It would be more useful to see these cleanup reactions as what they really are: adjustments by the body to keep itself whole and functioning. Major infections such as meningitis or pneumonia occur most frequently in the wake of minor infections, precisely because the minor infection's task has been incompletely fulfilled.

---

* Hauschka points out: "Fear of an 'impure state' leads to a body cult that easily degenerates into the worst kind of materialism. The frequent washings and irrigations of the outer and inner man actually reflect a lack of confidence in the power of the soul and spirit to work in an enlivening and healing way in body functions."[1]

Antibiotics and other medications are designed to arrest infections, regardless of whether or not the infection has done what it "set out to do."

A change of diet from the S.A.D. to any of the healing modes (fasting, vegetarianism, macrobiotics) will lighten the input load automatically and make it much easier for nature to take its course. Usually less food is taken in, less protein, less fat; in short, the healing diets utilize fewer buildup foods and more breakdown foods. They give the body a vacation, as it were, time off so that it can take care of the laundry and the mail and the cleaning out of closets. And invariably it will do so.

Michio Kushi has classified signs of such "housecleaning" by the body into ten precise categories of symptoms:

1. General fatigue
2. Pains and aches
3. Fever, chills, and coughs
4. Abnormal sweating and frequent urination
5. Skin discharges and unusual body odors
6. Diarrhea or constipation
7. Temporary decrease in sexual desire and vitality
8. Temporary cessation of menstruation
9. Mental irritability
10. Other minor transitory symptoms: restless dreams, minor hair loss, feeling of coldness

Only some of these will be experienced by each individual, and the healthier his or her general condition, the fewer symptoms there will be. The symptoms are also characteristically transitory, sometimes lasting only a few hours or maybe days. Steady and extensive physical activity will speed up the cleansing process, which is why all effective dietary regimes include exercise.

As I was writing the first draft of this section, I received a call from an old friend. Unaware of the subject I was immersed in, he urged me to write about what happens when one makes dietary changes and begins to heal! It turned out that four days earlier he had (once again) abruptly stopped consuming coffee, cheese, and sugar in order to get rid of a cyst he had developed at the back of his neck. He put himself on a regime that included flaxseed (to help bowel elimination), miso soup, vegetables, corn, and small amounts of whole grain. He also forced himself to walk a half hour daily through the hilly terrain of his neighborhood.

For the first day or two he was extremely tired, had difficulty walking, swallowing, and developed strange headaches that started at the base of his neck. By the fourth day the headaches and the swallowing difficulty had disappeared, and the walking had become much easier. Slowly he was beginning to feel like his old healthy self again. He pointed out to me that if he hadn't been aware of the reaction-and-discharge syndrome that accompanies healing, he would have panicked and perhaps stopped his semifast. His cyst was still there—it had only been four days!—but it didn't hurt anymore. He expected that after a month or two of careful eating it would open by itself and drain, as had happened to him already a few times before. (And that was indeed what eventually happened: Two months later his cyst had all but disappeared.)

Following is a table of possible symptoms that can arise when certain foods are eliminated. Think of what happens when you have a crutch taken away after you've used it for a while, even though your legs are perfectly good: Because the use of the crutch has weakened them, you will be a little wobbly until you regain your normal strength. The symptoms, then, are the wobbliness; they will go away once the body becomes strong again.

ELIMINATION AND SYMPTOM CHART

WHEN YOU ELIMINATE	YOU MAY ENCOUNTER	FOR
Sugar	Tiredness, drowsiness, depression, feelings of alienation, lack of coordination	1 to 5 days
Coffee	Headaches, shakiness, nervousness	1 to 10 days
Alcohol	Tension, inability to relax	2 to 5 days or more, depending on the extent of the drinking
Milk and Milk Products	Mucus elimination through skin, sinus, mucous membranes, lungs, sex organs	Starting up to 3 months after the food was stopped— for a year or two
Meats, Fats, Protein	Foul body odor, coated tongue, feelings of being toxic, skin eruptions	Varies: 1 to 4 weeks with a fast, 6 to 10 months for the deeper accumulations

If you have made a change in diet and are experiencing certain troubling symptoms, how can you tell whether they are signs of a healing crisis or of erroneous habits still persisting? A mistaken judgment in this situation could spell much additional trouble.

First of all, you can refer to Kushi's list of symptoms on page 216; if your symptom is on the list, and you feel OK about it, it's a healing reaction. Or you can consider a very helpful concept about the nature of healing symptoms noted by practitioners of homeopathy: They have found that discharge symptoms in the healing mode tend to follow a specific order, or progression, namely:

1. Symptoms move from the inside to the outside of the body (mucus in the lungs is coughed up; toxic matter from deep within the system comes out as boils or rashes).
2. Symptoms move from the upper part to the lower part of the body (medication that affects the kidneys, such as steroids, can be discharged by a rash on the legs).
3. Symptoms relating to chronic conditions disappear in the reverse order of their appearance; the ones that emerged latest leave first and the earlier ones reemerge and then leave last. This means that long after we set out on a healing path, we might relive symptoms of very old problems if these were suppressed or incorrectly treated. Their reemergence (sometimes known as retracing), if treated naturally and allowed to follow its course, would only mean that the body is healing itself. For example, if you used to cough a lot as a child and took medicine and then developed asthma, when you go into a healing mode, you may have a brief flare-up of the asthma, and later—even several years later—have a coughing episode that is in fact a "retracing" of your childhood condition.

The foregoing three rules comprise Hering's Law of Cure, after Constantine Hering (1800–1880), who formulated them. To these, John Garvy, N.D., has added two more:

4. A feeling of well-being precedes a healing crisis.
5. There is also a feeling of well-being at the core during the crisis; that is, deep down inside it feels OK.

The latter two are the key to differentiating a healing crisis from a sickness that we might be perpetuating: A sickness feels like something is definitely wrong. IF YOU ARE NOT SURE, CHECK WITH A

HEALTH PROFESSIONAL.

The more the body has to clean up, the stronger and/or longer will be the discharge reactions. They will also be more pronounced if the change in diet is abrupt, less so if it's gradual.

Some foods, notably sugar, meat, coffee, and milk products, will not be fully eliminated unless completely abstained from. That is, as long as you have even one teaspoon of sugar in your tea once a day and no sugar at any other time, the addiction is maintained and withdrawal does not occur.

Should withdrawal symptoms become too uncomfortable, they can sometimes be stopped by the "hair of the dog" method: A sip of coffee will miraculously eliminate a coffee-withdrawal headache. In fact, this is what keeps addictions going. The addictive substance (coffee, sugar, drugs) "cures" the discomfort produced as the body tries to clean out that same substance. Stopping the discharge may prolong the agony somewhat, as the healing process is arrested for a few days; however, this is preferable to throwing the whole healing program out the window because it is too difficult or painful to maintain.

It is easier to endure these apparent symptoms of illness at the start of a healing diet when you know their true nature. If you don't know that there is a difference between a tension headache and a withdrawal headache, you may panic and run for the medication. Fear can make us sicker than sickness itself.

Keep in mind also that not everyone will experience the same discharges, nor will they last the same length of time for everyone. Use the Elimination and Symptom Chart only to orient yourself, so that you know what to expect. And when well-intentioned friends want to know why you have a cold if you're eating so healthily, just smile and say, "Because I'm getting better!"

How Long, Oh, How Long?

When we shift into a healing mode, we have to unravel, like Penelope, what we have knitted so far. This takes time, a detail that can be bothersome to those whose liver congestion (as Chinese medicine will have it) makes them impatient. As a student once said to me, "I don't want to wait. I want to be better this minute!"

Perhaps deciding to heal ourselves, or to accept healing, does indeed make us instantly better on the spiritual level. The material side of our being, however, is denser and takes longer to react.

Although the body does follow the direction of the mind, it has its laws and progressions, which cannot be bypassed (except in the case of miracles). As the mind/spirit aspect of our being becomes whole, the body aspect, its complementary opposite, does so too—but at its own speed.

Our cells renew themselves continuously. The quickest changes occur in the blood and lymph, because they are in continuous flow. Blood sugar and the acid-alkaline balance may change as a result of diet in a matter of hours, perhaps less.*

Before any such changes can actually make us *feel* different, however, the new regime needs time to make a physiological impact. Eating more alkalinizing foods (see chapter three, page 73) than acid-forming ones can have a noticeable effect in one or two days. In cases of extreme "stuckness" it can take as long as seven to ten days to feel better because we have to allow for the withdrawal symptoms to come and go.

In general, within a week of a major change in diet—if it is a *good* change—you should feel:

- Better
- Positive about your new direction

It takes between 90 and 120 days to renew all the red blood cells. As the old red cells in the bloodstream are replaced with cells built with good-quality prime matter, you feel better and better. After about three to four months the healing process shifts deeper. It begins to pull debris out of the intercellular spaces, and very often a new spate of discharge symptoms show up at about this time. You will find this especially true if you have given up milk and milk products. Time and again, when one of my students has stopped eating these foods, I get a phone call, and the conversation runs more or less like this: "I have this terrible cold," I hear. So I ask, "How long since you changed your diet, or stopped eating dairy?" "About three months," is the answer. "Ah. And deep down inside, does it feel OK or not OK?" Thoughtful pause. "It feels OK. It feels like a clean-out."

I always take such communication at face value. For the one who is helping someone else heal, as well as for the one who's

---

* Carl Englund, of the Naval Health Research Center in San Diego, found that the "fluctuation of minerals, hormones, and other substances in the blood can vary throughout the day by as much as 500 percent."[2]

healing, it is essential to listen to all the healing body's feelings and signals. They will always tell us whether or not we're on the right track. In the case just illustrated, we obviously were. The only thing left to do was to take care of the externals—fasting, drinking ginger tea, or doing whatever facilitates the speedy completion of the mucus discharge—and wait till it stopped.

After the initial three- to four-month period there may be a few more discharges, on and off, for the following six months to a year. In each instance ask yourself how you feel deep down inside. Whenever the answer is, "Not OK. I'm worried," I recommend a visit to a doctor or other health professional for a more thorough diagnosis.

It has been estimated that it takes about seven years for every cell of our bodies to be renewed. That means that every seven years or so we are a new being, totally different, materially speaking, from what we were seven years before. In my experience, during the first seven years any transgression from a healing regime that suits us is keenly felt and results in some immediate reaction or discharge. (I used to get colds regularly after eating in restaurants.) After seven years, these reactions are less pronounced, and we can better cope with disturbances or deviations. After fourteen years, errors in diet are often felt more on the psychospiritual level than on the physical. For example, in the time period between twelve and fourteen years A.C. (After Change), if I ate meat and I didn't need it—which happened maybe once or twice a year—I didn't actually get sick, but I quarreled with people and had trouble concentrating. After twenty years—where I am now—I'm just grateful that there is food around when I need it, whatever it is. If I eat meat when I don't need it, I just feel a bit dense. I know what to stay away from always (milk, sugar, honey), what I must be careful with (spicy peppers, chili, fried foods, fatty or oily meals, vinegar, raw spinach, cheese, overcooked food, too much miso, soy sauce, or seaweeds, over 30 percent grain), and what I can indulge in when I feel like it (fish, chicken, butter, tunafish sandwiches, pizza, Chinese food). I'm curious to see what the situation will be after twenty-five or thirty years.

CAN HEALTH FOOD MAKE US SICK?

Just as too little or too much of an individual foodstuff can be detrimental to health, so can a health regime pursued beyond the balance point.

If someone with difficult digestion or other gastrointestinal disturbances goes on a diet entirely devoid of raw foods, that is wise. The absence of the irritating food will encourage the body to start the healing process; if the rest of the diet consists of whole foods that keep the system balanced and on track, that process will continue until completed. After a number of months, the body will have become stronger, and a bit of raw fruit or a salad here or there will cause no problems. Much later, when healing is completed, a more frequent intake of raw foods will prove as healthy for this person—and indeed, as recommended—as it is for the rest of us.

As you heal, you have to modify your food intake so as to adjust it to your changing condition. In other words, as you yourself change, you must make changes in your manner of eating. If you fail to do so, you will become stuck, regardless of how "good" your food is, and if you've read everything in this book so far, you know how that can be a problem.

It's the pendulum concept again. A "health regime" is one that we embark on with the express purpose of swinging into a comfortable pattern, and thereby (a) undoing the damage done so far; and/or (b) improving upon the present condition. The healing regime is successful insofar as it helps us achieve one or both of those goals.

In our society, healing regimes that undo the damage done by the modern diet and lifestyle are invariably based, as we have seen earlier, on fresh, natural foods, sometimes with supplements, but always high in vegetables, fruit, grains, beans, and low in or devoid of fat, meat, salt, sugar, coffee, dairy, canned and frozen foods. Yet the pendulum swings, and I've also seen many imbalances arising from the rigid application of these regimes. These imbalances occur for two principal reasons:

1. EXCESSES IN DOING—that is, overemphasis and overreliance on individual foods or substances that may indeed be quite healthy but are not, realistically speaking, endowed with superpowers.
2. IGNORING or explaining away the body's ALARM SYMPTOMS, because the intellect is saying "This *couldn't* possibly be bad for me." The tuning-in-to-self test (does it feel OK or not OK?) has generally not been done in these cases, or its warnings have been ignored.

EXCESS IN DOING	EFFECTS
Vitamins and supplements	Constant hunger, weight gain, skin cracks or discharges, other unexplained symptoms that don't go away even if the diet is changed but the pills are continued
Raw foods and juices	Excess weight loss, spaciness, brittle hair and nails, lack of concentration, depression
Grain	Bloating (this may be from not enough chewing), sluggishness, pallor or sallow skin, excess weight loss (not assimilating enough), weight gain, lassitude, cravings for coffee and cigarettes, overacidity, demineralization
Cooked food	Tightness, rigidity, lack of joy; possibly rickets in children

ALARM SYMPTOMS	POSSIBLE CAUSES
Constant hunger	Too many supplements; lack of protein foods; sugar
Excessive weight loss	Not enough calories, uncomplemented vegetable proteins, insufficient beans or animal protein
Binges and cravings	Excess sugar, salt, supplements; protein lack; one-sided eating

Keeping the foregoing in mind will help you avoid one of the major pitfalls of taking responsibility for your own health: that of making it worse, which can happen if you are overly theoretical and not enough in touch with your body's signals.

One young man who came to see me—let's call him George—was a perfect example of someone stuck in healing regimes that had swung him past the balance point. He had embarked upon a raw-foods regime to cure a strep throat. It had quick and excellent results, and he decided to stay with it, eating fruits, nuts, salads, figs, bananas, and other hot-weather foods. He had a wonderful time all summer and felt light, clear, healthy, spiritually uplifted.

Yet as soon as the fall rains and chills arrived, he fell ill. He felt depressed, extremely cold, and at times had to wear several sweaters to endure the weather. He was also constantly hungry, although he ate large portions of the foods mentioned above, and often. In spite of the amounts he ate, he lost weight, going from 145 pounds (not much to begin with for a man almost six feet tall) down to 120. His friends and family worried, feeling something was wrong; but George believed the regime was morally and philosophically right and stuck with it.

Eventually, when his pants wouldn't stay on his hips any longer and five layers of sweaters and undershirts were not enough to keep him warm, he changed his diet. From basic raw foods (all expansive) he flipped over into the macrobiotic regime of cooked foods: brown rice, beans, seaweed, root vegetables, miso (mostly contractive). He began to feel better, warmed up, and put on a few pounds, but not quite enough. He still became depressed and had coughs and bouts of anger. As with the raw-foods regime, he was told that his symptoms were still "discharges of toxins."

One day he took a good look at his bony frame and wondered how many toxins he still could have to get rid of. He also got in touch with his core feeling that "this is not OK." Coughing was something new for him; he had had no bronchial or lung problems before that could now have been undoing themselves. It was then that he decided to look for help elsewhere and came to see me.

We discussed the fact that he had no major health problem to cure except for that early strep throat and a bit of mucus accumulation. That had been taken care of months ago. He had restricted himself unnecessarily; and as his body didn't have too much excess matter to get rid of, it got rid of too much useful matter. To put it in Western scientific terms, he had become protein deficient.

Each food philosophy has its dogma and its devils, its sin and its salvation. When we think our dietary path is "true" and narrow, and we dare deviate from it, paranoia, fear, and guilt set in— emotions infinitely more damaging, and prophetically self-fulfilling, than minor dietary indiscretions.

For someone like George, the problem is not in the eating, but in the thinking. Fear of eating the wrong thing is the problem, not food itself. I concentrated on dispelling that fear. In addition, I suggested that he keep the macrobiotic regime to about 70 percent of his total diet and that little by little he add more beans, some fish, chicken, eggs, salad, and fruit, avoiding sugar and dairy foods most of the time. A person who goes through natural eating styles like he did becomes very conscious about food and about the effect of food on health, so I couldn't, and wouldn't, urge him to eat "everything." I did, however, encourage him to eat out often with friends, to have an occasional pizza or tunafish sandwich, and slowly to build himself up again by eating his God-given sustenance with joy and gratitude.

The day after he came to see me, he called with a cheerful voice, having had two tempeh burgers with lettuce and tomato the night before instead of his usual bowl of rice and steamed vegetables. He didn't feel hungry after the burgers, and was considerably happier already. I saw him several months later; he had put on fifteen pounds, didn't feel so depressed anymore, and had lots more energy.

George had exhibited two of the three alarm symptoms listed above: constant hunger and excessive weight loss. He had also followed first a diet high in breakdown foods and then switched to one in which he still consumed insufficient protein (his ratio of grains to beans was 7:1, instead of 2:1 as in most traditional diets). If he'd had a lot of old stuck protein and fats in his body to get rid of, he would have felt great. But he didn't have that problem, and thus the healing regime turned into its opposite and made him sick.

Hunger after a meal usually indicates that the nutrients are out of balance. Excess salt, sugar, or supplements, and low-protein, low-fat diets can all bring on this symptom. Beans, fish, eggs, chicken, and meat are the foods that will correct this most efficiently. Nuts will help somewhat, as they contain protein and fats, but they're seldom enough. Fat will get rid of the hunger, but it does not satisfy the specific nutrient need of which the hunger is an expression. Please note that adding balanced whole foods, namely vegetables and grains, does not correct this condition! Neither do sweets, cakes, or pastries, which are the first choice for many people.

Going 20 percent or more below ideal weight and not being able to correct it by quantity eating, if the cause is not organic illness, also indicates an imbalance in the food intake. I have seen very thin young men go for two and three huge helpings of grain and vegetables and found that even though they ate as abundantly each day and chewed very carefully, they still put on no weight.

Of course a certain amount of weight loss is to be expected when you embark on a healing regime. In almost all cases, it's beneficial. It means that the body is cleaning out old debris, getting rid of unwanted matter that could, conceivably, cause trouble later on. Often the weight discarded is made up of cells built with low-quality foods, to be replaced with cells built out of better quality foods. In many people starting off with normal weight, there is a dip below normal for a few months, then the weight comes back up to its proper level without any effort. The process usually takes about a year.

Weight loss that goes beyond the "it's OK" feeling is usually caused by a low or unbalanced intake of protein and fat. But not always. In many cases, a body used to consuming standard quantities of meat, bread, cake, cookies, and potatoes is unable to extract the nutrients it needs from grains and beans. This is either because the intestines are sluggish, coated with old fats or hardened stool, or lacking in the bacteria necessary to break down vegetable protein. Such a condition can be taken care of with intestinal cleansing with herbs or a few colonics, consumption of fermented foods (they aid digestion) together with the whole grains, and thorough chewing so as to insalivate every bite of food. The body should also be allowed time enough to adjust to the new fare. Meanwhile, there is no point in starving: Don't hesitate to eat animal protein if you like, according to your need.

Although practically all men will lose weight on a grain-and-bean regime, only about half of the women will; the other half will actually put on weight. This difference, I believe, has to do with different rates of assimilation, of excretion, and of buildup efficiency in men and women. If you are a woman and find yourself putting on unwanted weight after a switch to a healing diet, try lowering your intake of grains and beans and increasing your intake of raw and cooked vegetables. Also, avoid salt and salty seasonings, keep oil and fat intake very low, and consume broiled, poached, or baked fish, and occasionally fowl, for protein.

Another way in which food—both healthy *and* unhealthy—can make us unwell is when we eat the same thing, or the same flavor, all the time. According to the Five-Phase Theory, if we don't vary our foods or flavors, we overstimulate one energy phase while depleting another. For example, salty foods (Water Phase) will stimulate the kidneys when used sparingly; in excess, they will slow them down and cause water retention, while at the same time weaken the heart (Fire Phase). This happens to agree with modern nutritional knowledge: Salt is customarily restricted for people with heart trouble and/or high blood pressure (which involves the kidneys).

A similar situation occurs when we eat fats or oils (Wood Phase): A small amount will nourish the liver and gall bladder; too much, and those organs will be overburdened, while the stomach, spleen, and pancreas (Earth Phase) will be weakened. And indeed, some research points to high-fat diets as a causative factor in diabetes, a malfunction of the pancreas.[3] An excess of sweets (Earth) overstimulates the stomach, spleen, and pancreas and weakens the kidneys and adrenals (Water); perhaps that is another reason why sugar makes us tired.

Healthy food without variety can cause similar problems. I have seen many a case where heavy reliance on sour fruits and salad (Wood Phase) caused problems with the stomach or a strong craving for sweets (both Earth Phase). Too much rice, even brown rice (Metal Phase), will overwork and thereby slow down the lungs and large intestine, causing constipation and a sunken chest*; it will also create a tremendous craving for fats (Wood), such as tahini, peanut butter, and fried foods. Too much seaweed overstimulates the kidneys and thyroid (all water phase) and weakens the heart and small intestine (fire phase).

The best insurance against one-phase overload is to eat different grains and beans at each meal. Some possible combinations would be rice and kidney beans, barley and lentils, corn and black beans, split peas and millet, kasha and red lentils. A wide variety of vegetables of different colors, shapes, and flavors will help balance the meal. For nonvegetarians, consuming a different kind of fish or fowl each time is also helpful.

---

* I've heard rumors that it is called "rice chest"!

Ten:
Cravings and Binges: What Do They Mean?

How many times have we resolved to "be good," to take care of ourselves and eat properly, only to ruin the whole thing with some crazy binge? How long could we not stay on a healthy diet if it weren't for those uncontrollable cravings for "bad" yummies? And how often have we not had a craving that we've suppressed, considering it "unhealthy"? But in fact there are usually good reasons for cravings and binges. They are not the call of the devil, which we lack the will power to resist. Remember: The body, as a living system, will tend to conserve and protect, if not form, at least function. Most of its feelings and activities have the *purpose* of keeping it functioning in spite of obstacles or breakdowns. Freud has taught us that there are no *arbitrary* actions arising out of the subconscious, which in our model includes the physical as well as the psychological. The trick is to find out what our cravings are telling us.

From my own experience I've been able to discern three major categories, or causes, of cravings: ADDICTION/ALLERGY, DISCHARGE, and IMBALANCE OF SYSTEMS. When you start a healing regimen, you may find yourself subject to any one or all three. It will be helpful to you to understand what is happening in your body.

In order to change to a healthier way of eating effectively, we must distinguish between cravings that indicate a malfunction or misinterpretation of our appetite signals and those that indicate a true need. The first kind can be withstood or deflected, the second kind should be listened to. Addictions, allergies, and discharges make us crave precisely those foods that cause us unwanted physiological or psychological reactions. Cravings that arise out of an imbalance of expansive-contractive, acid-alkaline, or nutrient-proportion systems provide us with important information about how we're doing and, if not heeded, will provoke uncontrollable binges.

ADDICTION / ALLERGY

We are addicted to a food or drink (and thus crave it) when (a) the food creates symptoms of imbalance, such as headache, fatigue, skin problems, digestive disorders, or tension, some time after ingestion, and (b) the symptoms can be relieved by consuming more of the same food. If, for example, you give up sweets or coffee, you will initially crave them and feel generally depressed and tense. Eat a cookie, have a cup of coffee, and the symptoms go away—although not the addiction.

A food allergy is the opposite of addiction: Unpleasant symptoms appear almost immediately upon consumption of the offending substance[1] and are best controlled by avoiding that substance completely. There are many instances, however, when we do not connect our allergic symptoms with our food intake. We'll continue to crave the allergen and suffer through fatigue, tension, and headaches without realizing what their cause is or how simply they could be cured.

Addictions are harder to detect than allergies; it's not always clear to us that we are attracted to a specific food only because we ate it before and it hurts not to eat it. The most common offender in this category, sparing almost no one, is refined sugar.[2] One bite of cake—if we've had nothing with white sugar for a while—and the next day we want another; we think, "I must need this," or "I have a sweet tooth, that's just how I am," and we go for it. And then we want another, and another, and another. Today's sweet tooth is caused by yesterday's candy bar.

Getting off sugar is akin to getting off an addictive drug. People get cravings and headaches, feel depressed, fatigued, and generally dispirited. Fortunately, these symptoms rarely last more than three or four days after the last taste of the sweet stuff. After that, a remarkable lightness and clarity set in, eventually much more addictive, I feel, than sugar.

Addictions to stimulants such as coffee, chocolate, cigarettes, narcotics, and alcohol are common. Willpower is needed to break the addiction, as well as a few other tricks (see page 234 at the end of this chapter), and abstention for at least four days, if not more, before the craving subsides.

Physical cravings for addictive foods or stimulants will vanish after the withdrawal symptoms cease. However, every time you again consume even a bit of the offending substance, you should be very careful and watch yourself as if the addiction were back in full swing, or else it will easily creep up again. If you have been addicted to sugar, try such substitutes as dates, frozen bananas, semimoist dried fruit, or baked goods sweetened with barley malt or maple syrup, and especially sweet orange vegetables, like yams and winter squash; they satisfy the sweet tooth without restarting the addiction.

The most common food allergies are those to milk and milk products, eggs, wheat, corn, shellfish, nuts, chocolate, coffee, and alcohol. If the reactions are nonphysical, such as anxiety, sleeplessness, or extreme fatigue, you may not even be aware that you have a food allergy. A great deal of the time, people who are allergic to certain foods are also addicted to them; that is, they get symptoms when they *don't* consume them. Therefore, the elimination of allergenic foods will provoke a short period of unpleasant withdrawal symptoms (similar, in fact, to a "healing crisis"), which can be dealt with as discussed above regarding addictions. The most beneficial result of breaking the vicious cycle of addictions and allergies is the disappearance of unpleasant symptoms, both physical and psychological. Also, several of my students reported that a variety of unrelated allergies (to cats, feathers, even wheat) vanished when they eliminated just sugar and dairy from their diets.

DISCHARGE

Cravings can also arise from discharge, the cleansing the body undergoes when you start on a healing diet.

According to the holistically oriented natural-healing schools of thought, this is what probably happens: Over the years, you have stored toxins in the intercellular spaces of your body. These toxins can be by-products of metabolism that have not been excreted, or perhaps even electrical charges left by food. When you change your diet to a healing mode, it seems that the immune system begins to sweep out those toxins, dumping them into the bloodstream for eventual processing and disposal through kidneys, lungs, skin, or liver. Before they leave the body, these elements, or charges, get a free ride through the circulatory system. In the brain they pass by the hypothalamus, which acts like a tape recorder head, picking up information from the bloodstream as if the latter were a magnetic tape running by.* The information the hypothalamus picks up from the residue in the blood activates memories of hamburgers and mother's key lime pie, and cravings for the old familiar foods appear as if out of nowhere.

"I suddenly had this absolutely clear desire for a big, juicy steak, just like the kind I used to eat," one of my students once said in class. "I wanted it so badly I could taste it. So I ordered steak for dinner, and halfway through I realized that I didn't want it at all. In fact, I felt quite sick from it, that evening and the next day too. It was, now that I think of it, a memory more than a wish."

How do you recognize cravings of the discharge type? Often they are for something familiar, something you used to have a lot of. They also often disappear after a few hours. If they don't, and you're still not sure whether you actually need the steak or are just "remembering" it, try the "hair of the dog" method already mentioned. That is, when cravings or aches seem to be associated with the discharge of meat, sugar, dairy foods, processed foods, or stimulants, you should regard them as honest body needs and heed them. You should take what you want—IN SMALL AMOUNTS.[3] According to homeopathic medicine, "like cures like," but in opposite quantities; a small amount of the food you used to eat in large quantities will eliminate the craving for it. Thus, if my student had had only a bite or two of the steak, she would have been just fine.

IMBALANCE OF SYSTEMS

To understand the various cravings that can arise from imbalance we have to keep in mind the various models we've discussed in this book:

- Nutrient proportions
- The expansive and the contractive

* I was enchanted when I heard this concept explained by John Beaulieu of the Polarity Wellness Center in New York, during a course in Esoteric Anatomy, February 1983.

- The acid and the alkaline
- The Five-Phase dynamics

1. According to the chart of Nutrient Proportions in Food (see page 52), a craving for sweets (carbohydrates) could come from either an excessively high protein, fat, or mineral/vitamin (even salt) intake. Conversely, a craving for animal protein would have as its goal filling the space created by an excess of carbohydrates, minerals (including salt), fluids, or fats.

   However, I have also noticed that a craving for sweets, especially when accompanied by a craving for fats, often signals a minimal protein deficiency. I have seen this happen especially in boys and men who have switched to a vegetarian or a macrobiotic regime. They crave juices, sweets, bread and butter, peanut butter, nuts, tahini, and so on. Curiously enough, the craving for sweets and fats disappears when more protein foods (beans, fish, chicken, eggs) are added to the diet.

2. According to the expansive-contractive model (see page 69), a high intake of contractive foods (meat, salt, grain, cooked food) will create a demand for expansive things (fruit, sweets, alcohol, salads). If the craving is not heeded, the eventual result may be a big beer or ice cream binge. It works both ways: Too many expansive foods will create a desire for contractive ones, although from what I've seen, the cravings in that case will not be very strong. A high-fruit diet, for example, may make you wish for beans or meat, but the desire for those foods is somehow more easily ignored or rejected, and then the imbalance, unfortunately, is frequently maintained.

3. Cravings that result from an acid-alkaline imbalance are usually very strong, and almost impossible to resist. An excess of alkalizing food, such as fruit, salad, vegetables, and potatoes, will create a demand for acid-forming foods as balancers. If someone on a highly alkaline diet is eating no acid-forming meat, fish, fowl, or eggs, and very little grain, if any, then the need for acid-forming sweets will demolish all willpower. That need will not be satisfied entirely with sweet fruits, for these are also somewhat alkalizing; only the baked goods, the honey cakes, the natural or unnatural ice cream and candy bars will fill the bill. Many followers of yogic dis-

ciplines are familiar with this condition. It can be rectified simply by adding enough acid-forming whole grains, beans, and flour products to the diet, which will eliminate the craving for sugar.

It's interesting that the acid-alkaline balance will override the expansive-contractive relationship: Alkalizing, expansive fruit will not eliminate desire for the equally expansive honey or sugar-sweetened goodies—because they are acid-forming, and the alkaline demands it. The same holds true with contractive foods: A high intake of acid-forming grain, bean, or animal foods still creates a desire for salt, which is alkalizing, even though it is also highly contractive. Expansive but alkalizing vegetables, on the other hand, do not awaken a craving for salt, whose contractiveness would indeed balance the expansiveness of the vegetables, but, more important, would only alkalize the system further. This is why salt-free diets rely on them so heavily. Dietary approaches that emphasize one kind of food (protein, grain, fruit/salad) and ignore the power of the acid-alkaline system, rarely work in the long run: Cravings will arise for an opposite or complementary food or drink (coffee, sweets, fish, alcohol, sugar) to create the needed balance.

CRAVINGS THAT BALANCE ONE-SIDED DIETS

DIET	CRAVINGS
High meat (contractive, acid-forming)	Alcohol, sugar (expansive) Coffee (alkalizing)
High grain (contractive, acid-forming)	Salad, coffee (expansive, alkalizing)
High fruit, salad (expansive, alkalizing)	Salty food (contractive) Sweets (acid-forming) Protein (contractive, acid-forming)

4. Energetic imbalances that can be explained with the Five-Phase model sometimes show up as an attraction to unusual food combinations, yet not necessarily unhealthy foods. My own favorite instances of funny eating are the time when I decided I liked roasted red peppers for breakfast (Fire food), and a few days when I mostly ate whole wheat sourdough bread, sauerkraut, and beans (Wood and Water). If you want to find out what it is you're doing in terms of Five-Phase

CRAVINGS AND HOW TO DEAL WITH THEM

To Diminish Cravings For	The Food Must Be	Have More	Have Less	Substitute
SUGAR (cakes, cookies, pastries, candy, ice cream)	Eliminated	Whole grains; baked yams, squash, apples; dates; cooked fruit	Meat, salt, dairy products	Frozen bananas (for ice cream); desserts sweetened with barley malt, rice syrup, maple syrup
ALCOHOL	Diminished or eliminated	Complex carbohydrates, vegetables, corn, leafy bitter greens	Fats, salt, miso, soy sauce, animal protein	Nonalcoholic beer, fruit juices
COFFEE	Eliminated	Vegetables, salad	Acid-forming foods: meat, sugar, flour, grain Salt	Grain coffee, Postum
SALT	Diminished	Seaweed, black beans, vegetables	Sweets, fats, alcohol, meat, grain	Natural soy sauce, miso (small amounts), herbs and spices
MILK PRODUCTS	Diminished greatly or eliminated	Leafy greens, whole grains, beans, fish	Sugar, baked goods, fruit, meat	Tofu (small amounts), nut milk
FATS AND SWEETS (including baked goods made with natural sweeteners, whole wheat flour, oils)	Diminished	Protein: beans, fish, chicken, eggs	Grain, fruit, salad	

energetics, it's a good idea to consult with a health counselor who is familiar with that system. Meanwhile, you can trust yourself to balance the Five Phases automatically; as long as you stick with fresh, natural, wholesome food, you can follow your inclinations for variety with a fair degree of confidence. Just make sure to consume a different kind of bean and a different kind of grain every day.

Part Three:
HEALING

The seed of health is in illness, for illness contains information
—Marilyn Ferguson

Sickness is not what the body is for. —A Course in Miracles

Eleven:
Health and Illness:
New Definitions

If we look at ourselves from a systems point of view—as an organism comprised of physical elements and an energy field constantly in flux, the whole influenced at all times, endlessly, and in ways difficult to pinpoint, by countless disturbances and inputs, we must redefine our concepts of health and illness. Once we are aware of what represents health, and what illness—what is all right to feel, and what forebodes trouble—we can make more responsible choices about how to improve our condition.

WHAT IS HEALTH?

First, what it is not. It is not a condition we can attain once and for all. Just as our body changes by breathing, coughing, getting hungry, and all its other activities, so does our health. We don't "get there" and stay, as if we had arrived home and plunked down in our easy chair.[1] And even if we did, how long can we stay in an easy chair without getting up for something? How long can we stay anywhere without eventually moving on?

Our movement, our direction can be toward health, that is, toward wholeness and integration, oneness of body and mind, connectedness with fellow humans and with our environment. Or it can be toward illness, which manifests itself as alienation, disin-

239

tegration, and separateness. Almost invariably, if we are following the first path, we feel good and optimistic at our core. If we're on the second, we feel worried, sad, dissatisfied.

It is not enough to define health as the absence of disease. Rather, health is the aggregate of a series of specific conditions. These are ideal conditions and can in some way also be viewed as goals to be attained. Because we are looking at human beings as whole systems, internally complex and externally interactive, their appropriate functioning, or "health," must be manifested not only on the physical but also on the mental, emotional, social, and spiritual levels.

The descriptions following are based on the "Seven Conditions of Health," postulated by George Ohsawa (see page 33); they've been amplified with various observations of my own, and with those of Harold Gardner, M.D. on self-determination and controlling one's health choices. For clarity, I have classified the conditions of health into physical, psychological, social, and spiritual, even though each condition becomes manifest in all these levels.

PHYSICAL

1. NO FATIGUE. This means not waking up tired in the morning, or feeling "exhausted" all the time, a widespread condition nowadays, and a definite sign of imbalance. The feeling of "no fatigue" also applies to psychological outlook: It means being ready to accept challenges and work without saying, "Oh, it's too much for me, I can't handle it," and other such expressions.

2. GOOD APPETITE. This means enjoying food fully, whether it's a plain bowl of soup and some bread or an elaborate repast. In addition, it means an appetite for life, a thirst for knowledge, an eagerness for enriching new experiences, and a healthy and joyful appetite for sex.

3. GOOD SLEEP. Falling asleep within four or five minutes of lying down, sleeping deeply for five to seven hours, waking up at the right time with a clear head and without an alarm clock—those are the main characteristics. Good sleep also means a minimum of dreams (unless we explicitly wish to access our stores of subconscious information), no tossing and turning, no snoring, and no talking out loud. In short, this condition means having the ability to relax and rest completely in a clearly defined time period and to emerge from it totally alert and ready to go.

PSYCHOLOGICAL

4. GOOD MEMORY. Remembering what we have said and done, seen, heard, and read is crucial for good health. Without memory, we cannot learn and grow, for we are doomed to repeat our forgotten mistakes. A good memory will help us remember how we got to where we are, and if we're in a pickle, it will help us retrace and rethink our actions for a more satisfying result.

5. GOOD HUMOR. One of the trickier conditions. It means never getting impatient or angry—not repressing anger, just not feeling it. It means being genuinely cheerful, having a positive approach to life, seeing the good side of things, being able to laugh at ourselves and our foibles. In traditional Chinese medicine, anger is related to imbalanced energy in the liver; an angry outburst, chronic impatience, crankiness, and similar moods could be the expression of a congested liver. Conversely, the Chinese believe that allowing violent anger to be expressed regularly can injure that same organ.

6. PRECISION IN THOUGHT AND ACTION. Just like a cat that always lands on its feet, the healthy person is capable of making correct split-second decisions and of carrying them out accurately. This condition presupposes the existence of a sound nervous system and a strong and fluid body-mind connection. Knocking things over, dropping things, grazing the garage door with the car, even saying the wrong thing, are always indications that our judgment, perception, and movement are not correctly integrated—and thus our health less than what it could be.

SOCIAL

7. TAKING RESPONSIBILITY. This means that we realize the futility of blaming others for our problems. If we accept the fact that we are the creators of our lives, it follows that we also created whatever mess we are in, healthwise or otherwise. Guilt is unnecessary at this stage, for it paralyzes. A straightforward noting of the facts, on the other hand, helps us see the way out. If we made the mess, we can unmake it as well. Taking responsibility is the basis for personal power, for the ability to change ourselves, and thereby the world, in a positive and healing way.

8. MAKING CHOICES. Exercising our capacity to choose could

be the most crucial among the conditions of health. To fulfill it, we need (a) knowledge of the options available; and (b) the ability to communicate our decisions. And of course, to choose, we must accept responsibility for both the situation and the outcome. In the area of health, we should be able to make considered choices about the best healing technique to correct what ails us, with possibilities ranging from prayer and fasting to CAT scans and laser beam surgery. (It may be of interest to doctors and other healers that when the patient freely and knowingly chooses a particular therapy, with full knowledge of its limitations, malpractice is rarely an issue. It is so only in cases when the patient, instead of taking responsibility for his condition and his healing personally, blindly gives over that responsibility to the therapist.)

SPIRITUAL

9. HONESTY. When our health is good, we have no fear, and thus no need to lie. This does not mean that we have to say everything that comes to our minds—tact and discretion are not dispensable. It does mean not lying to ourselves, being fair and honorable, trustworthy and upright—it means, in fact, integrity.

10. GRATITUDE. This condition presupposes a good memory; as we remember how bad things can be, or how easily we can lose that which is dearest to us, we become very appreciative of all things around us. When our body is healthy and we feel good, everything seems magnificent and admirable. At the same time, a sense of wonder and appreciation can in itself be an expression of health, regardless of our physical condition.

11. HUMILITY. About this one condition of health, we can do little, for we cannot cure ourselves of arrogance, that intractable disease of the spirit. If we have it, only age, the memory of our mistakes, the "slings and arrows of outrageous fortune, the whips and storms of time," can heal us. Our humility, if it's genuine, must not be noticed by us— only by others.

12. LOVE. We may change our diet, clear our skin, heal our cancer—but if we have no charity, it's of little avail. Health is but an ego trip, vanity, and a striving after wind if we don't unconditionally *accept* life, ourselves, and our fellow

humans as they are—that is, love them. Finding fault with how our brother eats, judging him sick when he doesn't do as we do, disapproving of his lifestyle—all these only betray our own sense of incompleteness. Those who are capable of unconditional love at all times are forever healthy, no matter what their physical condition may be.

WHAT IS ILLNESS?

The conditions (or goals) of health listed above present us with a very precise model against which to measure ourselves. We will invariably fall short of some of them (if we think we don't, we fall short of numbers 9 and 11), but it is especially our shortcomings in the first six conditions that will quickly alert us that we are, in some way, ill. We are in fact right when we feel, for example, that being tired all the time is a sign that something is wrong, even if "nothing can be found." A loss of memory often accompanies hardening of the arteries, while habitual falling and dropping things can indicate the beginning of degenerative diseases of the nervous system. Even if there is no actual "disease" in the Western modern medical sense, this health model will help us to identify imbalances in our system that can be corrected.

Modern medicine recognizes mostly physical causes for our disorders: bacteria, viruses, genes, pollution, malnutrition. In cases where none of these seem to apply, the finger is pointed at psychological problems—stress, or "nerves." At times the latter seem simply catchall categories for "causes unknown," rather than actual causative agents.

"It appears to me that one ought to know what diseases arise in man from the powers [forces] and what from the structures," wrote Hippocrates. Ancient healing systems, folk medicine, and occult wisdom—all based on the premise that "all is one"—accept the nonphysical (the "powers") as coequal with the physical (the "structures"). Holistic healing (in accordance with the systems viewpoint) realigns itself with that venerable worldview; therefore, a listing of the causes of illness must encompass all levels of reality if it is to be accurate—just as health, as we have seen, is manifest in all aspects of human life.

Of all such listings, the one I have found most comprehensive and useful is that advanced by Paracelsus, the great sixteenth-century Swiss mystic and medical reformer. He recognized five major causes of illness:

1. *External and Environmental:* Heat, cold, wind, rain, trauma, and, in our modern terminology, bacteria, viruses, and pollution.
2. *Poisons and Impurities:* Spoiled food, wrong food, poisonous substances, chemicals of all kinds, herbs and medicines with undesirable side effects.
3. *Genetic and Hereditary:* We must include here not only long-standing genetic conditions, but also those caused by alcohol, drugs, medications, malnutrition, and an unhealthy diet in either parent, as well as during the mother's pregnancy.
4. *Psychological:* Stress, grief, psychological trauma, hysteria, and other emotional conditions.
5. *Spiritual or Karmic:* In the worldview of Paracelsus, as in that of many societies and philosophies, past lives are real, and we are accountable in our present life for our wrongdoing during past ones. Disdain for cripples in one life, according to this belief, may lead to being a cripple in another.

In this listing, wrong diet is only one among many causes of our disorders. We now know, however, that it can exacerbate the effects of the others by weakening our resistance and undermining our immune system.

Right diet is, then, not always a direct cure but works indirectly by strengthening the body once again and allowing the immune system to regain its power. For this reason, many different diets appear to be "cures" for any number of diseases; and people who experience them are neither mistaken nor lying about their stories. What happens is simply that each individual case history is the story of how one person's immune system was stimulated back into operation, rather than how a way of eating "cured" a disease. It's the relative viewpoint that we have to change: Mother's milk does not only "confer immunities," it also doesn't make the child sick. A diet free of nuts, nut butters, soda pop, fried foods, mayonnaise, and dairy products does not "cure" acne; it just doesn't cause acne, and therefore the body returns to normal and the acne disappears.*

* "It is assumed that we are ill and are made well," wrote British physician Thomas McKeown, "but it is nearer the truth to say that we are well and are made ill."[2]

All symptoms carry a message about conditions within our system. They are the only forceful method of communication between the body and the waking consciousness, which is usually focused outward. In fact, they are much like the red lights on the dashboard that indicate when the car is low on gas or oil. Early symptoms whose messages are not heeded will eventually give way to other, stronger ones; if we still don't understand what the body is trying to tell us, serious trouble is bound to ensue.

If only the symptom itself is eradicated, and its deeper, underlying cause is not found and attended to, it is akin to smashing the dashboard with a hammer instead of adding three quarts of oil to the engine. It is possible to do both—eliminate the symptom, or the area in which the symptom appears (e.g., as in tonsillectomy), and its cause (wrong diet). But that is like smashing the dashboard and then adding the three quarts of oil. The car will run well enough, but future communication between car and driver will be impaired—how will the car signal its need for oil the next time?

Symptoms are always a change in the function and eventually the structure of the body. What does this change mean? Change can be part of the movement of items through a system; it can be part of the structuring of the system; and it can be the system decaying.[3] Symptoms could, then, be classified into two opposite yet complementary categories, according to whether they indicate movement toward healing ("structuring") or away from it: (a) symptoms of the integration mode; or (b) symptoms of the disintegration mode.

This classification, as with most classifications of observed phenomena, is somewhat arbitrary, for all activities of the body are essentially designed to keep it functioning. It is when the symptom pits the body against itself that disintegration is hastened. For example, the formation of a cyst or tumor can be seen as the immune system's confinement and isolation of unexcreted cell waste or useless cells. But if the tumor begins to grow excessively, obstructing vessels and pressing on nerves, it is no longer useful; it has become detrimental to the system's functioning.

The integration mode is the one in which the body operates unconsciously most of the time. Paradoxically, consciousness can obstruct its smooth functioning by trying to "improve" things, through mechanical or chemical intervention. Often these interventions (surgery, drugs) seem perfectly rational and appropriate. But they end up having devastating side effects because they are based on the notion that without intervention things will get worse. This is rarely so: "The great secret, known to internists but still hidden from the general public," wrote Lewis Thomas, "is that most things get better by themselves. Most things, in fact, get better by morning."[4] When we don't acknowledge and co-operate with our body's inherent self-organizing abilities—with our immune system—our most elegant healing techniques invariably backfire.

I have come up with a classification of symptoms according to the degree, or stage, of illness they represent. It is based in part on the work of various natural healers, especially Michio Kushi,[5] as well as on my own observations. I do not intend it to stand as a definitive categorization of stages of disease, but rather as another aspect of the mental model of the human system—a practical model that is easy to use for lay people, and true only insofar as it is useful in making accurate appraisals and predictions.

This classification of symptoms has served me well in determining which disease conditions can be taken care of with food and home remedies, and which need the help of health professionals. Symptoms, then, can be seen as the following:

1. *Adjustment:* Minor symptoms, such as fevers and headaches, that can easily disappear without treatment or with simple natural remedies; they are the system's efforts to keep itself in homeostatic balance.

2. *Discharge:* This is the system's attempt to rid itself of useless or noxious matter through other than normal channels. These include sneezing, coughing, skin eruptions, mucus discharges. Most of these symptoms can and should be treated with diet and natural home remedies.

3. *Accumulation:* This stage ensues if the discharge is suppressed or is not adequate. It includes cysts, benign growths, excess weight, fatty deposits, stones. From here on, professional attention may be required.

4. *Malfunction:* When the accumulation gets in the way, or when the body's electric (energy) system goes awry, the organs and the immune system work less and less efficiently, as in diabetes, appendicitis, early cancer, heart attacks or fibrillation, hepatitis, kidney failure.

5. *Structural Change:* Eventually, the very shape of the organs or other body structures changes, sometimes irreversibly. Included here would be arthritis, cirrhosis, cataracts, enlarge-

ment of the heart, ruptured appendix, late cancer, advanced arteriosclerosis.

These five stages are handy for us to keep in mind, especially to delineate the limits of this book. In the following chapters, we are going to be examining how food can promote or assist in the healing of minor problems, of adjustments and discharges. On the basis of twenty years of practice, I am convinced that if these initial stages of imbalance are allowed or helped to heal gently and naturally, rather than being fought and suppressed with chemical medications, there is no need for the body to progress into more serious problems. In short, *the prevention of illness lies both in healthy diet, AND in the natural (nondrug) management of minor health imbalances.*

Twelve:
Food as Medicine

The infirmities of the flesh have given rise to as many varieties of medicine as there have been tribes, races, and societies. All manner of locally found substances have been used medicinally: barks, leaves, roots, insects, parts of animals, even mineral matter. Medicines have been physical, as in the drawing of blood, or spiritual, as in rituals to draw out evil spirits. And all of them, at some time or another, for one reason or another, have been, or have seemed to be, effective in some way. Whether this is because of the presence of a true healer, the right medicine, or a gullible patient is probably not relevant. What is relevant is that there are many systems of medicine, and modern Western healing techniques constitute just one of them, neither the ultimate nor necessarily the best one, although today perhaps the most powerful and influential[1]—as well as the most expensive.

CAN FOOD BE MEDICINE?

Food, if appropriate, as we have seen in this book, can continually heal our bodies, rebalancing them whenever they go slightly off-balance. It is thus a *healing* substance. But is it, strictly speaking, "medicine"? We usually think of medicines or remedies as strange or unusual substances, difficult to get, or specially prepared by experts, that will cure our sickness and eliminate our pain. We think of food as something that nourishes us, pleases us, and keeps us alive. But good doctors and healers throughout history have known that just as food continually builds our body, so it can alter it.*

This is not a new concept. Hippocrates taught, in a maxim oft repeated, that food should be our medicine and medicine should be our food. In most traditional medical systems on earth (except our own) food plays an integral part, and common foods are often used with medicinal purpose.

Although food is admittedly not the ultimate panacea, there is a power in it that we in our culture have barely begun to glimpse; food is, in ways yet unclear, "powerful medicine." Let's not forget that according to the Old Testament the knowledge of good and evil, as well as the possibility of immortality, were both conditioned upon eating something, in that case the fruit of a tree. One fairly amusing episode comes to my mind to illustrate this notion of the power of food.

In 1978, more than sixteen years after I had left Argentina, I returned for a visit. My high school friends were aware of my work with food and were curious. "What is it that you're teaching?" they wanted to know. So I offered to cook them a meal and explain some things. Gleefully, the offer was accepted, and a few days later I found myself making dinner for a party of twelve. I made a light, ample meal: carrot cream soup, brown rice, sautéed green squash with herbs, salad with lemon and olive oil dressing, broiled fish, homemade bread and spread, and baked apples with raisins and cinnamon.[3] Nothing terribly weird, I thought, but still quite a change from the Argentines' usual fare of steak or breaded fried veal cutlets with french fries, salads bound with mayonnaise, and cheese or custard for dessert.

Before dinner, my friends asked if they were allowed to have a little wine. Sure, I shrugged, they were used to it, why not. So during the meal the men went through their customary eight bottles of burgundy—and to everyone's amazement, they got roaring drunk. As this reaction was totally unexpected, they didn't quite notice their condition until the next day, when they realized how the evening had ended: one getting an outlandish haircut from another; one crashing his car (no big damage); one couple sleeping well into the morning so that they were late for work and the kids missed school; and other assorted mishaps and complications. In all, an unforgettable experience—they're still talking about it.

* Henry Bieler, M.D., wrote, "Since the body is, more or less, the product of the food fed it, altering body chemistry by diet is not only feasible but most desirable in disease states."[2]

What happened? Apparently, their usual high-fat, high-protein meals had been balanced by the wine that accompanied them, so drunkenness was never an issue. In fact, the expansive wine probably made those heavy contractive meals easier to take. But the light (low-fat, low-protein), high–complex-carbohydrate meal that I made completely altered my friends' physiological response to alcohol—with the result that what was normally a comfortable quantity of wine turned into an excess and made them drunk.

The episode greatly increased my respect for food's ability to change our metabolism very quickly. One meal, perhaps one bite, can have a pronounced effect. In many situations food is indeed, as American Indians traditionally believed, something that can "control nature," make us strong or weak, give or take away "power" (the ability to *do* or to have an effect), both cause and remedy many of our ills; therefore, a potent medicine.

The Law of Remedies

It is important to keep in mind that any remedy, whether drug, herb, or food, can indeed both *cause* a disorder and *heal* it. This, in fact, is one of the basic principles of the natural healing system called homeopathy, according to which the substance that causes a certain symptom will cure that symptom if consumed in a smaller quantity.[4]

An episode from my own experience illustrates this principle most clearly. One day when she was about nine, my oldest daughter suddenly developed a cough. There was no mucus, cold, illness, or any other problem associated with it; it was just a mysterious cough. As she hadn't eaten either dairy or ice cream during the past month—the usual culprits—I couldn't figure out where this was coming from. Then I remembered that three days before a friend of mine had returned from a trip to Europe and brought me some pure unsweetened licorice strings from Holland. I've never liked licorice, so I didn't eat it, but my daughter loved it and had finished the batch. On a hunch, I looked up licorice in an herb book.[5] I found that one of the conditions it helps heal is asthma, which of course entails coughing. Therefore I speculated that as my daughter had no cough or asthma that needed curing, the remedy, taken in a rather large dose, had flipped over and caused that very same condition it would normally cure. I felt that if such were the case, it would be out of her body within a day or two, with no further attention. And indeed within a couple of days there was not a trace of the cough left.

On the basis of this and other experiences, I have formulated the following Law of Remedies. I believe it applies equally to whatever remedies you may be using, be they pharmacological drugs, natural and synthetic vitamins and mineral supplements, homeopathic remedies, herbal remedies, or any food used medicinally:

1. Any substance (drug, supplement, or herb) that cures a symptom will cause that same symptom (a) in a different dosage, either larger or smaller; and/or (b) if used in the absence of that symptom. (Tranquilizers can cause anxiety; digitalis, an anti-arrhythmic, can cause cardiac arrhythmias.)
2. A remedy that has cured a symptom should be stopped once that symptom has vanished.
3. Symptoms caused by the excess of a remedy or medicine cannot be cured any more by the same remedy, even if the remedy originally did cure the symptom. Discontinuation of the remedy is mandatory; in most cases an antidote, or simply the passage of time, will eventually reestablish balance. This technique will minimize the development of resistance to remedies.

Foods, herbs, and other natural substances can be very potent remedies. They are also vast in number. Therefore, the healing systems based on them are as complex and sophisticated as that of modern medicine. Any detailed guide to these healing systems is beyond the scope of this book; my purpose here is to show how we can use food to heal ourselves continuously, every day, with the simplest of natural ways accessible to us. I have found a number of food remedies that are as easy to prepare as a bowl of oatmeal and that can help flip our balance if we've swung out too far in one direction or another. They are therefore very helpful in managing our health on a day-to-day basis. Please note that if you have a chronic, distressing problem, you will be best off consulting a professional healer who understands your needs.

HOME REMEDIES

Throughout history, every household has had its own remedies for various minor problems, handed down through the generations. Usually, these remedies reflected the healing system accepted in each particular society.

In our own society, we have a blend of many traditions. I myself am such a blend: European by birth and ancestry, South American by upbringing, North American by choice, Oriental by study. The remedies I've used at home for small health disorders are likewise a mixture of these traditions. Some are from the European school of natural health; some are from the Oriental system of macrobiotics; a few are from the "health food" movement; and my favorite digestive tea is an Argentine blend called Cachamai.

I have used the remedies listed below for fifteen, twenty years, some even longer, and found them effective in many different situations. I am not implying that only these remedies are worth using; just that these are the ones I understand best and have worked with most consistently. Also, I believe in simplifying life—it's complicated enough—so I use as few and as simple remedies as possible to avoid confusion. I hope that each reader of this book will add and subtract from the list and thereby end up with a highly personal and individualized home remedy kit, appropriate for his or her own situation. In the following sections of this chapter you will find information about how these remedies can be used to balance various conditions of imbalance. Please note that natural remedies of any kind may have less or no effect if you are also taking pharmacological drugs.

First, we'll list and categorize the remedies. After that, we'll look at different conditions and how these remedies can be used to counterbalance them.

CODE

E:	expansive	B-u:	Buildup
C:	Contractive	B-d:	Breakdown
Ac:	Acid-forming	+:	More
Alk:	Alkalinizing	-:	Less
W:	Warming	±:	More or less
K:	Cooling		

FRUIT JUICES (E/Alk/K/B-d), especially apple and apricot; grape, fresh grapefruit, and fresh orange juice can also be used, according to taste.

VEGETABLE JUICES (E/Alk/K/B-d), such as carrot, celery, greens, either straight or mixed.

LEMON TEA (E/Alk/W/B-d), cut a lemon in half, squeeze juice from one half and pour juice into a cup. Cut up the ½ juiced peel and set to simmer in 1¼ cups water for 8 to 10 minutes. Strain into the cup that holds the juice. If too tart or too bitter, add 1 tablespoon maple syrup or barley malt.

GINGER TEA (± C/Alk/W/b-d): Simmer 4 or 5 slices fresh ginger in 1 cup water, covered, for 10 to 15 minutes.

PEPPERMINT TEA with lemon (E/Alk/W/B-d): in some cases, with ½ teaspoon honey.

FIVE-PHASE DRINK (E/Alk/W/B-d): Mix 1 cup lemon tea with 1 tablespoon maple syrup or to taste. Add pinch of cayenne or five drops of Tabasco (cooling effect) OR ½ teaspoon fresh grated ginger (warming effect). Stir well, drink hot.

VEGETARIAN "CHICKEN" SOUP (C/Alk/W/B-d): Ingredients: 6 cups water, 1 carrot, 1 leek, 1 zucchini, 1 rib celery, handful of green beans, 1 bay leaf. Wash and chop the vegetables, and simmer them for about 30 minutes, covered. Remove bay leaf. Eat soup with vegetables, or use broth only. (Note: there is no salt in this soup.)

MISO SOUP (C/Alk/W/B-d): Miso is a paste of fermented soybeans, sea salt, and sometimes a grain such as rice or barley; it is used to flavor soups and sauces in Japanese cuisine. It is an excellent alkalizer and has a generally contractive effect. Miso soup must be made with unpasteurized barley or rice miso, preferably American-made or good-quality Japanese (obtainable in bulk from natural and macrobiotic-food suppliers). The simplest way to prepare it is to dissolve ½ to ⅔ teaspoon miso in 1 cup hot water. A small jar of miso can be taken on trips as a coffee replacement in the morning. A richer, more mineral-laden miso soup is obtained by shredding half a sheet of nori seaweed and simmering it in the water for 4 to 5 minutes, with perhaps a few cubes of tofu; the miso is added at the end, with a few chopped scallions for garnish. I have found no better counterbalance to a sugar binge or to the sour taste remaining after an excess of flour products, baked goods, sweets, or grains.

GRATED RADISH (± C/Alk/K/B-d): Finely grate daikon, black radish, or white (icicle) radish, adding a few drops of natural soy sauce (shoyu or tamari).

FRESHLY GRATED GINGER (± C/Alk/W/B-d): Horseradish is somewhat similar in nature.

GARLIC (± C/Alk/K/B-d): Use it fresh.

GOMASIO (C/Alk/K/B-d): A.k.a. sesame salt. Recipe: Grind 1 cup roasted sesame seeds, until half crushed, in a mortar, preferably the Japanese kind known as a suribachi, which has grooves. Add 2 teaspoons sea salt; then grind the salt well into the seeds. (Proportion of seeds to salt: 20:1.)

UMEBOSHI PLUMS, or umeboshi paste (C/Alk/ ± K/B-d): Also called plums pickled in brine, are obtainable in Japanese and health food stores. The plums are pickled in salt for about two months, sometimes with beefsteak (chiso) leaves, which give them a bright color. They taste salty-sour. Make sure that they have not been doctored up by checking the ingredients: Only plums, water, salt, and perhaps chiso or beefsteak leaves should be listed. The whole plum includes the pit, which some people like to suck on as if it were a candy. The paste made of these plums is in some sense more handy, because it is easier to adjust dosage, usually measured by dipping a chopstick or pinky into the jar; hence you will find suggestions for "a lick or two" of umeboshi plum paste. (Also available are UME concentrate, used as an alkalizing drink with hot water, and UMEBOSHI VINEGAR, wonderful with grains, especially cornmeal, and in salad dressings.)

KUZU (C/Alk/W/± B-d): This is a starch made from the root of the kudzu plant, which grows wild as a pest in the American South. The only kuzu starch obtainable in this country is imported from Japan and available in health food stores as kuzu arrowroot. Good kuzu is a bit on the expensive side. If you find very cheap kuzu that is not lumpy, it has probably been adulterated.

Kuzu is similar to arrowroot or cornstarch in that it must be dissolved in cold liquid and the mixture stirred while it heats, thickening as it reaches the boiling point. It has an alkalizing effect. One tablespoon kuzu starch will thicken 1 cup liquid to the consistency of Chinese vegetable sauce; 2½ tablespoons kuzu to 1 cup liquid makes pudding, which when cool is the consistency of soft tofu. As a remedy, kuzu can be used in two ways: shoyu-kuzu (salty, runny, like a thick broth) and apple juice–kuzu (thick and sweet like a pudding).

Shoyu-Kuzu can be prepared in any of three ways:
  1. Plain shoyu-kuzu: Dissolve 1 tablespoon kuzu in 1 cup cold

water and cook, stirring, until thick. Add 1 tablespoon natural soy sauce (shoyu or tamari), or enough so that it tastes
wonderful.

2. Shoyu-kuzu with umeboshi: To the mixture of kuzu and
   water as above, add 1 mashed-up umeboshi plum, or ± 1
   teaspoon umeboshi plum paste, and let the mixture simmer
   2 minutes longer. Add less soy sauce than for plain shoyu-
   kuzu, as the plums are already salty.
3. Shoyu-kuzu with umeboshi and ginger: To recipe number
   2, above, add ½ to 1 teaspoon freshly grated ginger at the
   beginning.

Apple Juice–Kuzu: In 1 cup apple juice, dissolve 2 tablespoons kuzu
starch and ± 1 teaspoon vanilla extract (optional). Cook until
thickened, stirring all the time. Swirl in 1 tablespoon tahini (sesame seed paste). Eat hot or cold. (This tastes like dessert, but it
is a remedy.)

BARLEY WATER (C/Ac/W/B-u): Two tablespoons barley cooked in
2 cups water for approximately 1 hour, covered. Mix.

SOFT RICE (C/Ac/W/B-u): Cook 1 cup washed brown rice in 4 cups
water for 2 hours; stir often. Soft rice can also be made by re-
cooking previously cooked rice in an equal volume of water, until
creamy, over a very low flame, stirring often.

ROASTED RICE CREAM (C/-Ac/W/B-u): or rice and millet, mixed
fifty-fifty. Wash 1 cup grain. Spread in a baking pan and roast at
350° F, stirring once or twice, until lightly browned and fragrant
(about fifteen to twenty minutes). Grind in a blender or coffee
grinder. Dissolve the roasted ground grain in water (use about 1
cup ground grain to two cups water) and bring to a boil while
stirring. Cover and cook from thirty-five to forty minutes over
the lowest heat, stirring often. Delicious—and more alkalizing—
with a few drops of natural soy sauce (shoyu or tamari) or umeboshi vinegar or with some gomasio. For a tangy flavor and a good
alkalizing effect, rice cream can also be cooked with a whole umeboshi plum mixed through it; no extra seasoning will then be
needed.

All the foregoing remedies have a distinct flavor. The advantage
of using foods as medicine is that the taste can guide us: It's quite
safe to live by the notion that if a food remedy tastes good to us,
it is good for us, and vice versa. Kuzu, in its various forms, is an

especially good example of this premise: The preparation that appeals to you at a given time is the one you should have at that time (and this can and will vary); the one that makes your throat close up will do you no good. The body knows what it needs, and it is unwise to force yourself to swallow any food remedy if you dislike it.

EXTERNAL REMEDIES

I've found that food remedies are very well complemented by external water treatments. Water is probably the oldest of healing tools; it is easily available, either from brook, sea, rain, or even tongue. It can be used:

- As ice
- Cold
- Lukewarm
- Hot
- As steam

in the form of:

- Packs
- Compresses
- Baths
- Sprays
- Steamings

A comprehensive review of water therapy is outside the scope of this book. There are several excellent works on the subject, which periodically appear and then go out of print, because the public in the United States, unlike that in Europe, is not familiar with this easy and highly effective form of natural healing.[6] There are, however, several simple treatments that I have used for a number of conditions—especially fevers and earaches—with great success; you will find the details in the individual section for each condition.

On the whole, please note the following:

- Cold water, in short applications, reduces fever, relieves pain, and tonifies the system. In a compress (a folded cloth dipped in water and wrung out), placed on abdomen or sprained muscle, covered by dry towels, cold water warms up and increases circulation; thereby it aids metabolism and the elimination of waste matter. Long cold-water applications are depressant and can chill the body. A cold foot bath can relieve congestion in the upper body, as blood rushes down to heat the feet.

• Hot water, in the form of compresses or baths, relaxes the muscles and combats tension. It also increases perspiration and surface circulation, thereby relieving congestion that is deep within the body. The eventual reaction to hot water will be cooling, as the perspiration evaporates; unless care is exercised, a hot-water application, if too prolonged, can both weaken and chill the body. For this reason, it is a very good idea to finish every hot shower with a few seconds of a cold one, to provoke the body into a warming reaction. CAUTION: Hot-water treatments should NEVER be used on:
  • Open wounds or injuries
  • Inflammations on the surface of the body
  • Sprains or broken bones
They could make the condition significantly worse.

FASTING

Perhaps nowhere is the power of food more evident than when food is abstained from. Entire religions have evolved from one man's fast, empires toppled, wars halted. For examples we need look no further than Jesus, Muhammad, the Buddha, Gandhi.

"Prayer and fasting" is the time-honored path toward understanding and enlightenment followed by spiritual masters East and West. Judaism, Christianity, and Islam all observe fast days; the Greek mystery schools, Jainism, Buddhism, South and North American Indian cultures, Siberian shamans, and practically all traditional cultures we know of use fasting for religious, spiritual, or health reasons.

In addition, not eating is probably the oldest and most universal food-related healing technique. Animals routinely stop eating if they don't feel well. And from the dawn of history, as well as from earliest infancy, human beings have also fasted when illness has struck.

The practice of fasting tacitly acknowledges the fact that ours is a self-healing organism. Healing occurs naturally *if it is allowed*; improper or excessive food simply thwarts the natural ongoing healing processes. Forcing a sick person to eat "to keep up his strength" overlooks the fact that digestion uses up strength too:

more often than not, the available strength is better used for heal-ing the problem at hand than for digestion. Also, as fasting appears to release a hormone that stimulates the immune system, it would indeed help speed recovery from fevers and infections. Not eating, in short, is as important as eating. For just as our bodies require both sleep and wakefulness, movement and rest, so we alternate between eating and not eating. Too much of either, and we go off-balance.

It is important to differentiate between fasting and starvation. Fasting is entirely voluntary and an individual choice; it has a be-ginning, an end, and a clear goal, be it healing, a political objective, or a spiritual vision. If prudently done, its effects are almost in-variably beneficial. Starvation, on the other hand, is involuntary; it involves no freedom of choice, but occurs as a result of external circumstances, such as war, drought, crop failure, poverty. It means not having enough to eat for a long time and results in a weakening and wasting away of the body. Today in our society there are also a number of people who starve themselves volun-tarily, thinking that they are either "too fat" and need to "diet" or that they are actually following a "healthy diet"; strong will-power, ideology, and fear keep them on a narrow food path, mak-ing them ignore their true hunger and think that their deepest instincts are somehow "wrong" or "bad." Such rigidity only brings misery and pain, and has nothing to do with using food as a healing tool.

How to Fast

There are various ways to fast. A fast can last from four hours to many days, and the reduction of food can be in terms of quantity and/or quality. In all cases, however, liquid intake must be abun-dant, or else dehydration and shrinkage will quickly set in.

We can fast:
a. Daily
b. Unto the ninth hour
c. One or more days
d. One or more weeks

We can follow:
1. A water fast
2. A juice and broth fast
3. A monodiet

Let's examine each of these possibilities in turn.

a. The most sensible and natural way to fast is once a day.[7] Ideally, this means abstaining from food for ten to fourteen hours, or from about 6:00 P.M. to 8:00 A.M., give or take an hour or two. This practice allows the body enough time to cleanse the waste products of metabolism; it also facilitates the release of the hormones that stimulate the immune system, which are released by both fasting and sleep. If such a fast is practiced regularly, there will be no buildup or backlog of metabolic debris in the body, the possibility of serious illness will be diminished, and prolonged fasts will be unnecessary.

b. With a small buildup, such as when you feel a fullness in the stomach, or are bloated and have overeaten, a few days of "fasting unto the ninth hour" will be sufficient to cleanse the system. It means avoiding solid food until 3:00 P.M., then eating a light snack of fruit, salad, or whole-grain bread or crackers, and a full, well-balanced vegetarian meal at about 6:00 P.M. Between dinner and 3:00 P.M. of the following day, only tea, water, or juice are to be taken. This type of fasting is excellent if it is necessary to keep up with daily work and normal activities. People whose metabolism is slow, but clean and efficient, can often live on this eating schedule for prolonged periods of time with excellent results. ·

c. A fast or monodiet from one to ten days, either abstaining from food or eating only one kind, can be safely followed by most people who feel slightly unbalanced. This has been called prophylactic (disease-preventing) fasting.[8] It is most effective when embarked upon following a deep inner urge. However, please note that anyone with chronic diagnosed ailments such as heart disease or diabetes should consult with a physician, especially if taking prescribed medication, before going on any fast. *It is not advisable to fast even for short periods of time if one is taking any kind of medication, or in cases of pregnancy or nursing.* It is advisable to discontinue vitamins and other supplements during a fast, as the body is unable to utilize supplements properly unless food is eaten as well.*

---

* Paavo Airola, a staunch supporter of supplementation, strongly recommended discontinuing it while fasting.[9]

Medication poses a problem because the body becomes supersensitive while fasting, and side effects can become quite pronounced. Fasting is not advisable during pregnancy or breast-feeding because food-energy supply to the baby will also diminish. (I tried fasting for a day or two at different times when I was nursing my children, to repair some minor cold or dietary indiscretion; invariably the babies protested, although my milk supply itself didn't seem to have decreased. They acted as if the same amount of milk didn't deliver the usual nourishment. I imagine its nutrient density must have diminished.)

d. Any therapeutic fast longer than ten days and embarked on to lose weight or overcome a chronic illness must be followed only under experienced supervision. A prolonged fast can precipitate an intense healing crisis around the fifteenth day, and it is strongly advisable to have someone around who understands the process. It is also advisable that such a fast be conducted away from energy-consuming daily obligations and work, in a supportive, relaxing, natural setting, surrounded by trees, greenery, and lots of sunlight. As there will be no energy input from food, what energy the system will need should come from warmth, light, and oxygen. (Recent theories hold that "light energy structures matter," and that we need light as much as food to build our body.[10]) A therapeutic fast is a time to direct attention inward, toward healing and reintegration; exercise, walking, and sunbathing will all enhance its effectiveness. A prolonged fast without these precautions can do much damage. One good friend of mine once followed a juice fast for twenty-eight days in the middle of a New York winter, continuing her normally stressful life and work. She wanted to stop at ten days, but the M.D. advising her pushed her to continue. She was freezing, exhausted, unable to walk uphill, and the fast did not cure the chronic cough that was her original problem. Today she estimates that it took her two years to undo the damage and feel normal once again.

However long a fast lasts, it involves a reduction not only in the quantity, but also in the quality of food intake. The following are the possible variations of fasts of reduced quality:

1. The Water Fast is what purists consider the only *true* fast. It consists of taking nothing but water. Healing reactions have been reported by people who have undertaken it, as well as weakness and fatigue. A water fast may have its drawbacks in our industrialized world. As long as twenty years ago it was pointed out that we all carry stores of insecticides, pesticides, strontium, and other poisonous substances in our bodies. These are usually stored in the places where they pose the least hazard: the body fat. A fast that breaks down fat stores also releases these poisons into the bloodstream, and they can cause illness, perhaps even death. Migrating birds have been known to die as a result of the insecticides released into their bloodstream from the breakdown of their body fat during long flights.[11] Not only does the water fast, especially if prolonged, offer no buffers to internally released pollutants, it also provides no minerals needed for continued nerve function. Therefore, only those with a strong constitution and plenty of reserves can safely undertake a water fast of more than two days' duration; and then it should always be under professional supervision.

2. To avoid the problem of stored pollutants being released internally too quickly, a number of nutritionists recommend the juice fast, that is, the drinking of fruit and vegetable juices instead of water. Cooked vegetable broth may also be used. It appears that as the energy of dissolved nutrients is taken in, whatever noxious substances are being released by the breakdown of body fat are buffered, diluted, or maybe released more slowly, thus causing fewer problems.

   A juice or broth fast is also quite alkalizing because of the minerals in the juice or broth. It therefore helps balance the acidifying effects of a diet that has been high in protein, flour, and sugar. It is most effective when combined with exercise and vigorous physical activity. In some health spas, a daily enema is mandatory with fasting to help clean out toxic matter that may remain in the intestines and be reabsorbed.

   Because fasting itself is highly contractive, the expansiveness of juices provides quite a good balance; that is one of the reasons for the popularity of this type of fast for countering the effects of overeating. In some cases, however, the juice fast (as well as the water fast) can overtax the kidneys because of the excess liquid intake. One of my students who had been going on regular three-day juice fasts every month, felt that her kidneys were becoming overworked because her back was hurting around the kidney area. At my suggesiton, she stopped fasting and thus drinking all that fluid, added some aduki beans (which have a diuretic effect) and seaweed to her diet, and began to feel much better.

3. Monodiets consist of eating only one category of food for a given period of time. Like other fasts, their goal is to give the metabolism less work to do. Monodiets are as varied as the people who invent them: Among the better known ones are the grape diet, the apple diet, and the macrobiotic all-grain "number seven" diet (which, as the last of a series of ten variations, for a long time was misunderstood as the ultimate goal of "pure" macrobiotic eating). In my experience, alkalizing monodiets based on fruits and vegetables—just as with juice fasting—are helpful in cases of protein and fat overload. The macrobiotic all-grain fast, because it is acid-forming, is most effective when cushioned by some alkalizing seaweed, miso, and sea salt; it has had some excellent results when followed for seven to ten days by people coming off sugar and recreational drugs. It should be considered a therapeutic fast and in no case followed for more than ten days, as it could be overly acidifying.

How Will It Feel?

Once a fast is under way, there is usually a small "healing crisis" on the second or third day: headache, stomachache, coated tongue, foul breath, and so forth. Those symptoms usually disappear after the fourth day, as do hunger pangs. Once you cease to feel the initial hunger, it is safe to fast until real hunger sets in. Real hunger is usually accompanied by feelings of deprivation, emptiness, and fatigue. Its onset will depend on the backlog of metabolic debris: Some people have been known to fast cheerfully for forty days, whereas the last time I fasted I couldn't go longer than four. I guess I have a nicely cleaned-out metabolism—but, on the other hand, I'd probably cave in quickly during a famine. Ironically, some people who survived starvation in concentration camps during World War II found that their aches, pains, and infirmities disappeared during their ordeal, only to return full force or worse once they resumed "normal" eating after the war. Several family members and friends of my parents had just such experiences. One of them was a pianist whose hands had been hurting for years, forcing her to curtail her career. The pain disappeared while she was imprisoned but returned after she came home. "I know that it has something to do with the food I'm eating," she repeatedly told my mother, "but I don't know *what* it is that's wrong."

Breaking the Fast

It's important to break a fast gently, eating small amounts of light (no fat, low protein) foods. *Take as much time as you spent fasting to return gradually to regular eating.* All the good done by a fast can be wiped out with hasty or excessive eating immediately afterward. In fact, you can make yourself quite sick that way. One friend of mine plunged back into normal eating two days after a week-long fast, she got so sick that she had to do the whole fast over again and come out of it very gradually. Then she was fine.

Basic Rules of Successful Fasting

1. Fast when you are ill and have no appetite.
2. Fast only when you really want to, not when you think you should.
3. Stop when you begin to feel deprived and empty.
4. Careful with reentry! Come back slowly, taking as many days to return to your usual diet as you spent fasting.
5. Fasts longer than ten days should be done in a sunny, natural setting, away from normal work activites and under professional supervision.
6. In warm weather, fast with juices, fruit, raw vegetables. In cold weather, fast with broth, cooked vegetables, grain.

Appropriate fasting is one of our greatest healing tools. Let's learn to use it wisely.

CONDITIONS THAT RESPOND TO DIETARY MANAGEMENT AND HOME REMEDIES

Now that we've looked at various dietary systems and natural remedies, we are ready to examine both the conditions to which they can be applied and the approximate time frames for the abatement or disappearance of symptoms. These timetables depend on the particulars of each case and certainly do not apply universally. On the whole, they are broad generalizations based on my observation of specific cases and on the rates of body-tissue regeneration (see page 221).

What follows then is a listing of specific conditions, the simplest remedies that I have found to help rebalance them, and approximately how long they will take to abate.

Headaches

The most common and at times the most debilitating of adjustment symptoms, headaches invariably herald a general systemic imbalance. Their prevalence is testified to by the myriad over-the-counter medicines designed to eliminate them, the headache clinics, the dates canceled, the love not made. We hear of sick headaches, tension headaches, migraines, hangovers.

According to the Bircher-Benner headache clinic in Zurich, Switzerland, headaches can be caused by metabolic overload, arteriosclerosis, heart ailments, disorders of the liver, of the gastrointestinal tract, and of the kidneys; but also by narrowed space in the skull, mental illness, heat and sunstroke, sinus congestion, infectious disease, tuberculosis, eye strain, misaligned cervical vertebrae, neuralgia, shingles, and allergies. In all these cases the underlying disorder must be healed before the headache disappears for good.[12]

What follows is a much simpler way to consider headaches, one that I have found to be extremely effective as a first attempt to deal with them.

According to medical science, headaches can only be caused by (a) expansion of the blood vessels in the head; or (b) tension or strain of the muscles in the neck, scalp, or face. The first kind are called *vascular* headaches; the second, *tension* headaches. I have found it most useful to classify most simple headaches into those of *expansion* and those of *contraction*, with side categories for "liver" headaches, caffeine-withdrawal headaches, and others.

Expansion headaches are usually the result of too much
- Liquid of any kind, including fruit juice
- Alcohol
- Ice cream and other cold and highly sugared foods

Remedies for these should take effect in two to fifteen minutes and will be found among contractive foods, especially salty ones:
- Gomasio (sesame salt) (page 254)
- Umeboshi plums or brine-cured olives (page 254)

Contraction headaches are usually the result of
- Tension, overwork
- Heat
- Meats and salty foods (especially on an empty stomach)
- Lack of food and/or fluids
- Excess mental concentration or physical activity in addition to the above

Remedies for these should work in five minutes to twenty-four hours and consist of something cool and liquid, sweet or sour, such as
- Apple or apricot juice (page 252)
- Cold unsweetened applesauce or other cooked fruit

Liver headaches are similar to contractive headaches, but stronger, more painful, and harder to turn around. They have also been called migraines. They arise two, four, even eight hours after the unbalancing food has been consumed and therefore are rarely linked to it. Usually, they are the result of consuming fatty foods on an empty stomach, including fried eggs or cheese for breakfast, fried tofu or tempeh, salads with oily dressings, avocados, and tempura.

Remedies for these are the same as those for headaches of contraction, and in addition
- Lemon tea
- Five-Phase Drink
- If all else fails, sleep (you can also cleanse the liver with a few days of juice fasting, followed by several days of fat-free vegetarian food)

Caffeine-withdrawal headaches, which occur within a day of giving up coffee, tea, or chocolate, can range from a mild background ache to a full-fledged migraine. Treat them as contraction headaches; however, sometimes they do not respond. That is the time to go back to bed and wait till they go away—which they eventually do. Try the "hair of the dog" method—one sip—if it's really bad.

In some cases, people with allergies will respond with a headache to allergenic substances. The most common of these are wheat, corn, milk and milk products, chocolate, tomatoes; household chemicals and exhaust fumes run a close second. This kind of condition is best diagnosed by a clinical nutritionist or allergist and treated by metabolic-strengthening therapies and withdrawal of the offending substances.

To find out which kind of headache you have, you can:
- Make a list of what you've eaten in the past six hours or so and see if it's expansive, contractive, or fatty.
- Have a tiny bite of umeboshi plum if you can't figure it out. If you remain the same, or get better, you have an expansive headache. If you get worse, you have a contractive or a liver headache.

Chronic headaches can be associated with a number of illnesses, organ malfunctions, and accumulations; if you have frequent headaches, and if all the aforementioned treatments fail, you can assume that there is an underlying disorder and that it is essential that you get a professional diagnosis.

Fevers

For thousands of years, an elevation in body temperature was considered beneficial; it was thought to speed up the disease process and help the disease condition clear up. But for the past eighty years or so, pharmacological medicine has insisted that fever is no good and must be lowered as soon as it appears—in other words, that the fever is the sickness.

Fortunately, science is becoming sophisticated enough to begin to discover through the scientific method what the ancients knew by dream, vision, or intuition. It has been found recently that bacteria cannot live at fever temperatures and that iron and zinc stores—which bacteria need for growth—are lowered during a fever. During a fever, therefore, bacteria are both cooked and starved.[13] Instead of being seen as an enemy, fever is now acknowledged as an ally in the treatment of disease.

Fever generally starts in the intestines, and in my experience it is almost invariably associated with the consumption of animal protein, such as meat, chicken, eggs, and milk products. An excess of this protein, if not moving fast enough through the intestines, will putrefy and invite bacteria as scavengers. Fevers then arise to burn up the putrefying matter as well as the bacteria. Interrupting this process with aspirin or antibiotics is akin to killing the cleaning lady in the midst of her spring cleaning, when everything is one big mess. Because the job doesn't get finished, all the debris is left lying around, including the corpses of the dead bacteria, and the stage is set for more extensive and complicated infections and illnesses later on. Witness the discovery, in recent years, that there is a relationship between Reye's syndrome and the administration of aspirin to children with simple viral infections; this discovery has already resulted in widespread injunctions against the use of aspirin for children's infections and fevers.[14]

Each interrupted infection leaves debris and residue in the body. Subsequent "illnesses" attempt to clean up not only whatever problem is then acute, but also the leftovers of prior unfinished business. Keeping this in mind, we can understand in a new light why people become sicker and sicker as they age. Every time the body has attempted to do housecleaning, the process has been interrupted with medication, and the body has become more and more overloaded. One day, the immune system takes a look at the mess and says, in effect, "This stuff doesn't belong here; let's take care of it," and turns around and attacks the whole body. This could be the beginning of autoimmune diseases such as allergies, Guillain-Barre syndrome, rheumatoid arthritis, Lou Gehrig's disease, multiple sclerosis, lupus, even cancer and AIDS.[15]

Treatment of a simple fever that does not exceed 104° F and is not accompanied by other symptoms will be most effective if it:
    (a) allows the fever to do its job; and
    (b) avoids exacerbating the condition that caused the fever.

This can be accomplished by observing the following measures:
- Keeping warm, to allow body temperature to build.
- Fasting, that is, eating no solid food or at least no protein or fats.
- Drinking hot fluids, perhaps with some spice, to encourage perspiration: Five-Phase Drink, vegetable broth, ginger tea.
- If the patient has chills or is restless, a fifteen-minute warm bath of the same temperature as the fever is very soothing and will banish the chills. This remedy is especially good for children.
- After the fever breaks—or if the patient is really hungry—

barley water, soft rice, (page 255) and salt-free vegetable soup (page 253) are the best choices in foods.

Because it is a beneficial physical reaction, a simple fever can be allowed, should even be encouraged, to run its course. Should it last longer than two or three days, or present any peculiar aspects, it's best to consult a competent health professional.

The Common Cold

One of the most widespread adjustments/discharges, the common cold is also commonly misunderstood. Viewed as a threat, it is, like most "sicknesses," more of a loving friend that comes to warn us about, and at the same time set aright, the misalignments, stresses, and dietary errors in our lives. Instead of heeding the message and making the corrections, we ignore or shoot the messenger—leaving ourselves open to repeat messages, which usually become more intense. Nature is persistent: If we don't respond to a tap on the shoulder, we'll eventually get a kick in the behind.

What, then, should we do about a cold?

First, we must find out what kind of cold it is. As with headaches, I've found it useful to classify colds into those that result from expansion and those that result from contraction.

Expansive colds can be caused by:
- Sugars, sweets, refined starches, and similar acid-forming foods
- Ice cream, milk, and other milk products
- Large quantities of liquids, juices, fruits

Their symptoms include an actively runny nose, plenty of mucus discharge, coughing, sneezing, and wheezing. There is usually no fever, and the patient is quite willing and able to continue with daily work and activities, taking time out for some nose blowing here or there.

A cold of this type can sometimes be caught and reversed right at the beginning by some quick contracting, with an umeboshi plum or two, for example. If that doesn't work, it's best just to let it go and allow the body to go through its cleaning process. A little stimulus and general noninterference work best, and these can be assisted by:

- Partial fasting, that is, no fats or protein for a few days. (The old adage "Feed a cold, starve a fever" has been distorted by word-of-mouth transmission: The original saying was "*If* you feed a cold, *you'll have to* starve a fever," that is, *you'll get worse if you keep eating.* My experience supports this.)
- Alkalizing foods, but on the contractive side: cooked vegetables, soups (including miso soup), baked potatoes.
- Fluids only when desired, or when there is a feeling of stuck mucus (in that case they should be abundant, to help loosen it). Caution: Large amounts of fluids in a cold of expansion will make it feel worse.
- Moderate activity.

Contraction colds are usually caused by:
- Tension, overwork, fatigue
- Salty, fatty foods
- Excess protein and sugar

Their symptoms include tightness in the chest and head, headache, fever, exhaustion, stuffiness in the sinuses, chills, aches. This condition is also known as the flu.

Remedies should aim to loosen and relax. Thus, the following are helpful:
- Partial fasting—no salt, fat, protein, or starches—until the fever disappears (if there is one).
- Plenty of hot fluids, in the form of juice (try hot apple or pear juice with cinnamon); chamomile, ginger, or lemon tea; or plain hot water with lemon, to help loosen the tightness. (page 252)
- Alkalizing foods, on the expansive side: fruits and salads, unsalted vegetable soup. (page 253)
- Rest. It is mandatory. In fact, often the rest alone will allow the body to recuperate easily.

As should be evident, these remedies are not intended to interrupt the process of a cold, but rather to relieve the discomfort of its symptoms.

Coughs

The treatment of a cough will depend on whether it is a useful cough that brings up mucus or a useless, dry one caused by local irritation (a "tickle in the chest"). The first kind should be encouraged and allowed to do its cleansing job; staying away from salty foods, which tend to tighten and hold back, will help speed up the process. This cough can be treated like chest tightness in a contractive cold: Drink hot lemon tea, perhaps with honey; try a hot chest compress; drink hot pear juice with a cinnamon stick.

The second kind of cough can be stopped with a lick or two of something salty, especially umeboshi plum paste. I was once doing a demonstration class at Artpark, an outdoor art exhibition near Niagara Falls, and mentioned this very subject. As if on cue, a woman in the audience had a dry-coughing attack. The fifty people present watched in silent anticipation as the jar of umeboshi paste was passed along from my table to the uncontrollably coughing woman. She dipped her pinky into the paste and licked it—and instantly stopped coughing. The crowd applauded. She took another lick for good measure and, smiling and nodding, sent the jar back to me.

If the umeboshi (page 254), which is quite contractive, doesn't do it, licorice tea, a bit more expansive, often works. Persistent, chronic coughs should be diagnosed by a physician.

Sore Throats

Ginger tea (page 253), slippery elm tea, and shoyu-kuzu with ginger (page 255) are very soothing to a sore throat. In addition, an effective external remedy is the cold-water compress: Dip a large cotton handkerchief in cold tap water, wring it out, fold lengthwise, and wrap around the throat. Fold a dry cotton dish cloth or hand towel in the same way and place it over the handkerchief, securing them in place with a woolen scarf that covers everything. The handkerchief will get warm from the body heat, which is fine. The compress should be left on for a minimum of two and a maximum of four hours. Then it can be either renewed or removed altogether.

Earaches

In Chinese medicine, the ear and the kidney are related; that is, disturbances in the ear reflect imbalances in the kidney-adrenal system. This concept gets some support from Western science, which has determined that, in the embryo, the ear and the kidney develop at about the same time and eventually turn out to be of similar shape and size. In my experience, the major causes for ear infections are:

- Dairy foods, such as milk, cheese, and ice cream
- A high-protein diet

The first one is by far the most common cause of ear problems in our society, especially with young children. The most effective short-term remedies are the following:

For mild earaches:
- Dairy-free vegetarian diet for at least a few days.
- Hot compress on the ear—a washcloth wrung out in very hot water, plus a woolen hat over it to keep it in place. This one works very well in the middle of the night when both parent and child want to go back to sleep.

For more severe earaches and ear infections:
- Shoyu-kuzu with umeboshi (page 255) once or twice a day for two days.
- Vegetarian chicken soup (page 253), grains, and vegetables; include ginger, garlic, and radishes in the meals (page 253).
- No dairy or animal protein.
- Hot compress on the kidney: Prepare a pot of very hot water, and make eucalyptus tea (use a handful of eucalyptus leaves tied in a cheesecloth for two quarts of hot water), or ginger tea (use a handful of grated ginger tied in a cheesecloth for two quarts of water). Take a dish towel and fold it lengthwise so that you have a four- to five-inch-wide strip. Hold it by the ends, dip the middle in the pot, wring out by twisting well, and place it on the back above the waist. It should be as hot as can be taken without undue discomfort. (CAUTION: DO NOT USE THIS COMPRESS ON PEOPLE WHO CANNOT ARTICULATE HOW THINGS FEEL TO THEM, such as infants, older people, or very sick people.) Place a couple of dry towels on top, changing the compress every two minutes or whenever it cools, for a total of twenty minutes. Do once a day for three days.
- In the case of infection, if the ear is discharging pus and fluids, place a cold compress (a washcloth wrung out in cold tap water) on the mastoid bone behind the ear, to keep the infection from spreading.

- Using a bulb syringe, wash out the ear with lukewarm chamomile tea.

If the earache lasts more than two days, or if it causes crying or extreme discomfort, consult a specialist. In the case of a persistent earache but no accompanying feeling of sickness, fever, or lack of appetite, don't overlook the possibility that there is a foreign object in the ear, such as a stone or insect. Neither hot compresses nor antibiotics are effective against an earache caused by a bedbug.

Skin Problems

In a systems view of the body, input of all kinds relates to output of all kinds. Food, therefore, would have a definite relationship to matter pushed out through the skin. I am continually amazed that dermatologists persist in viewing the skin as merely a protective envelope for the body, ascribing its eruptions to "viruses" and imprecise malfunctions and supporting the myth that "diet has nothing to do with acne."

In my experience, diet has everything to do with acne. Not only did I fix my own bad skin through correct eating but I have seen among my students a number of severe cases—the large purplish kind of acne on cheeks and chins—*completely cured* within three months by a change of diet.

The systems perspective that views the skin as an organ of elimination, as a "third lung" or a "third kidney," is much more useful and accurate than the one that sees it as separate from the rest of the body system. Toxic matter that is not eliminated through normal channels will often find its way out through the skin. Treating these discharges with external applications of chemical potions is seldom effective; lightening the load of the inner organs through a change in diet, on the other hand, can work wonders within ten days to three months.

Like many a teenager in our milk-and-sugar culture, I've had my share of skin problems. Thus, I've studied the subject at length. According to my observations (limited by my daily experience, which does not include rare and serious illnesses), there are at least three causes of skin disorders:

- Fat, protein, and sugar excess
- Mineral-water excess
- Organ malfunction (usually kidney or lung)

The simplest way to deal with skin discharges is by eliminating the cause, or the input that brings them about; then the skin will heal itself naturally. *Abstention* from certain foods becomes medicinal. Let's examine each of the three causes individually.

Fat-and-protein combinations are the most common cause of skin discharge in the form of fatty pimples, acne, and boils. If the body is overloaded with mucus and/or fat deposits, the kidneys, liver, and digestive organs cannot keep up with the disposal work, and the body therefore expels the stuff via the skin.* The foods responsible are usually milk, cheese, ice cream, fatty meats, nuts, and peanut butter. Those affected are not only people eating the SAD: I often see people who turn vegetarian increase their intake of cheese and nuts to "get enough protein," only to find themselves with skin problems they never had before. Sugar plays a role in that it appears to trigger the process, either by depressing the immune system, or because its expansive energy pushes the excess out.

According to Michio Kushi, excess protein and fats are also discharged in the form of warts, moles, callouses, and tumors. However, I find that these conditions can also at times point to a malfunction of protein metabolism. Beauty spots, freckles, and brown moles may be the result of too much sugar attracted to the surface of the skin by the heat of the sun.[17]

Sugar, especially in the form of fruit sugar, can make the blood smell sweet and attractive to insects and fungi. Thus, insect bites and fungal infections respond well to the elimination of sweet juices, and fruit, and to local applications of a natural antibiotic such as miso, green clay,† or brown-rice vinegar.

Excess fats can also affect the overall texture of the skin, making it oily or, surprisingly, very dry. Skin becomes oily when fat is discharged through large pores. Dry skin, which appears often with fine-grained complexions, is caused when fats accumulate under the skin and thus prevent the body's natural moisture from reaching the surface. Lowering dietary fat intake can therefore improve both oily and dry, cracked skin. However, dry skin can also be caused by an insufficient amount of fats in the diet.

Mineral-matter excess is a catchall category. I include in it all substances taken out of their natural context, such as extracts,

* It's interesting that the *A.M.A. Family Medical Guide* describes the content of boils as "cheesy."[16]

† Obtainable in health food stores.

concentrates, and anything in pill form. Salt, especialy iodized salt, also falls into this category. When the body cannot process these substances naturally, it will push them out through the skin. I've experienced this many a time. For example, when I first found out that seaweed is a good source of minerals, I decided to take kelp tablets, a concentrated natural source of those minerals, instead of eating the seaweed itself, for I had discovered, to my chagrin, that I didn't like the taste of it. Within a few days I had developed painful welts all over my arms, which disappeared as soon as I stopped taking the kelp. Kelp is implicated in acne because of its iodide content, and iodide irritates the pores' lining as it is excreted through the skin. Multivitamins and iodized salt can also cause problems for the acne-prone.[18]

Another example: My eldest daughter, when she was nineteen months old, suffered smoke inhalation due to a fire and was given steroids and other medication to combat the fluid accumulation in her lungs. When she was taken off the medications, she discharged those substances via a red pimply rash from her waist all the way down to her toes. And you may remember the case mentioned earlier of the young woman who had tiny painful pimples all over her chin, like a beard, which disappeared as soon as she stopped taking her twenty daily vitamin supplements.

The severe, purplish acne that develops on cheeks or chin seems to be related also to the intake of artificial sweeteners, especially in the form of soda pop, in addition to ice cream and peanut butter. At least I've seen it disappear when those foods were removed from the diet.

Pimples, welts, or rashes from mineral-matter excess can be recognized easily: They hurt if you press them with a finger (presumably because minerals are hard and crystalline and thus irritate the skin). They tend to be red and open, perhaps weeping, rather than pus-filled or fatty. The only true way to heal them is to discontinue the input of the substance being discharged. Clay poultices may help speed the discharge.

Some deep-seated mineral matter, often from drugs, strong medications, or artificial substances, can be pulled to and through the skin by the heat of the sun. The heat opens the pores and causes blood and fluids to expand and rise to the surface; this, in turn, can bring useless or toxic substances with it, attempting to expel the latter from the body. In some cases this could give rise to irritations or diseases, including skin cancer, which appears to be "caused" by the sun. But not all committed sunbathers get cancer, nor do all skin cancer sufferers lie regularly in the sun. Therefore, perhaps we should consider the possibility that the sun only causes skin diseases if the body gives it something to work with.

Organ malfunctions, or general metabolic imbalances, can manifest themselves in the form of chronic skin conditions, such as psoriasis, eczema, and other scaly, itchy, or weepy conditions. Allergic reactions and nutritional-deficiency symptoms also belong in this category. A switch to a simple, natural diet of whole grains, beans, and cooked vegetables, avoiding meats, milk products, refined sugar and grains, an excess of fruit, nut butters, and alcohol, often brings on almost miraculous cures as the body rebalances itself.

A word of caution: In certain cases, dietary management alone is not sufficient to heal skin problems, and other methods must be called upon. Each stubborn or complicated case should be evaluated individually and treated by a competent healer. It is beyond the scope of this book to deal specifically with anything other than simple everyday problems.*

Hair and Nails

These extensions of the skin are supposedly "dead," yet hair can be lustrous or dull, nails strong or brittle, a fact that suggests that there still is life—that is, the ability to change—in them. Because they grow and change, and because they are a form of output, we can affect their condition by varying the input. It may take time to see results, but there will definitely be results.

- Fuzzy, unruly, brittle hair on top front of the head—or at times all over—usually appears in people who consume considerable amounts of sugar, fruit, juices (including orange juice), raw vegetables, and/or smoke marijuana. Split ends (an expansive phenomenon) is another effect of these expansive foods.
- Loss of hair can be the result of various situations. On the crown, it may be from an excess of contractive foods, such as meat and salt. At the front of the head it could be from

* For a more detailed examination of skin disorders, see Michio Kushi's *How to See Your Health.*

expansive foods and drinks, as mentioned previously. Allover gradual thinning can be caused by faulty protein metabolism, malabsorption or lack of zinc, or possibly by some sluggishness or malfunction in the intestines.

Faulty protein metabolism that leads to hair loss can be the result of:

- Insufficient protein, too much sugar, or insufficient animal food (for those who are unable to absorb all the nutrients and protein they need from vegetarian sources). *Remedy:* Eat more beans, eggs, fish, chicken, even beef in some cases. Eliminate sugar.
- Uncomplemented vegetable proteins (too much grain and not enough beans; or too many vegetables, fruit, and nuts and not enough beans and grain; or too many beans and insufficient grain). *Remedy:* Pay more attention to complementary proteins, increasing beans, seeds, or grain, as needed.
- Too much protein, not enough minerals. *Remedy:* Add sea vegetables to the diet, decrease animal protein foods.
- Too many minerals, and proportionately insufficient protein (normal absorption of protein may be hampered when it's out of proportion with minerals; see chapter regarding nutrient proportions). *Remedy:* Increase protein intake and reduce seaweed, salt, or mineral supplements.

I have seen dramatic changes in the luster and quality of hair of some of my students as they changed from a diet high in meat, sugar, fruit juices, and dairy to one rich in whole grains, beans, fresh vegetables, and sea vegetables. Dull, frizzy, brittle hair became shiny and heavy. Most amusing is the stage when the new hair coming in is of that beautiful quality and has already grown three or four inches, and the rest of the hair is its old brittle self. One can actually see the change in diet, and in health, chronicled in the hair shaft.

Oily hair and dandruff are usually related to the intake of fats, milk, cheese, and ice cream. Reducing the intake of these foods and increasing salads and cooked vegetables usually brings improvement. (Dry hair and scalp can also be the result of too much fat in the diet, as is the case with dry skin generally (see page 273); dehydration may be another cause.)

The condition of the nails is affected by many internal factors, among them:

- Improper protein and calcium balance. *Remedy:* Increase protein and mineral intake: seaweed, fish, eggs.
- Dehydration. *Remedy:* Increase liquid intake.
- Stress (which may affect calcium balance). *Remedy:* Overcome stress with rest and relaxation.
- Excess expansive, sour foods, including vinegar, citrus and lemon juice. *Remedy:* Reduce the intake of sugar, salad dressings with vinegar, fruits, and fruit juices.
- Excess salt. *Remedy:* Reduce salt intake, increase fruit.

If the approach selected is the correct one, results will be noticeable in one to two weeks.

Digestive Problems

GENERAL DIGESTIVE DISTRESS
In order to keep ourselves balanced, as we have already established, we need to work with opposite forces. You will be able to appreciate just how effective this approach is if you put it to work after some enjoyable gastronomic excess that leaves you tottering the morning after. Here is a list of various food excesses and how you can balance them within one hour to two days if there is digestive distress:

IF YOU HAVE HAD TOO MUCH	NEUTRALIZE IT WITH
Fats, oily food	Radishes; lemon tea; peppermint tea with lemon
Acid-forming food	Vegetarian chicken soup; miso soup (best antidote to sweets); vegetable juice (best for flour and animal-protein excess)
Alcohol	Umeboshi (plum with pit if possible, or paste); gomasio (sesame salt)
Sugar	Miso soup; tamari kuzu with umeboshi; umeboshi paste
Fruit, salad, raw food	Roasted rice or rice cream; oatmeal, seasoned with shoyu or umeboshi vinegar; beans; millet or other grains; whole-grain bread

IF YOU HAVE HAD TOO MUCH	NEUTRALIZE IT WITH
Meats, eggs, cheese	Fruit; vegetable soup or stew; salads
Food	One day of fasting, with your favorite kuzu drink in the morning, and either vegetable juice or vegetarian chicken soup the rest of the day if desired. (See page 257 in this chapter for more on fasting.)

CONSTIPATION

Of all body parts, the colon seems to be the one that is most often the object of obsession. There is some good reason for that: If the garbage is not thrown out regularly, the house will be unclean no matter how stylish the living room. Most of us feel good if we have one easy bowel movement daily, although what is a healthy frequency will vary depending on the individual and the food intake. When the movement is significantly less frequent or involves difficulty and straining, alarm signals go off, and we try to fix the situation.

The large intestine operates by a rhythmic alternation of expansion and contraction. If it becomes very contracted and tight, it cannot expand and therefore stops working. If it becomes expanded and loose, it cannot contract, and the same thing happens. Thus, we can recognize two kinds of constipation: constipation from excess contraction, and constipation from excess expansion.

Constipation from contraction is caused by eating too much:
- Protein
- Fats
- Salt
- White flour

Generally, it responds well to
- Prune juice, salad, sprouts, fresh fruit
- Coffee, sometimes (although this is not a remedy I would recommend)
- Whole grains, well chewed, especially brown rice

Constipation from expansion is usually the result of consuming too much fruit, juices, and salads, as in some health diets. The standard way of treating constipation that does not respond to

prune juice is with laxatives or enemas. Pleasanter methods include:
- Increasing consumption of whole grains (especially brown rice), with their naturally occurring bran, and fibrous vegetables; and
- Decreasing intake of raw foods and juices.

For people who feel very blocked and stagnated, a few enemas or colonic irrigations may be of great help. However, it is not advisable to have these more than occasionally, as they can become habit forming and weaken the colon's normal peristaltic activity.[19] Irrigations also wash out the helpful intestinal flora, along with everything else, and these may take a while to become reestablished. In general, one of the best and most natural stimuli for proper intestinal function is a brisk walk, especially early in the morning.

DIARRHEA
A sudden and continuous diarrhea, if it lasts longer than an hour and especially if accompanied by vomiting, is a critical condition requiring immediate medical attention; dysentery, cholera, and toxic-shock syndrome all exhibit those symptoms, and fatal dehydration can set in quickly.

A mild diarrhea, however, if it occurs rarely and lasts no more than three or four days cleans out the system and is to be considered a temporary discharge. It is best left alone. If it lasts more than three days or so, it is becoming more of a malfunction. There are two very effective old remedies for this:

- Cooked white rice;
- Grated apple with skin, allowed to turn brown.

INFLAMMATION
In problems of inflammation of the digestive tract, such as ulcers, colitis, spastic colon, and so on, abstinence from raw vegetables and fruits is usually very helpful. One of my students, sent to me by her doctor, had a serious case of *reflux esophagitis*, which gave her attacks of palpitations and breathlessness similar to heart attacks. She invariably had one if she ate a large salad, but did fine, as we soon discovered, with cooked vegetables, grains, and beans—she even lost twenty-five pounds on this regime! Cases of colitis have also responded well to all-cooked-food diets, if they

included a high proportion of alkalizing foods such as cooked vegetables and soups; small amounts of beans, brown rice, and millet; maybe a bit of fish. Miso soup with seaweed and shoyu-kuzu are good support foods in these cases as well.

Kuzu, incidentally, is my preferred universal remedy for disorders of the digestive tract. I find that shoyu-kuzu on an empty stomach is excellent for cases of expansion, gassiness, or even bleeding ulcers.

Shoyu-kuzu with umeboshi (good as an antacid) is helpful for indigestion or overeating.

Apple-juice kuzu pudding (a relaxing concoction) helps counterbalance contraction, tightness, cramping, as well as tension, anger, and irritability.

In serious, persistent cases of digestive disorder, the kuzu should be taken first thing in the morning and just before retiring. Milder cases do well with kuzu once a day. My children, if they've eaten out too much and feel a bit under the weather, may refuse dinner and ask for a bowl of shoyu-kuzu with umeboshi; then they are fine the next morning.

The most important thing to remember in cases of ulcers at any point of the digestive tract is that they are a problem of excess acidity and therefore must be treated with alkalizing foods. The large amounts of milk and cream often used to treat ulcers would have an acidifying effect because of their high protein and fat content. Thus, in addition to avoiding milk and cream, it would be wise for ulcer patients to avoid acid-forming foods in general, such as meats, eggs, flour products, sugar and sweets, alcohol, and fats. They should also keep their grain intake low, chew everything thoroughly, and follow a dietary approach like the one indicated above for colitis.

Eating Disorders

Our appetite system consists of our taste and smell sensations, bodily feelings that indicate desire for food and drink, satiety, and so on. This system is the sentinel at the gates of our stomach, ideally allowing only healthful substances in and keeping noxious ones out.

It is a system both effective and efficient, as it has kept the human species alive for a few million years. In the past hundred or so, however, there have been some changes in our food supply that have wreaked havoc with the ability of our appetite system to understand what we're eating.

The most obvious of these changes has been the splitting up of foodstuffs into their separate chemical components. Extraction, concentration, isolation, and similar technological maneuvers have yielded nutritive substances that are out of context: white flour, white sugar, juices, soy-protein isolates, individual vitamins and minerals, and so on. Their wide use has completely changed the common diet of the Western world and is fast changing that of the rest.

These partial foods—as opposed to whole foods, such as whole wheat bread, sugar cane, fruit, whole soybeans—create relative deficiencies of the elements they don't have; for example, sugar, a pure carbohydrate, sets up a vitamin deficiency, among other things. As the body perceives itself unevenly nourished, it keeps on looking for the elements it needs to balance itself and therefore "gets the munchies." White bread and jam create a need for protein, fiber, and minerals; a potato chip and ice cream binge may be the attempt to meet that need.

In addition, the appetite is further confused by the increased use of chemical additives, whether they're made from petroleum or isolated from natural substances. Some foods that would normally be spoiled don't taste spoiled, others taste like what they're not, and some that are in fact harmful seem delicious. How's a body to know what to eat?

An increasingly common condition with varying degrees of severity, eating disorders indicate, above all, a breakdown of the appetite system's ability to monitor food intake. Hunger, in a body fed isolated foodstuffs, becomes unreliable or even disappears. One specific episode illustrated this phenomenon for me most dramatically.

Some months ago, my friend Judy was complaining about her insatiable hunger. "No matter what I eat," she said, "I'm hungry after every meal. I feel unsatisfied, and go munching on chips or crackers or whatever. And I know I don't need it! I just can't help myself. Do you have any thoughts on this?" I did indeed, for I'd seen many of my students go through the same experience and had found my solution to be amazingly effective: Look for the unbalanced food element and eliminate it. It's usually either sugar or supplements; second-level culprits are white flour and juices in large amounts. I knew that Judy didn't eat sweets except perhaps at a party. "Do you take vitamins?" I asked. "Of course," she said; they had not been prescribed. I suggested she eliminate them for a while and see if that made a difference.

That same evening in class, Maria, one of my students, mentioned that she was never hungry. "I eat because it's time, because I know I should, because I'm with others . . . but never because I'm hungry," she said. As she looked to be in reasonably good shape, not too thin nor too heavy, I was puzzled. I questioned her about her intake of food and found that she was eating mostly natural, wholesome foods, hardly any sweets, adequate amounts of protein—no problem there. I couldn't find the logic for a disappearance of the appetite. Finally, I asked whether she took vitamins, and yes, she did. I suggested she eliminate them for a while and see what happened.

A week later, while we were chatting about something else, Judy said to me, "By the way, it worked. My appetite is back to normal since I stopped the vitamins. I don't get the munchies anymore." Her experience had been the same as that of numbers of my students who had been in a similar situation and followed my suggestion.

That evening in class, Maria blurted out, "Guess what happened to me today!" "What?" chorused the class. She was obviously excited. "I *got hungry!* I actually woke up ravenous. Boy, did I enjoy breakfast!" We figured that the vitamins—superfluous in her well-balanced natural diet—had confused her appetite enough to keep it from signaling when it was time to go for real food.

There are many psychological components, usually associated with body image, in the more serious and chronic eating disorders such as anorexia and bulimia; it is not within the scope of this book to examine them. I also suspect that harsh birthing practices, bottle-feeding, a high sugar intake early in life, and perhaps even erroneous medication may all have some role in these conditions.

In terms of diet, a number of my students with bulimia—the binge-vomit syndrome—have found that consuming only whole foods, with special attention to complex carbohydrates such as grains and beans, has been very helpful. They don't feel stuffed eating that way and are better able to make the psychological adjustments that allow them to accept nourishment without guilt and the consequent compulsion to force vomiting. However, even the smallest bite of something with refined sugar can make them feel unstable again. For a sweet taste, they rely on orange vegetables such as yams, pumpkin, and winter squash, as well as cooked fruit desserts. They have also reported feeling better eating only small amounts of animal food, and not every day.

Anorexia, the pathological lack of appetite, is among other things a deep-seated fear of food; this can mean all food, or simply "unhealthy" food. True anorexics usually don't show up in my classes until after they've made the commitment to change, so my experience with them is limited, at best. I encountered a few cases in which a desire to eat healthfully had rigidified into a severely restricted way of eating; then, when the intellect dictated foods that the body wasn't attracted to, the appetite closed down and *all* food lost its appeal. Students in that situation responded very well to emphasis on sensory delight and the idea that food is our helper rather than our master, still within the context of healthful, but not rigid, eating.

Female Disorders

Without going into clinical detail, I can safely say that the first treatment for women with problems of the reproductive system is strictly to avoid all foodstuffs that relate to the reproductive system of animals or contain natural or artificial hormones. This includes milk and all milk products (they're a product of the cow's reproductive system), eggs (a product of the chicken's reproductive system), and the meat of animals that have been raised on estrogens. See chapter fourteen, "The Effects of Food on Sex," for a more extensive discussion.

In my experience, such abstentions, coupled with a hearty health-supportive diet, have helped ameliorate symptoms in cases of PMS, periodic swelling and tenderness of the breasts, cysts, tumors, discharges, endometriosis, and infertility. Endometriosis is further helped by sexual abstinence during menstruation. It seems that coitus can push the secretions back up and through the fallopian tubes into the pelvic cavity. This endometrial tissue then remains there and causes acute pain and discomfort. Orthodox Jewish women, whose traditional customs keep them from having intercourse while they show the least bit of bleeding, have an extremely low incidence of endometriosis. The time frame for the reversal of these conditions seems to be from one month to eighteen months, depending on the severity of the problem.

SERIOUS ILLNESS

In this category I would like to place, first, those conditions that involve substantial accumulation of matter, malfunction, and structural change of the organs (cancer, advanced hardening of the arteries, cirrhosis of the liver, tuberculosis, Bright's disease, advanced arthritis) and second, the insidious autoimmune diseases of neurological disintegration that are becoming increasingly frequent (Alzheimer's, ALS, multiple sclerosis, AIDS, rheumatoid arthritis, and similar problems).

Can a change in diet, or a cleansing fast, heal these disorders?

Many books have been written attempting to answer that question affirmatively, offering many different dietary systems, with or without additional medicines, herbs, supplements, and physical therapies. Each of these systems can point to a number of successful cures, at times well publicized. As with conventional medicine, the failures are not counted and not reported. Perhaps we'd do well to keep in mind Ohsawa's maxim: "All diseases can be cured, but not all people."

From what I've been able to discern, some diseases of accumulation, such as arthritis, cardiovascular problems, and early cancers, can and do respond well to changes in diet. The no-nightshades diet (see page 178), regardless of the disdain of official medicine, seems to be extremely effective for arthritic conditions, joint pains, and bursitis. The no-salt, no-fat approach is widely successful in treating accumulations in the blood vessels. Metabolic healing systems and macrobiotics point to a significant number of cancer cures, collectively as high as, if not higher than, those claimed by standard medicine.*

Unfortunately, I have not heard of any sustained success with dietary management for the disorders of neurological degeneration such as Parkinson's, MS, Alzheimer's, or Gehrig's disease (amyotrophic lateral sclerosis). After all the research I have done on dietary systems, I've come to the conclusion that improper food

* These are the systems delineated, respectively, by Norman F. Childers, Nathan Pritikin, Max Gerson, William Donald Kelly, and George Ohsawa. Incidentally, the *New York Times* has reported that a growing number of medical analysts are challenging the official position that great strides have been made in the cure of cancer by chemotherapy and radiation. In the opinion of Hayan Bush, director of a cancer center in Ontario, "We're not curing much more cancer now than we were a generation ago."[20]

is probably not the direct cause of these problems. They seem to arise, rather, after frequent suppression by chemical means of the minor imbalances and discharges caused by improper diet; among the most common of these is that of indigestion relieved by commercial antacids. I know of at least three cases, two of ALS and one of Alzheimer's, in which the patient consumed an over-the-counter antacid preparation daily for ten to twenty years. A possible culprit is aluminum, a heavy metal present in many of those medications;[21] this substance has apparently been detected, upon autopsy, in the brain tissue of patients with Alzheimer's disease. (Other common sources of aluminum include commercial salt if it includes sodium silico aluminate, baking powder and therefore all baked goods that contain it, antiperspirants, and aluminum cookware.)

It is my belief that the widespread use of antibiotics and vaccinations is probably among the main causes of immune system disorders.[22] As the defender and guardian of our body integrity, the immune system has as its main job to distinguish between self and nonself; it will therefore attack, destroy, and expel foreign bodies such as bacteria, viruses, grafts, and transplants (unless it is suppressed). In cases of disorder (allergies, asthma, lupus erythematosus, rheumatoid arthritis, cancer, AIDS, and many others), the immune system actually makes a mistake and attacks the body's own tissues.

When we add them all up, autoimmune disorders are probably the epidemic of our times, as a large proportion of the population suffers from at least one of these problems chronically. As a majority of the population of the Western world is also routinely immunized and frequently treated with antibiotics, both medical interventions that meddle with the immune system, I see a definite connection.*

Several cases appear to support this connection. All the people I've seen with AIDS also had an extensive history of antibiotic use. One of my students was diagnosed as suffering from lupus erythematosus, an autoimmune disorder; we traced the timing of her attacks and found that each and every one of them came right after a cold that had been treated with antibiotics. Another woman

* According to Robert Mendelsohn, M.D., "There is a growing suspicion that immunization against relatively harmless childhood diseases may be responsible for the dramatic increase in autoimmune diseases since mass inoculations were introduced."[23]

with melanoma and a brain tumor had had throughout her life a fair number of smallpox and other vaccinations due to her frequent travels abroad. A beautiful young girl developed MS a few months after a series of smallpox vaccinations that were given to try to "boost" her immune system; she tried every dietary and herbal cure on earth to stem the inexorable disease; but none worked. My heart ached as I saw her come to my classes each time weaker and weaker, and finally in a wheelchair, unable to focus her eyes or to write.

I think it's not unreasonable to suspect that all the tampering and the "boosting" and the chemical intervention in the immune system can cause that damage. When the damage is minor, a healing diet can allow self-healing to proceed. Unfortunately, when the immune system is seriously damaged by medication, it is often extremely difficult—though not impossible—to repair body function with food, for the efficacy of food as a medicine hinges solely on its ability to support and stimulate the immune system.

It never hurts, of course, to clean up the diet even if it seems unlikely that such a change will cure a major illness. If you've been eating much meat, sugar, fats, dairy, commercially prepared and salted foods, with few fresh vegetables or whole grains, a switch to a nondairy vegetarian, macrobiotic, or whole-grain regime will certainly help the organism clean itself up as much as possible. At least you will be assured that you're not continuing to make things worse. You may experience some surprising remissions or disappearances of long-standing small annoyances, such as dandruff or insomnia or hives. Pain, of any kind, will most often be alleviated.

Even when the outlook is grim, miracles are possible. All cures or long-lasting remissions of severe life-threatening illnesses as an apparent result of diet that have come to my attention include a profound change on the emotional-spiritual level, and a subsequent total change in the individual's attitude toward life. In cases of serious illness, the best diet in the world is only minimally effective without that inner change.

In Conclusion

If we panic at a headache or fever and suppress them with aspirin, if we worry about a minor infection and cart out the antibiotic artillery, we often get ourselves into a worse state simply out of fear. But if we welcome minor disturbances as early warning signals pointing out our mistakes and learn to interpret them, we will have plenty of time to make corrections and thereby avoid the escalation and aggravation of our health problems.

Because the body tends to heal itself if allowed to do so, most of the time all we have to do is get out of the way and let it carry on. Thus, through rest, fasting, appropriate food selection, and a few gentle nudges from natural remedies, we can easily regain our equilibrium and thereby stand a good chance of functioning joyfully and actively for many years.

Of course there are many of us who have made many mistakes and brought ourselves into a serious condition of ill health. If that is the case, it is no use feeling guilty; let us view the result of our actions as information rather than punishment. The best thing, then, is to undertake some lifestyle changes so as to avoid making things worse: change your diet, exercise, meditate, pay attention. In other words, become conscious. The approach to healing outlined in this book as a whole will cause no further harm, and quite possibly may help. However, food, or remedies, don't heal: If appropriate, they only allow the body to heal itself; or, if inappropriate, they may prevent it from doing so. That is why you will find no panacea here, no magic potion or elixir that will set everything aright, no single substance or remedy that will bring eternal deliverance from pain. There are only various ways of rebalancing the complex system that is our body, and it is up to each one of us to discover and make use of the ones that will be relevant and helpful to our own lives.

Thirteen:
The Effects of Food
on Mood

Not only could the absence of certain nutritional factors vitally impair mental health, but the excess of some of these very same factors in certain persons could also vitally impair mental health.
—George Watson, *Nutrition and Your Mind*

Psychosomatic illness, a long-accepted category of modern medicine and psychology, is one in which bodily dysfunction is seen as caused by mental or emotional conditions, rather than by a "virus," "bacteria," or other external physical causes, known or unknown. Unfortunately, if the physical illness appears to stem from mental causes, it is usually dismissed as somewhat "unreal," and so unworthy of attention. "It's all in your mind" is both a brush-off and a statement of ignorance.

All that is "in your mind" manifests itself via the body. Laughing, crying, blushing, shaking—all are physical reactions caused by mental or emotional states. This we know. Also, the notion that feelings are stored and experienced in the body, rather than in the "mind," has become the basis for such successful holistic therapies as rolfing and bioenergetics.[1]

But the reverse is equally true: Bodily conditions affect mental or emotional states with similar intensity. For example, hunger can cause crankiness, lack of sleep makes it difficult to concentrate, diuretics and a host of other pills can cause depression and suicidal tendencies.

When a destructive or overwhelming mood hits, it's not always necessarily psychological in origin. There is medical research indicating that substances in food or in the environment, including many modern household products, can cause brain-sensitivity reactions, producing fatigue, irritability, headaches, listlessness, anxiety, depression, and even psychotic behavior.[2] Another researcher suggests that in the case of unusual mental or emotional reactions we look at the following four areas:[3]

- Improper or inadequate nutrition
- Drugs, poisons, allergies, or infections
- Stress—expending energy beyond one's biochemical limits
- Lack of sleep, resulting in failure to repair tissues

Mood, it becomes clear, can be one of the first indicators that something is out of kilter with us. In keeping with the focus of this book, let's look at the first area mentioned above, from a systems viewpoint.

Body/mind is an infinity loop:*

Body   Mind

If there is anything we want to change, we can start at any point in this continuum and proceed from there: psychoanalysis, meditation, or seminars such as est or Relationships can help us lose weight, breathe more deeply, improve our digestion. Because we are rooted in the material world, however, it is usually easiest for us to manipulate physical things such as food. A change in diet, which can be embarked upon at any time, at any hour of the day, can make us feel more centered, improve our disposition and concentration, and even increase our joyfulness and good cheer.

If you feel depressed, yet nothing has actually *happened* that could have caused you to feel that way, and talking about it doesn't help, the cause may well be physical or physiological. Only a physiological approach would then be of help.

---

* As Marilyn Ferguson has said, "Intervention anywhere in the dynamic body/ mind loop affects the whole."[4]

For example, I had a call recently from Y., one of my cheeriest students. She called me, she sobbed, because "I've been lying on my bed all morning thinking of ways to kill myself." First I thought she was playing a joke on me, but after a few more sentences like that, I realized she was truly depressed. I thought something terrible must have happened, but when I asked, she said, "Nothing. Everything is fine. I don't know where this is coming from."

That response made me think that the problem was physical—which I tend to think of first anyway. I feel that with mental distress you should first clean up physiological imbalances, and then, if some distress still remains, you can deal with that core problem directly and efficiently through psychological means. As Y.'s depression had come on suddenly, it could have been an allergy response; apparently she used to get these attacks of the blues years ago, when she used to eat lots of chocolate. And indeed, she had had some chocolate the night before for the first time in years. For breakfast she had had some oatmeal and raisins—carbohydrates and a sweet taste, expansive, and not at all a balance for highly expansive chocolate.

Depression is a feeling of losing one's ground, losing grasp of reality, being unconnected, uncentered. It could also be classified as expansive. So I suggested to Y. that she go to the kitchen and take a good lick of salty umeboshi plum paste. The effect of umeboshi is instantly tightening and centering because of the salt, waking one up, so to speak. (If she hadn't had umeboshi in the house, I would have suggested Greek olives, anchovies, salami, brine pickles, or any other salt-cured food.) I've used umeboshi very successfully to snap my children out of crying jags, for example.

By the time Y. came back to the phone, she had already stopped crying. We talked some more, I told her to take a few more licks of the paste, and within a few minutes she sounded almost like her old self. "I feel much better now," she said, and I could tell by her voice that it was true. Then I suggested that she have some fish or chicken for lunch and that she stay away from sweets of any kind for a while. By the time we hung up, I was satisfied that she was quite out of the hole. The entire conversation didn't take more than fifteen or twenty minutes. I spoke to her again a week later, and she had been perfectly fine. She is also staying away from chocolate.

The most common foods to cause mental disturbances are sugar, milk, and milk products. Negative reactions to milk have often been called allergies, implying that these are isolated, abnormal cases. I would like to submit that negative reactions to milk products, including emotional reactions such as depression, weepiness, and feelings of helplessness and inability to cope, are so widespread that they almost could be considered the norm. The reactions are intensified when the diet also includes sugar.

Sugar is very closely linked to feelings of alienation, despair, and depression. As we saw in chapter six, sugar strengthens feelings of individuality; when those feelings are taken to an extreme, individuality becomes aloneness and alienation. I hope the day will come when, if we suffer from any of these feelings, we'll all know to first stop eating cake, ice cream, candy, pastries, chocolate, sugared cereals, and so on. Then we will wait four days, and only then, if the feelings still persist unabated, accept them as psychologically generated and explore them through therapy.

Wheat, once revered as the staff of life, now causes unpleasant allergic reactions in many people, often in the form of moodiness and depression. Obviously, wheat today is not what it once was. Perhaps the agricultural growing methods currently in use, which involve considerable use of pesticides and chemical fertilizers, might be part of the problem. I've not run across any research done on this subject, but you may want to keep this in mind if you consume large quantities of wheat products, such as bread, noodles, and crackers. If wheat is consumed with sugar, as it would be in the case of cakes, cookies, or pastries, it would make sense to eliminate the sugar first—and dairy too, if used—before the wheat is accused and found guilty.

For more detailed information and guidelines about the effects of various foods on mood, please turn to chapter six. The chart on the next page, however, will give you a quick and handy overview of what moods may be related to which food excesses or deficiencies. It's up to you to decide where the shoe fits, if anywhere. The chart is a map of possibilities,* not of fixed and immutable facts. You must experiment to see where, when, and to what degree the guidelines apply to your personal condition.

---

* Based on Five-phase theory and my own observations.

FOOD AND MOOD CHART

Mood	See If the Diet Has a Lot Of	And/or Not Enough Of	Possible Quick Remedy	Organs Involved (Five-phase Theory)
Depression, melancholy	Sugar, honey, maple syrup; milk and milk products; allergenic foods; over 70 percent grains	Beans, fish, fowl, meat, whole grains	Something salty: umeboshi, olives, anchovies. Also aromatic spices	Lungs, large intestines, adrenal insufficiency
Fear	As above; also, meat, fats	Brown rice, barley, beans, cooked vegetables	Apple juice kuzu (if tension); shoyu-umeboshi-kuzu (if uncentered)	Kidney-adrenals, weakness in the heart
Anger, short temper	Fats, salt, brown rice, cheese, meat, fried eggs	Salad, sprouts, sour food, kasha, cornmeal	Bananas, fruit juice, apple-juice-kuzu	Liver-gall bladder, weakness in stomach
Overexcitement, excessive laughter; anxiety	Wheat, greens, raw food; stimulants such as coffee, chocolate, alcohol, strong spcies, sugar	Seaweeds, kasha, salty foods, millet	Something salty (see above)	Heart-small intestines, weakness in lungs
Worry; lack of sympathy	Dairy products, sugar, sweets, honey, salads, sour foods	Sweet vegetables, millet, corn, cooked greens, fats, oils	Bread and butter	Stomach-spleen-pancreas; weakness in kidney-adrenals

Fourteen:
The Effects of Food on Sex

Eating can bind a pair together more effectively than sex, simply because people eat more often and predictably than they have sexual relations.
—Peter Farb and George Armelagos,
Consuming Passions: The Anthropology of Eating

LEVELS OF EXPERIENCE

The connection between food and sex is pervasive and intimate. The language and metaphors of love and erotica are heavily dependent on food-related words: *cheesecake, beefcake, I could eat you up, She's a dish, melons, nuts,* and many others with denser second meanings. Sex in some ways entails the incorporating or partaking of a partner's energy; when we eat, we also incorporate an external entity, and so the parallel exists in literal fact as well. This is particularly true for women. Perhaps that is why women who don't have an active or satisfying sex life turn to overeating, thus replacing one type of input with another.

Eating can also be a sociable precursor to sex, as introductory ceremony, or a ritual signifying agreement. It may often be a biological necessity afterward, as people need to replenish the expended calories.

Food relates to sex, then, on several different levels. They are:

- SENSORY: texture, color, taste, aroma, moisture content
- ROMANTIC, SENTIMENTAL: defined by surroundings and memories
- CHEMICAL: nutrients and other chemical substances in foods that have an effect on the reproductive system
- SOCIAL: foods that social beliefs, rituals, and customs decree to be preparatory to, suggestive of, enhancing, or inhibiting sex
- ENERGETIC: foods that relax the body or firm it up, expand or contract it

A distinction can also be made between foods that affect the sex act itself and those that have an effect on reproduction.

Let's examine each of these in turn.

THE SENSORY
Foods can affect sexuality when their appearance or texture are suggestive of the physical aspects of sex. These foods include bananas, carrots, asparagus, fresh ripe figs, and raw foods that drip. Anything eaten with the fingers can be sexy—movies such as *Tom Jones* and *Flashdance* showed scenes in which the act of eating itself was intensely eroticized. Seafoods such as sea urchins, raw oysters, and clams, especially when freshly dug up and immediately eaten, are also highly sensuous and suggestive. (Please note that the levels intersect: Sensuous foods can also have a *chemical* effect on sexual behavior, or a *social* meaning that relates them to sex.)

SENTIMENTAL OR ROMANTIC
A special person, a special place, soft lighting, pleasing music and aromas, can all imbue a meal with the connotations that lead to sex. Any one of the foodstuffs eaten at that time, when encountered at a later date, can have a similar effect simply by remembrance and association.

CHEMICAL
Scientific studies have found that individual foodstuffs have an effect on sexuality via their chemical constituents.

Zinc, the most popularly known of these elements, is an important component of the male ejaculate; its deficiency in men has been associated with infantilism of the sex organs and the loss of sexual potency. Casanova's purported habit of eating fifty oysters as his daily dinner may well have been one of the secrets of his success, for oysters are very rich in zinc.[1] Other sources are the germ and bran of grains, oatmeal, onions, seeds (pumpkin, sesame, sunflower), eggs, herring, liver, and beef. The refining and processing of foods removes this mineral; white flour, polished rice, and sugar all are zinc-deficient. Consuming such refined foods can create a zinc deficiency in the body, which can cause a variety of symptoms, including whitening of the hair and nails, loss of hair, poor circulation, impotence, lack of ovulation or menstruation, psychotic symptoms, slow wound healing, and hyperactivity in children. It must be noted that a habitual diet high in whole grains and low in animal products may also cause, in some cases, eventual signs of zinc deficiency.[2] This is because whole grains contain phytates, a substance that inhibits the absorption of zinc.

Certain foods, such as ginseng and sarsparilla, are known to stimulate the adrenal cortex, which is involved in the production of male sexual hormones. These foods contain elements similar to cortisone. Apparently, in the minuscule quantities in which they appear in these foods, cortisone-like elements stimulate the adrenal cortex. (In larger quantities, as when used as medicine, cortisone has the opposite effect, suppressing the adrenals.) Carrots, yams, and pomegranate seeds have estrogen-related factors and could supplement deficiencies in women.[3]

A lack of substances called histamines, in either blood or tissues, has been linked with an inability to reach orgasm in both men and women.[4] Histamine production appears to be triggered by the presence of folic acid and vitamins B_6 and B_{12}. Foods rich in folic acid include organ meats, asparagus, leafy greens, peanuts, mushrooms, whole-grain cereals, lean beef, and egg yolk—all of which, in one dietary tradition or another, have been considered aphrodisiacs.

Other foods, if eaten in large quantities, may have a cooling effect on sexual ardor. Turnips, kale, cabbage, and soybeans (including tofu) contain traces of antithyroid factors; as the thyroid regulates sexual desire, activity, and fertility, when consumed in large enough quantities these foods could possibly inhibit sexuality by lowering thyroid energy.[5] Oriental folk rumor, which I've been unable to verify, has it that tofu "cools the sex organs" and is used by monks for the specific purpose of aiding them in maintaining celibacy. In this light, it's interesting to note that the traditional Japanese diet, high in thyroid-depressing soybean products, also contains appreciable amounts of seaweeds, rich in thyroid-stimulating iodine.

SOCIAL

Feasts and exchanges of food are an integral part of marriage ceremonies the world over. In Tikopia, one of the Santa Cruz Islands in the Pacific, the ritual includes a meal with unmarried friends; in the Trobriand Islands, there are complex exchanges of food between the two families. In Sri Lanka, when a woman cooks for a man, it indicates that she has a sexual relationship with him, and she refers to her mate as "the one I cook for."[6]

In all traditional cultures it is taken as a matter of course that food affects sexual performance and health. Carrots and leeks were considered "love medicine" by the ancient Greeks; asparagus with egg yolks was a potion recommended in the Arabian *Perfumed Garden for the Soul's Delectation*; seventeenth-century Frenchmen noted that fish and shellfish encourage lovemaking.[7] Other foods considered sexually stimulating include camel's hump and sea slugs (for the Arabs), shark's fin and bird's-nest soup (in China), and prunes (in Elizabethan England). When the potato and tomato were first introduced in Europe, they were considered poisonous; eventually, in a curious switch, they gained a reputation as aphrodisiacs. In our own society, caviar and champagne are the stereotyped seduction foods, and, as we'll see in the next section, the choice is quite reasonable.

ENERGETIC

All of life is an interplay of opposites, powered by the yearning of their ultimate unification. When the outer and the inner, expansion and contraction, become one, time disappears, and we glimpse infinity. The sexual act is perhaps the only moment in which most humans are in fact able to unify these opposites, even if only for a few moments, and, if there is a true union, reach an instant of timelessness and ecstasy.

Sex is an energetic exchange, a delicate balance between expansive and contractive forces. In broad terms, the male embodies expansiveness, because of his external sex organs and his traditional mode of action in the world. The female embodies contractiveness, with her internal sexual organs and her traditional home and child-centered activities. Both the male and the female, however, manifest expansion and contraction during the sex act, and both male and female secrete small amounts of hormones of the opposite sex.

Food affects sexuality because of its own expansive and contractive properties. It is no accident that some classic food combinations of romance combine the extremes of expansiveness and contractiveness: champagne (expansive) and caviar (contractive), for example, or honey and eggs, and beer and oysters. I've even heard of coffee and buckwheat as being particularly effective!

Keeping this in mind, we can see the role of aphrodisiacs in a new light: An aphrodisiac is a substance that will expand and relax someone who is sexually too tight, or contract and strengthen someone who is too spacy and scattered. Aside from their chemical and nutritional components, it may be for that reason that foods as diverse as eggs, fish roe, beef, and hard cheeses (contractive), and asparagus, honey, hot spices, mushrooms, and tomatoes (expansive) have all at one time or another been found to have "aphrodisiac" effects. What many of us have come to dismiss as nonsense makes perfect sense if we accept a broader view of how food affects us.

Because the effect of a food, drink, or herb varies with the condition of the individual, the effectiveness of "aphrodisiacs" is neither universal nor generally testable. Much depends on the customary diet: If you consume two eggs daily, another egg will not necessarily have a sex-enhancing effect. But if you rarely eat them, a single egg may indeed have a powerful influence. Cultural factors must also be taken into account: Europeans will possibly be only minimally sensitive to bird's-nest soup, the traditional Chinese aphrodisiac, while the Masai may shrug off cocoa, a favorite of Aztec lovers.

If there is either too much expansive force or too much contractive, sexual energy and performance are thwarted. For example: Alcohol or "mind-expanding" drugs could, in small and precise measure, help expand and loosen someone who is too tight. In large doses, or if there's not enough contraction or tension to begin with, they'll create so much expansion that the power of contraction is lost, and with it the tension necessary to achieve orgasm. Another example of excessive expansiveness would be a vegetarian dinner of curries, yogurt, ice cream, plus three beers and two glasses of wine—hardly conducive to an amorous night. Circe's meal of cheese and barley, honey and wine, quickly put Odysseus to sleep.

Conversely, meat and eggs, in discreet amounts, may pull together someone whose energy is scattered and unfocused. But as major and steady components of the diet, they can lead to tightness, tension, an inability to relax. (Then a drink or two are needed, and we go around again.) In short, though foods and drinks of extreme expansiveness or contractiveness may, in small amounts, enhance sexual satisfaction, in larger amounts they will reduce it.[8] According to a friend of mine who has had much experience, hamburgers and whisky make for dull sex; she found that the most satisfying encounters come after a few days' fast in the heat of summer, after a meal of fresh fish, fruit, and wine.

Food can work both ways, and at times it may be desirable to cool an overardent lover, or an oversexed teenager. Then such foods as citrus, cucumbers, tofu, raw salads, and cold cooked fruit desserts—baked apples, poached pears—would be the best choice.

Now that we've looked at the various levels on which food and sex relate, let's look at specific foods and diets and their effect on both sexuality and reproductive health.

THE EFFECTS OF VEGETARIANISM

Men's interest in sex, and to a lesser degree that of women, may be reduced or in some cases eliminated by a totally vegetarian diet, a fact quite useful to celibate spiritual groups. This occurs most frequently with vegetarian diets that emphasize expansive foods, such as raw fruits, salads, sweets and baked goods, and perhaps yogurt and cheeses. One medical observer even maintains that vegetarians as a group have a high rate of impotence and problems with libido.[9] A macrobiotic vegetarian diet, on the other hand, which includes enough contractive foods, such as whole grains, beans, and fermented soy products, may prolong endurance and increase sensitivity.

Because animal protein promotes a higher production of sexual secretions,* large amounts of meat daily could lead to a need for more frequent orgasmic release. A vegetarian or semivegetarian regime would therefore prolong endurance, because there would be less stimulus for frequent discharge. We thus have the possibility of choosing the quality of our sexual exchanges: short and

---

* Semen and vaginal lubricants.

frequent, or long and intense, depending on whether we choose to be meat eaters or vegetarians.

THE EFFECTS OF SUGAR AND DAIRY

Of all the foods that may create problems in either sexual performance or the health of the reproductive organs, the two greatest offenders are refined sugar and processed milk products.

There is some evidence that a high consumption of sugar-sweetened foods may lead not only to impotence and premature ejaculation, but to unrealistic sexual attitudes and expectations, strong urges, strange fantasies, and even crimes of sexual violence.[10] This is not as farfetched an idea as at first glance it may appear: Sugar consumption and criminal behavior have been linked by a growing number of researchers.[11] Sugar, especially in men, will also lower the sex drive if it is part of a low-protein diet, and play havoc with performance indirectly by causing diabetes.

The experiences reported by many of my students have convinced me that one of the major dietary factors in female reproductive problems is dairy food. By dairy I mean pasteurized, homogenized, vitamin D—fortified milk, cheeses, ice cream, and even yogurt.

At least one gynecologist has found that the patients with the most severe problems—cysts, tumors, discharges, infections—invariably eat large amounts of milk products.[12] Any problems of accumulation or malfunction of the reproductive organs, in both male and female, would automatically interfere with our vitality and our overall enjoyment of sex.

Yogurt, because of its antibiotic properties, is supposed to help in cases of vaginal infection. Yet I know scores of cases in which vaginal infections disappeared after the elimination of both yogurt and other milk products. One woman who had a large uterine tumor called me, elated, three months after she had eliminated dairy products from her diet, to tell me that she had discharged the tumor with her menses.

Women with problems of the ovaries often do well to eliminate eggs from their diet; eggs are a product of the chicken's ovaries, and could therefore overload the woman's system. In fact, several of my vegetarian female students who relied on eggs for protein complained of repeated hormonal problems. Conversely, if a woman who has had no eggs for years has ovarian trouble, an egg or two may prove helpful as a stimulant remedy. Another of my students reported that she had lost her period (without the weight-loss usually associated with that condition) when she became a complete vegetarian; as soon as she started eating a few eggs, two years later, it came back.

For comments on the effects of artificial sex hormones added to animal feed or implanted in cattle, see the section on meat, chapter six, page 163.

THE EFFECTS OF A CHANGE IN DIET

Switching from a regimen based on meat, sugar, dairy, and white flour to one consisting mostly of whole grains, beans, vegetables, fruit, and smaller amounts of fish, poultry, and maybe eggs on occasion—what in this book I call a health-supportive whole-foods diet—often has interesting effects on sex. Some people may find that their desire diminishes or even temporarily disappears. Frequently this means that the body is concentrating its energy on repairing other, more vital organs and functions. However, if after six or eight months on a mostly vegetarian diet, sexual desire has not returned, it may be wise to increase the intake of animal protein, especially if you're a man.

People who turn vegetarian after puberty may experience some changes in their sexuality as well as in their personality. These are some of the possibilities:

- CLEANOUT: Sexual energy vanishes for a while, then returns stronger and clearer.
- DECLINE: Desire gradually diminishes toward celibacy.
- DELAYED REACTION: There may be no noticeable effect for a year or two, then either of the above.

After the body has cleansed and rebalanced itself, sex becomes easier, more sensitive, and less demanding of effort. It's important to note here that a healthy sex life does not depend on magical foods, but emerges naturally in a generally healthy body. Whole, wholesome, natural foods, both expansive and contractive ones, will support satisfying, well-integrated sexual function,[13] just as they will support good health in general.

Women with hormonal problems, or who have had difficulty conceiving, often find that such a way of eating will correct their condition. At times, acupuncture or hot compresses on the abdomen will further enhance the healing.* Going by the cases that I'm familiar with, it appears to me that the process may take from one year to eighteen months to complete; that is about the time it took several of my students to get pregnant. In some cases, a chronic vaginal discharge may stop, then return for a while—as a cleanout—and then stop again. However, women who get too thin on a largely vegetarian diet may lose their menses due to malnutrition: Female hormones are synthesized from substances obtained from body fat and cholesterol, and if there is not enough fat under the skin, the hormones cannot be produced.

FOOD FOR MEN AND WOMEN: SHOULD IT BE DIFFERENT?

Much has been made, of late, of the ways in which men and women are the same. Yet let's not forget that they also are different— and that is why they are attracted to each other, like magnets of opposite polarities. If we even out the differences and increase the equality, the attraction diminishes, just as it would with magnets. In business settings, this may be quite convenient. In personal relationships, however, it's preferable to keep the polarity alive. It's certainly more fun. Therefore, rather than eating exactly alike, a couple might be wise to allow for dietary variations for each party. According to Japanese folklore, for example, men should eat more animal-protein foods, women more vegetables, and if they share the same meal, the male's portions should be larger; he should also be given a small dish of salted fish or beans, to forestall any tendency to overexpansion or weakness. As we will see, rather than being an expression of "sexism," such customs make a great deal of sense when we look at them from a systems viewpoint.

In our relativistic reality, the opposites in a pair are rarely, if ever, exactly equal or symmetrical. The buildup and breakdown of body cells—our metabolism—although different for every individual, also exhibits a certain gender-related asymmetry. In women, it's tilted toward anabolism; that is, women are more ef-

* See Kushi, *The Macrobiotic Way of Natural Healing*, for a thorough description of compresses, douches, and tampons to help eliminate stagnation in the reproductive organs.

ficient at *building up* tissue, because they must create babies within their bodies. They also tend to put weight on easily and have a harder time shedding it if they want to. In men, metabolism is tilted toward catabolism; that is, men are more efficient at *breaking down* tissue, perhaps because they discharge protein, carbohydrates, and minerals during sex.[14] They also tend to lose weight with greater ease, much to the chagrin of the strenuously dieting mates.

As a result of this metabolic "inequality," men do need more protein than women, in general, though individual needs may vary. Vegetarian men who do not convert protein efficiently will often meet their need for protein through quantity eating. I can always count on the men in my cooking classes to come back for thirds, or to finish all the food in the pot. If the body is working well, and assimilates its food, that will work out fine. But if that is not the case, the body will grow thinner and thinner, regardless of how much grain or salad is consumed. A bit of fish, chicken, or even meat—each with its attendant fats—will easily remedy this dangerous situation.

Women are favored by nature in that they are extremely efficient assimilators of nutrients; in time of scarcity or famine, their bodies can still extract and convert what they need from whatever meager foods are available, and bear or nurse children. In our society of affluence, that evolutionary advantage has turned into a curse. The overabundance of food, the reliance on nutrient-dense foods such as meat and cheese, the sedentary lifestyles, and the tendency to have few or no children—more input than output, in other words—have put a crimp in their energy flow, and women find themselves accumulating excess matter in their bodies. By their nature, women receive energy, then convert and enlarge it, creating life. If that natural creative need is not fully expressed, either by having children or by other acts of creativity, there is physical, mental, emotional, and spiritual stagnation.

Because of their efficiency as food convertors, women in general need to eat little volume and are often content with the children's leftovers or some scraps of this or that lying around. For the same reason, they also need less protein than men. However, at least according to my observations, they don't seem to do well with long spiritual fasts: A feeling of emptiness and deprivation sets in quickly unless the original condition was one of serious excess. There are some men of normal or even low weight who can fast for many days for spiritual reasons, and feel great; witness the statements of such vegetarian spokesmen as Dick Gregory, Paul Bragg, Max Warmbrand, Herbert Sheldon, Arnold Ehret, and spiritual masters of many persuasions. I have found almost no women who can do the same.

The family cook, therefore, need not be distraught if the man of the house eats three portions and the lady only half, if he eats the meat and she doesn't, or if he'll have dessert and she won't. If such dietary food choices are natural and unforced, they are only the expression of some very real, and common, metabolic variations.

Fifteen:
A Health Nut in the Hospital

One thing that we all learn as we grow older is that no matter how hard we try to do things right, something invariably trips us up. It is as if there were an automatic response from the universe whenever we get complacent and think we have it all figured out: "Ha! Now let's see how you get out of *this* one!"

I've had quite a few of those situations. One of them in particular is relevant to the subject of this book, so I'd like to share it with you. The relationship between natural healing and necessary hospitalization is not one I've studied at length, nor have I had—fortunately—much experience with. So, I do not have enough material to make general recommendations. What follows will perforce be intensely personal, but nevertheless, I hope, helpful.

As you know, I've been working for years on the whys and hows of natural healing. I've applied what I learned to my own life and to the people in it, with generally satisfying results. And I usually feel quite confident that I can handle practically anything except broken bones and third-degree burns. Living as I do outside the established medical system, I have developed some distant respect for the craftsmanship of modern medicine, but also quite a bit of disdain for its shortcomings and arrogance. On the whole, I have little personal use for doctors and hospitals, except in the case of rare physical emergencies.

Imagine, then, my surprise and shock to find myself, at the age

304

of forty, with an ectopic pregnancy.* I knew enough to know that it could be dangerous. I had also never heard of any kind of natural remedy for such a condition. Surgery, quite clearly, was the only way out. What a way to be shown my *own* shortcomings and arrogance!

Still, for my own peace of mind, I had to explore whether there was any possibility at all of an alternative treatment. I was fortunate to have found a caring and competent gynecologist, Dr. David Sherman, who was patient with me and sympathetic to my philosophical anguish.

I refused immediate surgery after the diagnosis, as I was not in pain. Dr. Sherman was concerned, worried that something might happen to me and that he would be blamed. Yet he spent much time patiently answering all the questions my husband and I kept asking. I also discussed the matter at length with Christiane Northrup, a Maine gynecologist whose understanding of both macrobiotics and medicine allowed her to speak my language as well as that of Dr. Sherman.

For a week, I talked to every alternative healer I could find. They all said, "Operate." I fasted, just in case—perhaps it would just starve? or shrink and fall out? Lino Stanchich, an experienced macrobiotic teacher, helped me with exercises, mustard plasters, and ginger compresses. My husband and I prayed a lot, visualizing all manner of healing possibilities. Both Dr. Sherman and Dr. Northrup mentioned that there had been autopsies of women showing signs of old ectopics that had apparently been reabsorbed, but no case had been documented in the literature, and the doctor was definitely not willing to let me try to be the first: The sonogram showed the lump in my Fallopian tube to be already the size of a hen's egg. I just couldn't believe that my body would be stupid enough to let this thing grow any further, let alone explode; I felt it would either stop it, accommodate it, or make it disappear. But I had no proof, no assurances, no case histories, no backup—and no support for what I wanted to believe.

"That which I feared hath come to pass," goes a biblical saying, and so it was with me. After a week of rage and denial, I had exhausted all my sources of information and had to come to grips

---

* This is a pregnancy that remains in the Fallopian tube and grows there; it can eventually rupture the tube and cause internal bleeding, which in some cases is fatal. The only current treatment is surgery to remove the pregnancy.

with my situation. There was no exit. Even my children, when they were told what was going on, wanted me to have the operation, and they are even more terrified of hospitals than I am. So I decided to accept the inevitable and face it as well as I could, drawing on all the resources at my disposal.

First of all, I reasoned, I was going to be opened up, and to heal I had to close up again correctly. Therefore I should encourage the contractive forces of my body. Having spent the week on a juice and vegetable fast, I was quite thin and contracted already. On the day I was to be operated on I ate kasha (buckwheat groats) and miso soup for breakfast. (Surgery was scheduled for 9:00 P.M. It's important not to eat for a good eight hours before receiving anesthesia, to avoid vomiting and possibly aspirating the vomit while unconscious.) And I packed miso, seaweed, and umeboshi plum paste in my bag along with a book, some magazines, and the good luck charms my daughters gave me.

As I was lying outside the operating theater waiting, butterflies in my stomach, I decided to do a little positive programming on myself and have a serious talk with my subconscious. There are many stories of people hearing what is said around them while they are supposedly unconscious under anesthesia; that fact, and my common sense, made me think that there would still be someone in charge of my ship, during the operation, even if the speaking, thinking "I" was temporarily off duty. To that entity, then, I addressed myself, admonishing it to make sure that all systems were kept working properly and to cooperate with the doctor and whoever else would be working with him. I also decided to trust fully in the competence of the surgeon and the anesthesiologist, as my life would literally be in their hands for a couple of hours. The last thought I allowed to cross my mind just before I went under anesthesia was that these people knew what they were doing and that I was in good hands.

Having major abdominal surgery hurts. There is no getting around it, because the abdominal muscles are cut and sewn back together again. But more than the pain, I was bothered by the feeling of having an opening in my body where I shouldn't have had one. The fact that it was sewn up only made it feel like a sewn-up opening. My first body image when I came to was a memory of the shrunken heads made by the Jivaro head hunters of South America, with the mouths sewn shut. I felt as if I had had one of those mouths put in a few inches below my navel.

The pain, bad as it was, made sense, and so it didn't scare me.

Painkillers scared me, so I didn't ask for any. I didn't want to mess up my nervous system on top of everything else. It was a pleasant surprise for me that not only was I not given any medication against my wishes, I wasn't even offered any! I didn't have to expend any energy refusing and explaining. In my dazed state, I felt very distinctly that the medical establishment was becoming a little bit less drug-happy; soon, perhaps very soon, there would be real cooperation between the different healing methods.

I set my energy to the task of healing myself. As soon as I could, I had a few licks of umeboshi paste (highly contractive), to strengthen my adrenal system—the seat of vitality—and generally pull me together. After I was allowed to eat, I refused the Jell-O and the milk and asked instead for hot water, which I used to make myself some miso soup with seaweed, for the trace minerals in it. My husband brought me grains and vegetables, I ate oatmeal, toast, and salad from the hospital meals, and on the fourth day I was out.

The next six weeks I spent eating beans, grains, and vegetables, and avoiding sweets, fruits, and juices, so as to encourage contractiveness. In addition, I ate about three or four ounces of fish, chicken, or turkey daily; several times I even ate meat. After all, I was wounded, not sick; I needed protein for tissue repair. And repair I did—very quickly, according to the doctor. Also, it seems that my contractive energy worked very well during the operation itself, for the surgeon said my tissues had practically snapped back together of their own accord. Within two weeks I was on my feet and teaching again.

The most important thing I learned from my hospital experience was a reaffirmation of an old cliché: It takes two to tango. Healing, be it with herb teas or laser beam surgery, is a cooperation between the healer and the "healee," between the doctor and the patient. It cannot be done to us without our consent. In American Indian medicine, the shaman first asks permission "to change the course of this one's life."[1] The doctor can be the most consummate expert, cutting and sewing with great accuracy and precision, keeping all life-support systems precisely tuned—but unless the patient cooperates and heals, all the craftsmanship is to no avail. *There is nothing in heaven or on earth that any medicine can do if the body refuses to heal itself.* But if the body does want to heal, it will do so with, without, and at times even in spite of medicine.

In one episode of his TV series, *The Body in Question* (based on the book of the same title), Jonathan Miller showed open-heart surgery being performed on a woman with a defective valve. He said in conclusion, "If we hadn't treated her like a mechanism, we couldn't have restored her humanity." Apart from the fact that dying is every bit as human as living, there is a fallacy in that statement: Although the doctor indeed works like a mechanic, a mechanism doesn't heal. His work *fails* without the active cooperation of the patient's system. Perhaps the major philosophical flaw of modern medicine has been precisely that it has been treating the human organism, which is self-healing, as if it were a mechanism, which tends to break down if left alone. It is important and helpful to change a heart valve surgically, and it *is* right for the surgeon to take pride in his work. Yet regardless of the elegant mechanical maneuvers of which medicine is capable today, the doctor still does only half the work. The other half, equally intricate and subtle, is done by the patient. And much as the doctor needs acknowledgment and respect for his work, the patient needs it for his. I felt wonderful and competent when Dr. Sherman commented on how fast I had healed.

Fortunately, respect for the patient is fast becoming the norm, especially thanks to the work of such people as Norman Cousins, Dr. Bernard Siegel, and O. Carl Simonton, the concern of many enlightened physicians, and the growing willingness of patients to be responsible for their own condition.

A Proposal for Unifying the Opposites

Man is one, and our salvation lies eventually in a mutual sharing of all knowledge. —Richard Grossinger, *Planet Medicine*

It is becoming increasingly evident that, whatever our individual preference is in healing matters, our horizons must be broadened. "Holistic" or naturalistic types like myself must recognize the valuable aspects of technological medicine. Doctors and hospitals must admit that there are areas in which old-fashioned, noninvasive approaches to healing are more effective than their own. How can this dialogue be encouraged?

If I lived in a fairy-tale world and all my dreams could come true, I'd like to see a worldwide meeting of M.D.s, chiropractors, acupuncturists, iridologists, bodywork professionals, and food people (including myself) during which we would agree on the following:

- A concept of the human being as a fully integrated, self-healing organism that can, at times, be treated like a mechanism and survive
- A concept of health and disease as outlined in this book: briefly, health as the optimum functioning of human beings on physical, emotional, social, and spiritual levels; disease as information and an initially positive attempt to preserve function
- Our respective areas of true competence, ineffectiveness, and overlap
- The value of anecdotal evidence—what the patient feels and describes—because of the infinite amount of uncontrollable, scientifically unknowable variables that comprise a human being
- Declaring allegiance to the uncertainty of practice rather than the certainty of theory
- The fact that the patient's subconscious knows whether his or her condition is dangerous or not; that this subconscious can be consulted regularly through precise questioning and the "focusing" technique; and that, if its responses are carefully considered, it can be the healing professional's best ally both in choosing treatment and in evaluating its effectiveness
- The fact that the healer's most valuable tool is intuition rather than knowledge—although knowledge and practice are absolutely essential to sharpen and focus the intuition
- The fact that no one has The Answer, but that each healing method will solve part of the puzzle; and that serious professionals in any healing field have the obligation to know about others in related fields, so as to be able to refer patients to them
- The need to educate the public about the different healing methods available, so that each "health consumer" may in fact pick among them as he or she now picks among the different foods in a supermarket

Once we had some sort of consensus, we would establish which conditions should be treated with which healing method first. I cannot begin to enumerate all of the many variations of diseases afflicting human beings, nor present a full listing of all the healing systems. But here is a tentative and sketchy list of what I think would work:

- All conditions, but especially fatigue, mental fuzziness, colds, skin eruptions, recurrent infections in any part of the body, respiratory and digestive ailments, and other adjustments and discharges, as well as chronic conditions such as arteriosclerosis, arthritis, allergies, cancer, and so on, should first be treated by dietary management.
- Exercise should be routinely prescribed, especially for conditions of stagnation, sluggishness, and accumulation, such as cardiovascular diseases, slow digestion, overweight, malabsorption.
- All minor problems such as headaches, fevers, colds, and digestive disorders would best be treated with medicinal foods, herbs, and drinks. (See chapter twelve for some simple approaches to such conditions.)
- Problems with absorption and transformation of food can be treated with herbs and dietary supplements.
- Malfunctions such as diabetes and hypothyroidism, after dietary treatment has done all it can, could possibly benefit from chemical medications, moderately used.
- Backaches and problems with the skeleton are probably best handled initially by chiropractors and osteopaths, rather than surgeons.
- Pregnancy should be treated as a normal event and not a disease, and should be managed by midwives in homelike settings. Only in the event of abnormal conditions or special risks—the mother's illness, or structural defects—would it become a medical affair.
- Female complaints would first be treated by removing all hormone-related foods from the diet (dairy products, hormone-treated chicken or beef). Whatever complaints remain after ten or twelve months could then be treated by other methods.
- Malfunctions of cycles and movement (menstrual irregularities, glandular misfirings, sluggishness in any organ) could benefit from energy manipulations such as acupuncture, polarity, bodywork treatments, shiatsu massage, or psychic healing.
- Structural problems and mechanical traumas, such as multiple fractures or tumors that impede the functioning of some organ, will need to be treated with surgery when indicated.
- Psychological disorders, including depression, would first be treated by removing sweets, sugar, milk products, and ice

cream from the diet; by ascertaining that the patient is not protein starved or overmineralized; by investigating the possibility of chemical allergies; and additionally by talk, inner reflection, vigorous exercise, therapy, psychic healing.
* Physical problems that resist diet, supplements, medicine, or other material manipulations could be dealt with by the same methods as the nonmaterial ones applied to psychological disorders.

If technological medicine admits its limits and makes room for other healing systems that in many cases are more successful; if the naturalistic/holistic movements accept and recognize the value of the vast knowledge and extraordinary craftsmanship of modern medicine; and if we can integrate the two approaches to healing, then we will truly have found the medicine of the New Age. I hope I live long enough to see that day.[2]

Afterword

*Health is nothing more than united purpose—if the body is
brought under the purpose of the mind, it becomes whole because
the mind's purpose is one. Apart from the mind, the body has no
purpose at all.*   —A Course in Miracles

Some final words of caution: Food is our helper, our ally, our
support, at times our undoing. But it is not our salvation. A change
in diet can help us—but if we remain concentrated only on the
food aspect of health and well-being, after a while the pendulum
will swing back and we'll get sick again from the very same food
that once made us "well."

We have no right to be healed unless we are prepared to return
that gift a thousandfold. Health for its own sake is an ego trip. It
is wasted as a goal; but it gains meaning as a means, an instrument
to further the evolution of our consciousness. We must ask ourselves, if we wish to be healthy, WHAT FOR? To what use will we
put our health?

Regardless of what we eat, our bodies will automatically be
healthy when we are aimed in a positive direction, following our
individual path, centered and undivided in attention, doing our
chosen work, grateful for life, and living with love.

Chapter Notes

ONE: HEALTH TODAY

1. *Healthy People: The Surgeon General's Report on Health Promotion and Disease Prevention*.
2. Thomas McKeown, "Determinants of Health."
3. *Healthy People*.
4. Melvin Page, *Your Body Is Your Best Doctor*, pp. 111–17.
5. Alexander G. Schauss, *Diet, Crime, and Delinquency*, p. 91. See also Schauss, Bland, and Simonsen, "A Critical Analysis of the Diets of Chronic Juvenile Offenders."
6. René Dubos, *Mirage of Health*.
7. McKeown.
8. Ibid.
9. Robert Mendelsohn, *How to Raise a Healthy Child*, pp. 228–229.
10. Maryann Napoli, *Health Facts: A Critical Evaluation of the Major Problems, Treatments, and Alternatives Facing Medical Consumers*. p. 110.
11. Ivan Illich, *Medical Nemesis*, p. 26.
12. Robert Mendelsohn compared the yearly number of deaths due to unnecessary surgery (12,000) with that of knife murders (3,000) in *Malepractice: How Doctors Manipulate Women*, p. 82.
13. Sidney M. Wolfe and the Public Citizen Research Group (founded by Ralph Nader), *Pills That Don't Work*, pp. 18–19.
14. Illich.
15. Richard Grossinger, *Planet Medicine*, p. 23.

TWO: A NEW WORLDVIEW

1. Jonathan Miller, *The Body in Question*, p. 187.
2. See Fritjof Capra, *The Tao of Physics* and *The Turning Point*, for an exhaustive discussion of these ideas.
3. Fritjof Capra, "The Turning Point: A New Vision of Reality." Interview, *New Age* magazine, Feb. 1982.
4. See "Objectivity in Social Science and Social Policy," in *The Methodology of the Social Sciences*, translated by Edward A. Shils and Henry A. Finch.
5. Erno Laszlo, *Introduction to Systems Philosophy*.
6. *Brain/Mind Bulletin* 4, no. 13, discussing the theories of Ilya Prigogine.
7. Three Initiates, *The Kybalion*. Also, George Ohsawa, "Seven Principles of the Order of the Universe," *The Book of Judgment*.
8. Harold Saxton Burr, "Electro-Dynamic Theory of Development."
9. Rupert Sheldrake, *A New Science of Life*, p. 76.
10. "Exploring the Microworld."
11. Fritjof Capra, interview in *New Age* magazine.
12. Paavo Airola, *Are You Confused?*
13. Robert Mendelsohn, *How to Raise a Healthy Child*, p. 228.
14. "F.D.A. Asks Wyeth to Recall Infant Food Short on Vitamin."
15. Carl C. Pfeiffer, *Mental and Elemental Nutrients*, p. 24.
16. Robert Harris and Edel Karmas, *Nutritional Evaluation of Food Processing*, p. 316.
17. *Fact-Book on Fermented Foods and Beverages*, p. 7.
18. William Shurtleff and Akiko Aoyagi, *The Book of Miso*, p. 26; *The Book of Tempeh*, p. 35.
19. Harris and Karmas, pp. 339–40.
20. Harris and Karmas, pp. 364–75.
21. Isaac Asimov, *The Chemicals of Life*, p. 131.
22. William Longgood, *The Poisons in Your Food*, p. 3.
23. Ruth Winter, *Poisons in Your Food*, p. 4.
24. Jacqueline Verret and Jean Carper, *Eating May Be Hazardous to Your Health*, p. 19.
25. Rudolf Hauschka, *The Nature of Substance*, pp. 108–109.
26. Harold Saxton Burr, *Blueprint for Immortality: The Electric Patterns of Life*, pp. 63 and 75.
27. Rupert Sheldrake, *A New Science of Life*, p. 98.
28. Gary Null with Judy Trupin, "The Food Irradiation Threat", *Whole Life Times*, February 1986.
29. U.S. Department of Agriculture Handbook No. 8.
30. Hara Marano, "The Problem with Protein."

THREE: FOOD AND THE LAW OF OPPOSITES

1. Ilza Veith, trans. *The Yellow Emperor's Classic of Internal Medicine*, p. 13.

2. Richard Wilhelm and Cory R. Baynes, trans., *The I Ching*, p. lvi.
3. Walter B. Cannon, *The Wisdom of the Body*, pp. 168–75.
4. Karen MacNeil, *The Book of Whole Foods: Nutrition and Cuisine*, p. 213.
5. Michael Weiner, *The Way of the Skeptical Nutritionist*, p. 174.
6. Herman Aihara, *Acid and Alkaline*, p. 9.
7. Arnold Ehret, *Mucusless Diet Healing System*.
8. Paavo Airola, *Are You Confused?*, p. 79.
9. Alice Chase, *Nutrition for Health*, p. 326.
10. See the Atkins and Stillman diets, for example.
11. Stephan Pálos, *The Chinese Art of Healing*, p. 91.
12. Yanny Ting Hartmann, "Hot and Cold," unpublished paper, December 1983.
13. Rudolph Ballentine, *Diet and Nutrition*, p. 431.
14. Walter Cannon, *The Wisdom of the Body*.
15. Durk Pearson and Sandy Shaw, *Life Extension*, p. 373.

FOUR: MODERN DIETS: A REEVALUATION

1. U.S. Senate, Select Committee on Nutrition and Human Needs, *Dietary Goals for the United States*.
2. Weston A. Price, *Nutrition and Physical Degeneration*.
3. Mark Hegsted, M.D., professor of nutrition, Harvard School of Public Health, statement for *Dietary Goals* report.
4. Henry Schroeder, personal correspondence with the author, 1972.
5. "Are Health Foods Healthier?"
6. Nathan Pritikin, with Patrick McGrady, *The Pritikin Program for Diet and Exercise*.
7. George Watson, *Nutrition and Your Mind*, p. 33.
8. Ibid., p. 109.
9. Nikki and David Goldbeck, *The Dieter's Companion*.
10. Roger J. Williams, *Nutrition Against Disease*, p. 108.
11. Linda Clark, *Get Well Naturally*, p. 131.
12. Mark Bricklin, ed., *The Practical Encyclopedia of Natural Healing*, pp. 157 and 404.
13. Ibid., pp. 365–66.
14. Stanley W. Jacob, Clarice Ashworth Francone, and Walter J. Lossow, *Structure and Function in Man*, pp. 580–92.
15. Jane Brody, *Jane Brody's Nutrition Book*, p. 160.
16. Leslie J. Kaslof, editor, *Wholistic Dimensions in Healing: A Resource Guide*, "Parts or Wholes: An Introduction to the Use of Whole Plant Substances in Healing," p. 112.
17. "No society has been discovered that is exclusively vegetarian," state anthropologists Farb and Armelagos in *Consuming Passions: The Anthropology of Eating*, p. 35.
18. Karen MacEwan and David Stone, "Living Without Meat."

19. David A. Phillips, *From Soil to Psyche*.
20. "Andes Evidence Indicts Cholesterol." *The New York Times*, April 22, 1971.
21. *Dietary Goals*, p. 33.
22. Rudolf Hauschka, *Nutrition*, p. 18–25.
23. Janet Barkas, *The Vegetable Passion*, pp. 119–30.
24. Elliot D. Abravanel and Elizabeth A. King, *Dr. Abravanel's Body Type Diet and Lifetime Nutrition Plan*, pp. 27, 31–32, 104.
25. William Donald Kelley, *Metabolic Typing*.
26. Milton Hildebrand, *Analysis of Vertebrate Structure*, p. 232.
27. Benjamin T. Burton, Ph.D., *Human Nutrition*, p. 123.
28. Irene Liem, Keith Sternkraus, and Ted Cronk, "Production of Vitamin B_{12} in Tempeh."
29. Personal communication with the author, November 7, 1985.
30. Ronald Kotsch, Ph.D. doctoral thesis, p. xiii.
31. Herman Aihara, *Seven Macrobiotic Principles*, p. 15.
32. This and the following are taken from *Macrobiotics: Standard Dietary and Way of Life Suggestions*, a pamphlet published by the East-West Foundation of Boston.
33. Anthony J. Sattilaro, with Tom Monte, *Recalled by Life: The Story of My Recovery from Cancer*. East-West Foundation of Boston, *Case Histories*.
34. "Diagnosing Macrobiotics," *Macromuse* magazine.

FIVE: THE HEALTH-SUPPORTIVE WHOLE-FOODS EATING STYLE

1. Arnold DeVries, *Primitive Man and His Food*, p. 108.
2. Weston A. Price, *Nutrition and Physical Degeneration*.
3. Jane Goodall, *In the Shadow of Man*.
4. Reay Tannahil, *Food in History*, p. 155.
5. Alexander Leaf, "Every Day Is a Gift If You're Over 100."
6. Jane E. Brody, "Eating Less May Be the Key to Living Beyond 100 Years."

SIX: THE EFFECTS OF DIFFERENT FOODS

1. Rudolph Ballentine, *Diet and Nutrition*, p. 547.
2. Rudolf Hauschka, *Nutrition*, p. 83.
3. Oski, *Don't Drink Your Milk*, p. 60.
4. Ballentine, p. 132.
5. Helen B. Taussig, "Possible Injury to the Cardiovascular System from Vitamin D"; D. C. Anderson, et al., "Vitamin D Intoxication, with Hypernatremia, Potassium and Water Depletion and Mental Depression"; W. H. Taylor, "Renal Calculi and Self-Medication with Multivitamin Preparations Containing Vitamin D."

6. "Hormones in Milk."

7. "Nutrition—Applied Personally." Quoted in *The Book of Whole Foods—Nutrition and Cuisine* by Karen MacNeil, p. 213.

8. K. A. Oster, "Treatment of Angina Pectoris According to a New Theory of Its Origin." See also N. Sampsidis, *Heart Disease Explained*. The Federation of American Societies for Experimental Biology prepared a critique of the Oster theory for the FDA in 1975: "A Review of the Significance of Bovine Milk Xanthine Oxidase in the Etiology of Atherosclerosis"; some merit was found in the theory, but the results were deemed inconclusive.

9. Rubenberg, et al., "Myocardial Infarction in Patients Treated with Sippy and Other High-Milk Diets."

10. Benjamin T. Burton, *Human Nutrition*, p. 131; Ballentine, p. 228.

11. Jane Brody, *Jane Brody's Nutrition Book*, p. 232; Carl Pfeiffer, *Mental and Elemental Nutrients*, p. 376.

12. George Schwartz, *Food Power*.

13. William Dufty, *Sugar Blues*, p. 198.

14. Herman Aihara, *Acid and Alkaline*, p. 30.

15. Melvin Page and Leon Abrams, *Your Body is Your Best Doctor*, p. 196.

16. "Nutrition Report."

17. Jane E. Brody, "Osteoporosis."

18. George K. Davis, "Effect of a Nightshade on Livestock," in Norman F. Childers, *A Diet to Stop Arthritis*.

19. Brody, "Osteoporosis."

20. "Losers Weepers."

21. Hebrews 5:14.

22. Rudolf Hauschka, *Nutrition*, p. 55.

23. Hara Marano, "The Problem with Protein."

24. Orville Schell, *Modern Meat*, pp. 28–40.

25. Ibid., pp. 184–85.

26. Ibid., pp. 272–73.

27. Schwartz, p. 24.

28. Paul C. Mangelsdorf, "Wheat."

29. John Garvy, *The Five Phases of Food*, p. 16.

30. Schwartz, p. 95.

31. Judy Brown, "Soyfoods Are Catching On."

32. Ballentine, p. 140.

33. For a deeper discussion of this subject, see Rudolf Steiner, *Spiritual Science and Medicine*.

34. See Ballentine, p. 470; Jethro Kloss, *Back to Eden*, p. 243; Michio Kushi, *Book of Macrobiotics*, p. 133.

35. Saul Miller, *Food for Thought*, p. 22.

36. Hauschka, *Nutrition*.

37. Norman F. Childers, *Childers' Diet to Stop Arthritis: The Nightshades and Ill Health*.

38. George K. Davis, "Effect of a Nightshade on Livestock," in Childers.
39. J. Yogamundi Moon, *A Macrobiotic Explanation of Pathological Cal-cification*, pp. 3–5. See also Hans Selye, *Calciphylaxis*.
40. Childers, p. 92.
41. Ibid., p. 1.
42. Hauschka, *Nutrition*, pp. 104–109.
43. Rhoads, *Cooking with Sea Vegetables*; see also Price, *Nutrition and Physical Degeneration*.
44. Hauschka, *Nutrition*, p. 101–103.
45. See John Lust, *The Herb Book*; Kloss; Paul Twitchell, *Herbs: The Magic Healers*.
46. Kushi, *Book of Macrobiotics*, p. 52.
47. Dufty, p. 29.
48. Henry Schroeder, *The Trace Elements and Man*, p. 29.
49. Burton, pp. 147–48.
50. *Nutrition*, p. 68.
51. U.S. Senate Select Committee on Nutrition and Human Needs, *Dietary Goals*, p. 49.
52. Janice Fillip, "Salt, With a Grain Of."
53. Hauschka, *Nutrition*, p. 170.
54. Dufty, p. 42.
55. John Yudkin, *Pure, White, and Deadly*.
56. Price.
57. Lendon Smith, *Improving Your Child's Behavior Chemistry*.
58. Dufty, *Sugar Blues*.
59. Schauss, *Diet, Crime, and Delinquency*.
60. Benson J. Horowitz, Stanley W. Epstein, and Leonard Lippman, "Sugar Chromatography Studies in Recurrent Candida Vulvo-vaginitis."
61. Study done by Dr. C. Keith Conners, of Children's Hospital in Washington, D.C., quoted by Jane Brody in "Diet Therapy for Be-havior is Criticized as Premature."
62. Schauss, pp. 3–10.
63. Watson, *Nutrition and Your Mind*, p. 33.
64. Jane Brody, *Jane Brody's Nutrition Book*, p. 73.
65. Weiner, *The Way of the Skeptical Nutritionist*, p. 64.
66. D. E. Kosland, "Protein Shape and Biological Control."
67. Brody, *Jane Brody's Nutrition Book*, p. 72.
68. Michio Kushi, *How to See Your Health*, p. 151.

SEVEN: THE EFFECTS OF FOOD PREPARATION

1. Peter Farb and George Armelagos, *Consuming Passions*, p. 52.
2. Reay Tannahil, *Food in History*, p. 25.
3. Michio Kushi, *Book of Macrobiotics*, p. 64.

4. Ballentine, *Diet and Nutrition*, p. 34.
5. Weiner, *The Skeptical Nutritionist*, p. 24.
6. Henry Bieler, *Food Is Your Best Medicine*, pp. 186–98.
7. Reay Tannahil, p. 131–36.
8. Beatrice Trum Hunter, *Fact-Book on Fermented Foods and Beverages*, pp. 6–7.

NINE: WHAT TO EXPECT FROM A CHANGE IN DIET

1. Rudolf Hauschka, *Nutrition*, p. 168.
2. Carl Englund, "Chronopsychology Links Brain Function to Cycles."
3. Nathan Pritikin, *The Pritikin Program*.

TEN: CRAVINGS AND BINGES: WHAT DO THEY MEAN?

1. Carl Pfeiffer, *Mental and Elemental Nutrients*, p. 416.
2. For thorough discussions of the effects of white, refined cane sugar, see William Dufty, *Sugar Blues*; John Yudkin, *Pure, White, and Deadly*; and F. A. Abramson, *Body, Mind, and Sugar*.
3. John Garvy, "How Homeopathy Works."

ELEVEN: HEALTH AND ILLNESS: A NEW DEFINITION

1. As John Garvy pointed out in a seminar entitled "The Five Phases of Food" (Boston, June 1982), "Health is a direction, not a state." Elson Haas wrote, "Healing is a process, not a destination" (*Staying Healthy with the Seasons*, p. 4).
2. Thomas McKeown, *Determinants of Health*.
3. Alasdair MacIntyre, *Against the Self-Images of the Age*, p. 179.
4. Lewis Thomas, "Your Very Good Health," in *Lives of a Cell*, p. 85.
5. Michio Kushi, *The Macrobiotic Way of Natural Healing*, pp. 3–9.

TWELVE: FOOD AS MEDICINE

1. Grossinger, *Planet Medicine*.
2. Henry Bieler, *Food Is Your Best Medicine*, p. 60.
3. For recipes, see Annemarie Colbin, *The Book of Whole Meals*.
4. For more on this, see Harris Coulter, *Homeopathic Medicine*; Dana Ullman, "Principles of Homoeopathy," *Co-Evolution Quarterly*; and other works on the subject.
5. Mildred Jackson and Terri Teague, *The Handbook of Alternatives to Chemical Medicine*, p. 41.
6. See Dian Dincin Buchman, *The Complete Book of Water Therapy*; J. V. Cerney, *Modern Magic of Natural Healing with Water Therapy*;

Russell Sneddon, *About the Water Cure*; Jeanne Keller, *Healing with Water*.

7. Rudolph Ballentine, *Diet and Nutrition*, p. 303.
8. Paavo Airola, *Are You Confused?*
9. Ibid., p. 137.
10. Frank Barr and Arthur Young, quoted in *Brain/Mind Bulletin* 8 (July 11—August 1, 1983), p. 4. For more on the effects of light, see Richard J. Wurtman, Michael J. Baum, and John T. Potts, Jr., eds., *The Medical and Biological Effects of Light*.
11. Linda Clark, *Get Well Naturally*, pp. 365—56.
12. Bircher-Benner Clinic Staff, *Bircher-Benner Nutrition Plan for Headache and Migraine Sufferers*.
13. Jane Brody, "Fever: New View Stresses Its Healing Benefits."
14. Centers for Disease Control, *Morbidity and Mortality Weekly Report*.
15. For a scholarly and scientific explanation of this process, see Dr. Med. Hans-Heinrich Reckeweg, *Homotoxicology: Illness and Healing by Antihomotoxic Therapy*.
16. *AMA Family Medical Guide*.
17. Michio Kushi, *How to See Your Health*, pp. 145—49.
18. Noted by James E. Fulton, M.D., of the Acne Research Institute and author of *Dr. Fulton's Step by Step Program for Clearing Acne*.
19. Paavo Airola, *Are You Confused?*, p. 128.
20. *New York Times*, September 18, 1984.
21. Richard Carlton, M.D., personal communication, April 1984.
22. See *Homotoxicology* for the theories of Reckeweg on this subject.
23. Robert Mendelsohn, *How to Raise a Healthy Child*, p. 211.

THIRTEEN: THE EFFECTS OF FOOD ON MOOD

1. See Ken Dychtwald, *Bodymind*.
2. David Sheinkin, M.D., and Michael Schachter, M.D., *Food, Mind, and Mood*.
3. Watson, *Nutrition and Your Mind*, p. 59.
4. Marilyn Ferguson, *The Aquarian Conspiracy*.

FOURTEEN: THE EFFECTS OF FOOD ON SEX

1. George Schwartz, *Food Power*, pp. 112—13.
2. Carl Pfeiffer, *Mental and Elemental Nutrients*, pp. 215 and 244.
3. Schwartz, p. 95.
4. Pfeiffer, p. 469—71.
5. Schwartz, p. 95.
6. Peter Farb and George Armelagos, pp. 81—83.
7. James Trager, *The Foodbook*, pp. 477—83.
8. Saul Miller, *Food for Thought*, p. 137.

9. Guillermo Asis, interview in *East-West Journal*, February 1984.
10. Miller, p. 139.
11. Alexander Schauss, *Diet, Crime, and Delinquency*, pp. 19–29, including his list of seventy references; J. I. Rodale, *Natural Health, Sugar, and the Criminal Mind*; William Dufty, *Sugar Blues*.
12. Christiane Northrup, personal communication with the author, March 1983.
13. Miller, p. 139.
14. Pfeiffer, p. 472.

FIFTEEN: A HEALTH NUT IN THE HOSPITAL

1. Michael Braveheart, "The Great Medicine—In Theory and Practice," unpublished paper, December 1983.
2. Richard Grossinger, *Planet Medicine*.

References

Abehsera, Michel. *The Healing Clay: Ancient Treatments for Modern Times*. Brooklyn, New York: Swan House Publishing.

Aihara, Herman. *Acid and Alkaline*. Rev. ed. Oroville, Calif.: The Georges Ohsawa Macrobiotic Foundation, 1982.

Aihara, Herman. *Seven Macrobiotic Principles*. Oroville, Calif.: The Georges Ohsawa Macrobiotic Foundation, 1977.

Airola, Paavo. *Are You Confused?* Phoenix, Ariz.: Health Plus, 1971.

Anderson, D. C., et al. "Vitamin D Intoxication, with Hypernatremia, Potassium and Water Depletion, and Mental Depression." *British Medical Journal* 4 (December 21, 1968):744.

"Andes Diet Indicts Cholesterol." *New York Times*, April 22, 1971.

"Are Health Foods Healthier?" Panel Discussion, *Glamour* Magazine, July 1971.

Asimov, Isaac. *The Chemicals of Life*. New York: Signet-NAL, 1954.

Asis, Guillermo, M.D. "Men's Sexual Health: Body and Mind," Interview *East-West Journal*, February 1984.

Atkins, Robert, M.D., with Shirley Linde. *Dr. Atkins' Superenergy Diet*. New York: Bantam Books, 1980.

"Baby Robbying." *New York Times*, November 1, 1981.

Ballentine, Rudolph, M.D. *Diet and Nutrition: A Holistic Approach*. Honesdale, Pa.: The Himalayan International Institute, 1978.

Barkas, Janet. *The Vegetable Passion: A History of the Vegetarian State of Mind*. New York: Charles Scribner's Sons, 1975.

Baynes, Cary F., trans. *The I Ching or Book of Changes*. The Richard Wilhelm translation. Rendered into English by Cary F. Baynes. Bollingen Series 19. Princeton, N.J.: Princeton University Press, 1969.

Beaulieu, John, personal communication, February 1983.

Becker, Robert O., M.D., and Selden, Gary. *The Body Electric: Electromagnetism and the Foundation of Life*. New York: William Morrow and Co., 1985.

Bieler, Henry, M.D. *Food Is Your Best Medicine*. New York: Ballantine Books, 1982.

Bircher-Benner Clinic Staff. Trans. by Timothy McManus. *Bircher-Benner Nu-*

trition Plan for Headache and Migraine Sufferers. New York: Pyramid Books, 1972.

Brain/Mind Bulletin 4, no. 7 (February 19, 1979).

Brain/Mind Bulletin 4, no. 13 (May 21, 1979).

Brain/Mind Bulletin 7, no. 2 (December 14, 1981).

Brain/Mind Bulletin 7, no. 6 (March 8, 1982).

Brain/Mind Bulletin 8, no. 12–13 (July 11–August 1, 1983).

Bravenheart, Michael. "The Great Medicine—In Theory and Practice." Unpublished paper, December 1983.

Bricklin, Mark, ed. *The Practical Encyclopedia of Natural Healing*. Emmaus, Pa.: Rodale Press, 1976.

Brody, Jane E. "Diet Therapy for Behaviors Criticized as Premature." *New York Times*, December 4, 1984.

——————. "Eating Less May Be the Key to Living Beyond 100 Years." *New York Times*, June 8, 1982.

——————. "Fever: New View Stresses Its Healing Benefits." *New York Times*, December 28, 1982.

——————. "Osteoporosis." *New York Times*, January 11, 1984.

——————. *Jane Brody's Nutrition Book: A Lifetime Guide to Good Eating for Better Health and Weight Control*. New York: W. W. Norton & Co., 1981.

Brown, Judy. "Soyfoods Are Catching On." *Whole Life Times*, July-August 1982.

Buchman, Dian Dincin. *The Complete Book of Water Therapy*. New York: E. P. Dutton, 1979.

Burr, Harold Saxton, Ph.D. *Blueprint for Immortality: The Electric Patterns of Life*. London: Neville Spearman, 1972.

Burr, Harold Saxton, Ph.D. "Electro-Dynamic Theory of Development." *Journal of Comparative Neurology* 56 (1932):347–71.

Burr, Harold Saxton, Ph.D., and Northrop, F. S. C. "The Electro-Dynamic Theory of Life." *Quarterly Review of Biology* 10 (1935):322–33.

Burton, Benjamin T., Ph.D. *Human Nutrition*. New York: McGraw-Hill, 1976.

Buttram, Harold E., M.D., and Hoffman, John Chriss. *Vaccinations and Immune Malfunction*. Quakertown, Pa.: The Humanitarian Publishing Co., 1982.

Cannon, Walter, M.D., Sc.D. *The Wisdom of the Body*. New York: W. W. Norton & Co., 1939, 1963.

Capra, Fritjof. Interview, *New Age*, February 1982.

——————. *The Tao of Physics: An Exploration of the Parallels Between Modern Physics and Eastern Mysticism*. New York: Bantam, New Age Books, 1976.

——————. *The Turning Point: Science, Society, and the Rising Culture*. New York: Simon and Schuster, 1982.

Carlton, Richard, M.D., personal communication with the author, April 1984.

Center for Science in the Public Interest. "Losers Weepers." *Nutrition Action Newsletter* 12, no. 6 (July-August 1985).

Centers for Disease Control (Atlanta, Ga.). *Morbidity and Mortality Weekly Report*, February 12, 1982.

Cerney, J. V. *Modern Magic of Natural Healing with Water Therapy*. West Nyack, N.Y.: Parker Publishing Co., 1975.

Chase, Alice, M.D. *Nutrition for Health*. New York: Lancer Books, 1954.

Childers, Norman Franklin, Ph.D. *Childers' Diet to Stop Arthritis: The Nightshades and Ill Health*. Somerville, N.J.: Horticulture Publications, 1981.

"Chronopsychology Links Brain Function to Cycles." *Brain/Mind Bulletin* 7, no. 1 (November 23, 1981).

Clark, Linda. *Get Well Naturally—Nature's Way to Health*. New York: The Devin-Adair Co., 1965.

Cobb, Vicki. *Science Experiments You Can Eat.* Philadelphia and New York: J. B. Lippincott Co., 1972.

Colbin, Annemarie. *The Book of Whole Meals.* New York: Ballantine Books, 1983.

Connelly, Dianne M., Ph.D., M.Ac. *Traditional Acupuncture: The Law of the Five Elements.* Columbia, Md.: The Centre for Traditional Acupuncture, 1979.

Coulter, Harris L., Ph.D. *Homeopathic Medicine.* St. Louis: Formur, 1975.

——————————. *Homeopathic Science and Modern Medicine: The Physics of Healing with Microdoses.* Berkeley, Calif.: North Atlantic, 1981.

DeVries, Arnold. *Primitive Man and His Food.* Chicago: Chandler Books, 1952.

Dextreit, Raymond. *Our Earth, Our Cure.* Translated and edited by Michael Abehsera. Brooklyn, New York: Swan House, 1974.

"Does Diet Affect Criminal Behavior?" *Whole Foods* Magazine, October 1983.

Dossey, Larry, M.D. *Space, Time, and Medicine.* Boulder and London: Shambhala, 1982.

Dubos, René. *Mirage of Health: Utopias, Progress, and Biological Change.* New York: Harper & Row, 1959.

Dufty, William. *Sugar Blues.* New York: Warner Books, 1975.

Dychtwald, Ken. *Bodymind.* New York: Jove Publications, 1984.

East-West Foundation of Boston. *Case Histories.* Brookline, Mass.

——————————————————. *Macrobiotics: Standard Dietary and Way of Life Suggestions.* Brookline, Mass., 1983.

East West Journal. Interview, Guillermo Asis, M.D.: "Men's Sexual Health, Body and Mind," February 1984.

Ehret, Arnold. *Mucusless Diet Healing System.* Beaumont, Calif.: Ehret Literature Publishing Co., 1953.

Englund, Carl. "Chronopsychology Links Brain Function to Cycles." *Brain/Mind Bulletin* 7, no. 1 (November 23, 1981).

Esko, Wendy. *Introduction to Macrobiotic Cooking.* Tokyo: Japan Publications, 1983.

"Exploring the Microworld." *Newsweek,* October 23, 1981, p. 85.

Farb, Peter, and Armelagos, George. *Consuming Passions: The Anthropology of Eating.* Boston: Houghton Mifflin, 1980.

"FDA Asks Wyeth to Recall Infant Food Short on Vitamins." *New York Times,* March 12, 1982.

Ferguson, Marilyn. *The Aquarian Conspiracy.* Los Angeles: J. P. Tarcher, 1980.

Fillip, Janice. "Salt, With a Grain Of." *Whole Foods,* April 1980.

France, Richard, with Canty, Jerome. *Healing Naturally: The Commonsense Macrobiotic Approach to Cancer and Other Diseases.* Boulder, Colo.: Amaizeing Books, 1982.

Fulton, James E., M.D. *Dr. Fulton's Step by Step Program for Clearing Acne.* New York: Harper & Row, 1983.

Garvy, Jack. "How Homeopathy Works." *East West Journal,* August 1978.

Garvy, John W., N.D., D.Ac. *The Five Phases of Food: How to Begin.* Brookline, Mass.: Wellbeing Books, 1983.

Gendlin, Eugene, Ph.D. *Focusing.* New York: Everest House, 1978.

Goldbeck, Nikki and David. *The Dieter's Companion: How to Choose and Maintain the Diet Best Suited to You.* New York: Signet Books, New American Library, 1975.

Goodall, Jane van Lawick. *In the Shadow of Man.* New York: Dell Publishing Co., 1971.

Grollman, Sigmund. *The Human Body, Its Structure and Physiology.* New York: Macmillan, 1969.

Grossinger, Richard. *Planet Medicine*. Boulder, Colo.: Shambhala Publications, 1982.

Guirdham, Arthur. *A Theory of Disease*. London: Neville Spearman, 1957.

Gusick, Diane B. *A Course in Miracles*. New York: Foundation for Inner Peace, 1975.

Haas, Elson M., M.D. *Staying Healthy with the Seasons*. Millbrae, Calif.: Celestial Arts, 1981.

Harris, Robert, Ph.D., and Karmas, Ednel, Ph.D., eds. *Nutritional Evaluation of Food Processing*. Westport, Conn.: Avi Publishing Co., 1975.

Hartmann, Yanny Ting. "Hot and Cold." Unpublished paper, December 1983.

Hauschka, Rudolf. *The Nature of Substance*. London: Vincent Stuart Ltd., 1966.

——————. *Nutrition*. London: Stuart & Watkins, 1967.

Hildebrand, Milton. *Analysis of Vertebrate Structure*. New York: John Wiley, 1974.

Hoffman, Enid. *Huna—A Beginner's Guide*. Gloucester, Mass.: Para Research, 1976.

Horowitz, Benson J., M.D.; Epstein, Stanley W., M.D.; and Lippman, Leonard, M.D. "Sugar Chromatography Studies in Recurrent Candida Vulvovaginitis." *Journal of Reproductive Medicine* 29, no. 1 (July 1984).

Hunter, Beatrice Trum. *Fact-Book on Fermented Foods and Beverages: An Old Tradition*. New Canaan, Conn.: Keats Publishing Co., 1973.

Illich, Ivan. *Medical Nemesis—The Expropriation of Health*. New York: Pantheon Books, 1976.

International College of Applied Nutrition. *Nutrition, Applied Personally*. La Habra, Calif.: International College of Applied Nutrition, 1973. Quoted by Karen MacNeil, *The Book of Whole Foods, Nutrition and Cuisine*.

Jackson, Mildred, N.D., and Teague, Terri. *The Handbook of Alternatives to Chemical Medicine*. Oakland, Calif.: Lawton-Teague Publications, 1975.

Jacob, Stanley W., M.D., F.A.C.S.; Francone, Clarice Ashworth; and Lossow, Walter J., Ph.D. *Structure and Function in Man*. Philadelphia: W. B. Saunders Co., 1982.

Jacobson, Michael. *Eater's Digest: The Consumer's Fact Book of Food Additives*. New York: Anchor Books/Doubleday, 1976.

Jain, K. K. *Health Care in New China and What We Can Learn From It*. Emmaus, Pa.: Rodale Press, 1973.

Kaptchuk, Ted J., O.M.D. *The Web That Has No Weaver: Understanding Chinese Medicine*. New York: Congdon & Weed, 1983.

Kaslof, Leslie J. "Parts or Wholes: An Introduction to the Use of Whole Plant Substances in Healing." In *Wholistic Dimensions in Healing: A Resource Guide*. Leslie J. Kaslof, ed. Garden City, N.Y.: Doubleday & Co., 1978.

Keeton, William T. *Biological Science*. New York: W. W. Norton, 1980.

Keller, Jeanne. *Healing with Water*. West Nyack, N.Y.: Parker Publishing Co., 1968.

Kelley, William Donald, M.D., D.D.S. "Dr. Kelley's Self Test for the Different Metabolic Types." *Healthview Newsletter* (Charlottesville, Va.), 1977.

Kelley, William, M.S., D.D.S. *Metabolic Typing*. Winthrop, Wash.: International Health Institute, 1982.

Kervran, Louis. *Biological Transmutations*. Binghamton, N.Y.: Swan House Publishing Co., 1972.

Kloss, Jethro. *Back to Eden*. New York: Lancer Books, 1971.

Kosland, D. E., Jr. "Protein Shape and Biological Control." *Scientific American*, October 1973.

Kotsch, Ronald E., Ph.D. "Georges Ohsawa and the Japanese Religious Tradition—A Study of the Life and Thought of the Founder of Macrobiotics." Doctoral thesis, Harvard School of Divinity. North Chelmsford, Mass.: Sorbengeist Publications, 1981.

Kushi, Michio. *The Book of Macrobiotics—The Universal Way of Health and Happiness.* Tokyo: Japan Publications, 1977.

——————. *How to See Your Health: The Book of Oriental Diagnosis.* Tokyo: Japan Publications, 1980.

——————. *Natural Healing Through Macrobiotics.* Tokyo: Japan Publications, 1984; first published as *The Macrobiotic Way of Natural Healing*, edited by Eduard Esko. Boston, Mass.: East West Publications, 1978.

Langley, I. L., Ph.D.; Telfor, Ira, Ph.D.; and Christensen, John B., Ph.D. *Dynamic Anatomy and Physiology.* New York: McGraw-Hill, 1964.

Lappé, Frances Moore. *Diet for a Small Planet.* New York: Ballantine Books, 1975.

Laszlo, Erno. *Introduction to Systems Philosophy.* New York: Harper & Row, 1972.

Leaf, Alexander, M.D. "Every Day Is a Gift If You're Over 100," *National Geographic*, January 1973.

Levy, Jerre. "Sex and the Brain." A review of *Sexual Differentiations of the Brain*, by Robert W. Goy and Bruce McEwen. *The Sciences*, March 1981.

Lewison, Edwin F. "An Appraisal of Long-Term Results in Surgical Treatment of Breast Cancer." *Journal of the American Medical Association* 186 (1963):975–78.

Liem, Irene T. H.; Sternkraus, Keith H.; and Cronk, Ted C. "Production of Vitamin B_{12} in Tempeh." *Applied and Environmental Microbiology*, December 1977.

Longgood, William. *The Poisons in Your Food.* New York: Grove Press, 1960.

Lucas, Richard. *Nature's Medicines.* New York and London: Award Books and Tandem Books, 1966.

Lust, John. *The Herb Book.* New York: Bantam Books, 1974.

MacEwan, Karen, and Stone, David. "Living Without Meat." *Runner's World*, October 1977.

MacIntyre, Alasdair. *Against the Self-Images of the Age.* London: Duckworth, 1979.

McKeown, Thomas, Ph.D., M.D. "Determinants of Health." *Human Nature*, April 1978.

MacLeish, Kenneth. "Stone Age Cavemen of Mindanao." *National Geographic*, August 1972.

MacNeil, Karen. *The Book of Whole Foods: Nutrition and Cuisine.* New York: Vintage Books, 1981.

Mangelsdorf, Paul C. "Wheat." *Scientific American*, July 1953.

Marano, Hara. "The Problem with Protein." *New York*, March 5, 1978.

Mendelsohn, Robert, M.D. *How to Raise a Healthy Child . . . In Spite of Your Doctor.* Chicago: Contemporary Books, 1984.

Mendelsohn, Robert, M.D. *Malepractice: How Doctors Manipulate Women.* Chicago: Contemporary Books, 1981.

Miller, Jonathan, M.D. *The Body in Question.* New York: Random House, 1978.

Miller, Saul. *Food for Thought: A New Look at Food and Behavior.* Englewood Cliffs, N.J.: Prentice Hall, 1979.

Moon, J. Yogamundi. *A Macrobiotic Explanation of Pathological Calcification, the Great Industrial Epidemic.* San Francisco: G.O.M.F., 1984.

Morris, Martin. "A Drug from a Disease-Causing Plant (Solanum Malocoxylon)?" *New Scientist*, January 20, 1977.

Motoyama, Hiroshi, M.D. *Science and the Evolution of Consciousness*. Brookline, Mass.: Autumn Press, 1979.

Muramoto, Naboru. *Healing Ourselves*. New York: Avon Books, 1973.

Napoli, Maryann. *Health Facts: A Critical Evaluation of the Major Problems, Treatments, and Alternatives Facing Medical Consumers*. Woodstock, N.Y.: Center for Medical Consumers and Health Care Information, Overlook Press, 1982.

Northrup, Christiane, M.D., personal communication with the author, March 1983.

"Nutrition Report." *American Health*, September 1984.

Ohsawa, Georges. *The Book of Judgment*. Los Angeles: Ignoramus Press, 1966.

——————. *Zen Macrobiotics*. Los Angeles: The Ohsawa Foundation, 1965.

Oski, Frank A., M.D. *Don't Drink Your Milk*. Syracuse, N.Y.: Mollica Press, 1983.

Oster, K. A. "Treatment of Angina Pectoris According to a New Theory of Its Origin." *Cardiology Digest* 3 (1968):29–34.

Ostrander, Sheila, and Schroeder, Lynn. *Psychic Discoveries Behind the Iron Curtain*. New York: Bantam Books, 1970.

Page, Melvin, D.D.S., and Abrams, H. Leon, Jr. *Your Body Is Your Best Doctor*. New Canaan, Conn.: Keats Publishing, 1972.

Palos, Stephan. *The Chinese Art of Healing*. New York: Herder and Herder, 1971; Bantam Books, 1972.

Pearson, Durk, and Shaw, Sandy. *Life Extension: A Practical Scientific Approach*. New York: Warner Books, 1982.

Pescar, Susan C. *Medical Reference Library: Symptoms and Illnesses*. New York: Facts on File, *Time* Magazine, 1983.

Pfeiffer, Carl C., M.D., Ph.D. *Mental and Elemental Nutrients—A Physician's Guide to Nutrition and Health Care*. New Canaan, Conn.: Keats Publishing Co., 1975.

Phillips, David A., Ph.D. *From Soil to Psyche—A Total Plan of Natural Living for the New Age*. Santa Barbara, Calif.: Woodbridge Press, 1977.

Price, Weston A., D.D.S. *Nutrition and Physical Degeneration: A Comparison of Primitive and Modern Diets and Their Effects*. Los Angeles: The American Academy of Applied Nutrition, 1948.

Prigogine, Ilya. *From Being to Becoming: Time and Complexity in the Physical Sciences*. San Francisco: W. H. Freeman and Co., 1980.

Pritikin, Nathan, with Patrick McGrady, Jr. *The Pritikin Program for Diet and Exercise*. New York: Grosset & Dunlap, 1973.

Reckeweg, Hans-Heinrich, M.D. *Homotoxicology: Illness and Healing by Antihomotoxic Therapy*. Albuquerque, N.M.: Menaco Publishing Co., 1980.

A Review of the Significance of Bovine Milk Xanthine Oxidase in the Etiology of Atherosclerosis. Prepared for Division of Nutrition, Bureau of Foods, FDA, by C. Jeleff Carr, Ph.D.; John M. Talbot, M.D.; Kenneth D. Fisher, Ph.D. Bethesda, Md.: Life Sciences Research Office, Federation of American Societies for Experimental Biology, 1975.

Rhoads, Sharon Ann, with Zunic, Patricia. *Cooking with Sea Vegetables*. Brookline, Mass.: Autumn Press, 1978.

Rodale, J. I. *Natural Health, Sugar, and the Criminal Mind*. New York: Pyramid Books, 1971.

Roe, Daphne, M.D. Handbook: *Interaction of Selected Drugs with Nutritional Status in Man*. Chicago: American Dietetic Association, 1982.

Rubenberg, R. D. Briggs, et al. "Myocardial Infarction in Patients Treated with Sippy and Other High-Milk Diets: An Autopsy Study of Fifteen Hospitals in the U.S.A. and Great Britain." *Circulation* 21 (April 1960).

Sampsidis, N. *Heart Disease Explained.* Glen Head, N.Y.: Sunflower Publishing, 1981.

Sattilaro, Anthony J., M.D., with Monte, Tom. *Living Well Naturally.* Boston, Mass.: Houghton Mifflin, 1984.

Sattilaro, Anthony J., M.D., with Monte, Tom. *Recalled by Life.* Boston, Mass.: Houghton Mifflin, 1982.

Schauss, Alexander G. *Diet, Crime, and Delinquency.* Berkeley, Calif.: Parker House, 1981.

——————————., and Simonsen, Clifford E. "A Critical Analysis of the Diets of Chronic Juvenile Offenders," Part 1. *Journal of Orthomolecular Psychiatry* 8, no. 3 (1979). See also Alexander G. Schauss, M.A.; Jeffrey Bland, Ph.D.; Clifford E. Simonsen, Ph.D., "A Critical Analysis of the Diets of Chronic Juvenile Offenders," Part 2. *Journal of Orthomolecular Psychiatry* 8, no. 4 (December 1979).

Schell, Orville. *Modern Meat: Antibiotics, Hormones, and the Pharmaceutical Farm.* New York: Random House, 1984.

Schroeder, Henry A., M.D. personal correspondence with the author, 1972.

——————————. *The Trace Elements and Man.* Old Greenwich, Conn.: The Devin-Adair Co., 1973.

Schwartz, George, M.D. *Food Power—How Foods Can Change Your Mind, Your Personality, and Your Life.* New York: McGraw-Hill, 1979.

Selye, Hans. *Calciphylaxis.* Chicago: University of Chicago Press, 1962.

Sheinkin, David, M.D.; Schachter, Michael, M.D.; and Hutton, Richard. *Food, Mind and Mood.* New York: Warner Books, 1979.

Sheldrake, Rupert. *A New Science of Life: The Hypothesis of Formative Causation.* Los Angeles: J. P. Tarcher, 1981.

Shils, Edward A., and Finch, Henry A., trans. "Objectivity in Social Science and Social Policy," in *The Methodology of the Social Sciences.* New York: Macmillan Publishing Co., 1949.

Shurtleff, William, and Aoyagi, Akiko. *The Book of Miso.* New York: Ballantine Books, 1981.

——————————————————. *The Book of Tempeh.* New York: Harper & Row, 1979.

Smith, Lendon, M.D. *Improving Your Child's Behavior Chemistry.* New York: Wallaby-Pocket Books, 1980.

Smuts, Jan Christian. *Holism and Evolution.* New York: The Viking Press, 1961.

Sneddon, Russell. *About the Water Cure: An Explanation of Hydrotherapy.* London: Thorsons Publishers, 1965.

Spear, Bill, personal communication with the author, November 7, 1985.

Stamps, Jeffrey. *Holonomy: A Human Systems Theory.* Seaside, Calif.: Intersystems Publications, 1980.

Steiner, Rudolf. *Spiritual Science and Medicine.* London: Rudolf Steiner Press, 1948, 1975.

Sullivan, Jerome L. "Iron and the Sex Difference in Heart Disease Risk." *The Lancet* (June 13, 1981):1, 293–94.

Surgeon General of the United States. *Healthy People: The Surgeon General's Report on Health Promotion and Disease Prevention.* Washington, D.C.: Department of Health, Education and Welfare Publication no. 79-55011 (1979).

Tannahil, Reay. *Food in History.* New York: Stein and Day, 1973.

Taussig, Helen B., M.D. "Possible Injury to the Cardiovascular System from Vitamin D." *Annals of Internal Medicine* 65, no. 6 (December 1966):1195–1200.

Taylor, W. H. "Renal Calculi and Self-Medication with Multivitamin Preparations Containing Vitamin D." *Clinical Science* 42 (1972):515–22.

Thomas, Lewis. *Lives of a Cell: Notes of a Biology Watcher*. New York: Viking, 1974.

Three Initiates. *The Kybalion: A Study of the Hermetic Philosophy of Egypt and Greece*. Chicago: The Yogi Publication Society, 1912, 1940.

Trager, James. *The Enriched, Fortified, Concentrated, Country-Fresh, Lip-Smacking, Finger-Licking, International Unexpurgated Foodbook*. New York: Grossman Publishers, 1970.

Twitchell, Paul. *Herbs: The Magic Healers*. Menlo Park, Calif.: IWP Publishers, 1971.

Ullman, Dana, Ph.D. "Principles of Homeopathy." *Co-Evolution Quarterly* (Sausalito, Calif.), Spring 1981.

United States Department of Agriculture Handbook No. 8. *Composition of Foods*.

United States Department of Health, Education and Welfare. *Healthy People: The Surgeon General's Report on Health Promotion and Disease Prevention*. Washington, D.C., 1979.

United States Department of Health, Education and Welfare, Public Health Service. *Living Well: An Introduction to Health Promotion and Disease Prevention*. Washington, D.C., 1979.

United States Department of Health and Human Services. *Promoting Health, Preventing Disease—Objectives for the Nation*. Washington, D.C., Fall 1980.

United States Senate, Select Committee on Nutrition and Human Needs. *Dietary Goals for the United States*. Washington, D.C., 1977.

United States Senate, Select Committee on Nutrition and Human Needs. *Nutrition and Mental Health*. Washington, D.C., June 22, 1977, 1980 (update).

Veith, Ilza, trans. *The Yellow Emperor's Classic of Internal Medicine*. Chicago: The Yogi Publication Society, 1940.

Verret, Jacqueline, Ph.D., and Carper, Jean. *Eating May Be Hazardous to Your Health: How Your Government Fails to Protect You from the Dangers in Your Food*. New York: Simon and Schuster, 1974.

Watson, George, Ph.D. *Nutrition and Your Mind—The Psychochemical Response*. New York: Harper & Row, 1972.

Watts, Alan. *The Book on the Taboo Against Knowing Who You Are*. New York: Vintage Books, Random House, 1972.

Weiner, Michael. *The Way of the Skeptical Nutritionist—A Strategy for Designing Your Own Nutritional Profile*. New York: Macmillan Publishing Co., 1981.

Wilhelm, Richard, and Baynes, Cary F., trans. *The I Ching, or Book of Changes*. Bollinger Series 19. Princeton, N.J.: Princeton University Press, 1967.

Williams, Roger J. *Nutrition Against Disease: Environmental Prevention*. New York: Pitman Publishing Corp., 1971.

Winter, Ruth. *Poisons in Your Food*. New York: Crown Publishers, 1969.

Wolfe, Sidney M., and the Public Citizen Research Group founded by Ralph Nader. *Pills That Don't Work*. New York: Warner Books, 1980.

Wurtman, Richard J.; Baum, Michael J.; and Potts, John T., Jr., eds. *The Medical and Biological Effects of Light*. Annals of the New York Academy of Sciences, 453 (New York, 1983).

Yudkin, John, M.D. *Pure, White, and Deadly (Sweet and Dangerous)*. New York: Peter Wyden, 1972.

Index

Abkhazians, 135
Abortions, 164
Accidents, universal law of, 33
Accumulation of matter, problems of, 152, 163, 194, 195, 215, 310
  interrupted infections and, 267; loss of weight and, 225–26; as serious illness, 284; as symptom, 246; withdrawal symptoms and, *see* Withdrawal symptoms (diet change)
Acetates, 104
Acid and alkaline foods, 73–80
  acids, 74; alkalis, 74; blood and, 75; buffer foods, 76, 78*n*., 80; calcium and, 160–62
    coffee, alcohol, and salt, 162; high-protein foods, 160; milk and dairy products, 149; nightshades, 161; sugar, 160; wine, vinegar, and citrus, 161
  changing diets and:
    signs indicating the need for, 206; time frame for effects of, 220
  cravings and, 79, 232–33; effect on the body of, 75–76; expansive or contractive food and, 77, 233; fluids and, 74; fruits, 175; grain, 168; home remedies and, 252–87 *passim*; hydrogen ions and, 74–75; imbalance in, 78–79, 113; intrinsic sensitivity to, 79–80; nightshades, 177–78; pH and, 74–75; proportion of consumption, 77–78; salt, 185; sugar, 76, 77, 80, 187–88; various diets and:
    Fortified Natural-Foods, 96, 110; health-supportive whole foods, 138; high-protein, 106, 107; Italian, 79; Japanese, 79; macrobiotics, 127; Pritikin, 102; Recommended American, 97; Standard American, 93; vegetarian variations, 118; Western, 79; yogic, 79 which is "better?," 77–78
Acne, 65, 129, 152, 181, 244, 272
  diet and, 272, 273, 274
Acupuncture, 301, 310
Adaptive sel-organization, 29
Adaptive self-stabilization, 29
Adapting diet to individual circumstance, 128
Addiction, 189, 219, 229–30
  allergies and, 230; breaking the, 229–30, 234; defined, 229; to stimulants, 229–30; to sugar, 189, 191, 229, 230; withdrawal from, *see* Withdrawal symptoms (diet change)

Additives, food, *see* Chemical preservatives and other food additives
Adjustment as symptom, 246
Adrenal cortex, 295
Adrenal glands, 121, 227, 270, 307
Aduki beans, 5, 169, 262
African people, 133–34, 193
Agar, 171, 180
Aging process, 194
AIDS, 23, 267, 284, 285
Aihara, Herman, 125, 131
  seven macrobiotic principles of, 125–26
Airola, Paavo, 77–78, 214, 259*n*.
Alaria, 180
Alarm systems, 222–27
Alcohol, 17, 107, 175, 230, 297
  addiction to, 229–30, 234; calcium and, 162; excess, 277; fermentation and, 201, 202; high-fat, high-protein meals and, 249–50; withdrawal from, 217
Alkaline foods, *see* Acid and alkaline foods
Allergies, 17, 23, 40, 49, 98, 152, 275, 285, 310
  addiction and, 230; common, 230; defined, 229; depression and, 290–91; headaches and, 266; milk and cheese and, 119, 153, 156, 230, 290–91
ALS (Lou Gehrig's disease), 23, 267, 284–85
Aluminum, 186
  as cause of diseases, 285
Alzheimers disease, 23, 284–85
American Academy of Pediatrics, 149
American diet, *see* Recommended American Diet (R.A.D.); Standard American Diet (S.A.D.)
American Dietetic Association, 141
American Heart Association, 24
American Indians, 133, 135, 250, 257, 307
American Institute for Cancer Research, 193
American Medical Association Family Medical Guide, 273*n*.
Ammonia, 155–56
Amino acids, 170, 171, 202
Anabolism, 84–88
  women and, 301–2
Anemia, 113
  pernicious, 122–23, 124
Anesthesia, 306
Anger, 241, 280
  food chart for, 292
Anise, 182
Anorexia, 67, 283

Peter Roth

About the Author:

Annemarie Colbin was born in Holland and brought up in Argentina on a European vegetarian diet. After her arrival in the United States in 1961, she was introduced to macrobiotics. Her professional cooking career grew as much out of curiosity as from her search for optimum health; she was intrigued by the idea of being able to control the way one feels by what one eats.

Ms. Colbin, who practices what she preaches, founded and still directs the Natural Gourmet Cookery School in New York City, where many of her students are referred by doctors and other health practitioners. She is the author of *The Book of Whole Meals* and often writes articles for *East-West Journal* and *Whole Life Times.* Her work has also been featured in publications such as the *New York Times,* the *New York Daily News,* and *Cosmopolitan.*

Ms. Colbin travels regularly to major cities throughout the United States and Canada, lecturing and teaching cooking classes. She lives in New York City with her two daughters.

If you would like more information on Annemarie Colbin's new videocassette, VIDEO GUIDE TO THE BASICS OF HEALTHY COOKING, please write:

VIDEO DEPARTMENT
THE NATURAL GOURMET COOKERY SCHOOL
48 WEST 21st STREET
NEW YORK, NY 10010